The Anthropocene

For Paul Crutzen, John McNeill, and Will Steffen, who first discerned the Anthropocene and the Great Acceleration, and opened the way for others.

The Anthropocene
A Multidisciplinary Approach

Julia Adeney Thomas
Mark Williams
Jan Zalasiewicz

polity

The right of Julia Adeney Thomas, Mark Williams, and Jan Zalasiewicz to be identified as Authors of this Work has been asserted in accordance with the UK Copyright, Designs and Patents Act 1988.
First published in 2020 by Polity Press

Polity Press
65 Bridge Street
Cambridge CB2 1UR, UK

Polity Press
101 Station Landing
Suite 300
Medford, MA 02155, USA

ISBN-13: 978-1-5095-3459-3
ISBN-13: 978-1-5095-3460-9 (pb)

A catalogue record for this book is available from the British Library.

Typeset in 10.5 on 12pt Plantin
by Fakenham Prepress Solutions, Fakenham, Norfolk NR21 8NL
Printed and bound in Great Britain by CPI Group (UK) Ltd, Croydon

The publisher has used its best endeavors to ensure that the URLs for external websites referred to in this book are correct and active at the time of going to press. However, the publisher has no responsibility for the websites and can make no guarantee that a site will remain live or that the content is or will remain appropriate.

For further information on Polity, visit our website:
politybooks.com

Contents

About the Authors

Julia Adeney Thomas is Associate Professor of History at the University of Notre Dame. Her publications include *Reconfiguring modernity: Concepts of nature in Japanese political ideology* (winner of the AHA John K. Fairbank Prize) (2001), *Japan at nature's edge: The environmental context of a global power* (2013), *Rethinking historical distance* (2013), and *Visualizing fascism: The twentieth-century rise of the global right* (2020). Her areas of expertise are the intellectual history of Japan, global history, photography, and the environment.

Mark Williams is Professor of Palaeobiology at the University of Leicester. He was a founding member, with Jan Zalasiewicz, of the Anthropocene Working Group, where much of his work now focuses on quantifying human-induced changes to the biosphere. With Jan, he is the author of *The Goldilocks planet* (2012), *Ocean worlds* (2014), and *Skeletons: The frame of life* (2018).

Jan Zalasiewicz is Professor of Palaeobiology at the University of Leicester, and was Chair of the Anthropocene Working Group of the International Commission on Stratigraphy. He is a field geologist and paleontologist who has studied rocks and fossils ranging across more than half a billion years of geological time. He is the author of *The Earth after us* (2008), *The planet in a pebble* (2010), and *Rocks: A very short introduction* (2016), as well as of books co-authored with Mark Williams.

Preface

The "Anthropocene" is not the same as "climate change," "global warming," "environmental problems," "pollution," or a host of other terms that refer to changes on our planet. Instead, at its core, the Anthropocene is a geological concept. It integrates all these and many other phenomena and places them within the context of deep planetary time to indicate Earth's recent, abrupt transformation. Suggested informally in 2000 by the Nobel Laureate and atmospheric chemist Paul Crutzen (1933–), and independently by biologist Eugene Stoermer (1934–2012), this term designates a proposed new geological epoch, set in train by human activities. Indeed, there is overwhelming evidence, laid out in this book, that in the mid twentieth century, our planet entered a distinct new chapter in its ~4.54-billion-year history. The complex, integrated Earth System has moved away from the relative stability of the Holocene Epoch, which began ~11,700 years ago, to another less stable, and still evolving, phase. This new phase has, in many ways, no precedent in Earth's long history. It is also not as conducive to human wellbeing as the Holocene Epoch. In fact, evidence is mounting that life as we have experienced it for the last ten millennia is going to be changing very rapidly, and largely for the worse: the seas are rising; the air carries more carbon dioxide and particulates; global biodiversity is collapsing; the climate will, almost certainly, soon be hotter than it has ever been in the history of *Homo sapiens*. The pressure on the systems that nurture, shelter, and fuel us will become ever more intense in the years to come.

Currently, the geological community is in the process of accumulating evidence toward a formal proposal on the Anthropocene. In 2016, an overwhelming majority of members of the Anthropocene

Working Group (AWG) voted in favor of pursuing this proposal. In 2019, a binding vote by 88 percent of the AWG confirmed the earlier consensus that Earth has entered a new phase marked by a distinctive, near-global stratum. The causes of the recent transformation of our planet are the sudden rise in human population, globalization, and industrialization over the last 70 or 80 years. Should the Anthropocene be formally adopted, it would join the Eocene, the Pleistocene, and other such units on the great canvas of the Geological Time Scale (GTS).

The Geological Time Scale is the way geologists visualize the Earth's deep past. This tool for understanding changes over time shows the hierarchical arrangement of units, from relatively short ages to longer epochs, then to yet longer periods, which are encompassed within immensely long eras and finally organized into eons that may last more than a billion years. The Anthropocene, as currently proposed, is a potential epoch, which means it marks a bigger alteration in Earth processes than an age, but represents less change than a period. If confirmed by the International Commission on Stratigraphy, it would be the top line of figure 1, just above "Holocene." If you wanted to address a letter not to a place on Earth, but to a point in geological time, our temporal abode today is the early part of the newly proposed Anthropocene Epoch, in the Quaternary Period within the Cenozoic Era of the Phanerozoic Eon. That temporal address is cumbersome, but it would give clear directions for the planetary post.

Although the Anthropocene is a very new part of Earth's history, to make sense of it we need to place it in the context of our planet's past, beginning 4.54 billion years ago, then tracing the emergence of different life forms over many millions of years. The main protagonist of this story, *Homo sapiens*, evolved a mere ~300,000 years ago, slowly emerged as a dominant force, and ultimately became a planet-changing species by the mid twentieth century. The extraordinary transformations of the Earth System that we are seeing today occurred, effectively, within a single human lifetime, driven by cultural, political, and socioeconomic factors and fueled by technological changes that continue to press the planet beyond Holocene norms at an ever-accelerating rate. Understanding this recent human impact also requires a deep human history that, while shallower than planetary deep history, witnessed the rise of powerful forces. The ideas, inventions, and political and economic systems accelerating Earth's transformation, and those that resisted this destructive trajectory, are also stories of the Anthropocene. In other words,

Eon	Era	Period	Epoch	
Phanerozoic	Cenozoic	Quaternary	Holocene	←Present time ←11,700 years
			Pleistocene	
		Neogene	Pliocene	
			Miocene	
		Paleogene	Oligocene	
			Eocene	
			Paleocene	←66 million years
	Mesozoic	Cretaceous		
		Jurassic		
		Triassic		←252 million years
	Paleozoic	Permian		
		Carboni-ferous — Pennsylvanian / Mississippian		
		Devonian		
		Silurian		
		Ordovician		
		Cambrian		
Proterozoic				←541 million years
Archean				←2500 million years
Hadean				←4000 million years
				←4540 million years

Figure 1 Simplified Geological Time Scale. The figure shows the beginning of the Holocene Epoch commencing 11,700 years ago. Epochs are only shown for the Cenozoic Era.

to come to grips with the Anthropocene, one needs to span the enormity of geological time and its processes, and also delve into the complexities and sheer quirkiness of human behavior and institutions on more intimate timescales – hence, our plea for a multidisciplinary understanding.

Our book begins by explaining why the clunky term "multidisciplinary" is more precise than "interdisciplinary" for what we do here (Jensenius 2012). Interdisciplinarity synthesizes and harmonizes approaches. The result is that everyone, ultimately, asks the same questions and comes up with the same coordinated and coherent way of knowing. For instance, myrmecologist E. O. Wilson (1998) has argued for an interdisciplinary unity of knowledge that he calls "consilience." On the other hand, "multidisciplinarity" means that people from different disciplines work together to address the same issue, which in our case is the geological reality of the Anthropocene. Participants in a multidisciplinary conversation will always have to contend with the friction among their perspectives, because they bring to the table distinct methods, questions, and archives, with differing scales of time and space. No single story can ever capture the complex whole. To us, a multidisciplinary approach makes sense because the Anthropocene itself is multifaceted, multiscalar, and the product of a recent coalescence of human activities – some having very deep origins, such as the mastery of fire by our ancestral species, and others which are very recent, such as the rise of mass tourism. To assume that the Earth System and human systems operate separately is to misunderstand what is happening. Yet to suggest that no difference exists between the scales, methods, and questions important to geologists, social scientists, and humanists is to oversimplify the situation and suggest that a single understanding – and even a solution to this problem – is within reach.

After explaining our approach, our narrative opens with the deep history of the Earth, the fundamental context of the Anthropocene. In chapters 2 and 3, we discuss the Anthropocene in its geological context and as a time unit, explaining how the concept arose and the weight of the evidence behind it. Chapters 4 and 5 explore two crucial facets of the Earth System: climate and the biosphere, respectively. Both climate and the biosphere impact – and are impacted by – human activities. Indeed, according to Earth System science, Earth is one, integrated system where the atmosphere, hydrosphere, cryosphere, lithosphere, pedosphere, and biosphere (including, of course, human beings) mutually impact one another in complex ways. From this holistic perspective, the tomatoes you ate on Saturday can't be separated from the formation and movement of soil, rocks, ice, water, and air over billions of years. Earth System scientist Tim Lenton dates the contemporary idea of an integrated Earth System to the 1960s and early 1970s, with the Gaia hypothesis of scientist James Lovelock and microbiologist Lynn Margulis, though it had many forerunners (2016, p. 5). This application of systems science to Earth acquired the name "Earth Systems science" in the 1980s when NASA became interested in "human-driven ozone depletion and climate change" (Steffen et al. 2020, p. 56). In 1986, NASA developed the Bretherton Diagram showing that human activities play an integral role in the physical and biological processes of our planet (National Research Council 1986). This schematic diagram became "an important driving force for the conceptualization of subsequent Earth system research programs" (Mooney et al. 2013, p. 3666). Beginning in the 1990s, powerful computers allowed scientists to begin to model Earth's complexity with greater sophistication, though there is still much work to be done. Gradually, as the evidence piled up, it began to dawn on some Earth System scientists that Earth was no longer functioning within Holocene norms. Tellingly, in 2000, when Crutzen improvised the term "Anthropocene," it was at a meeting in Mexico City of Earth System scientists, rather than at a gathering of geologists.

The geological community became involved a few years later, initial analysis showing that the idea was feasible. As interest in the idea grew, the AWG was formed and went to work in 2009. Along with an array of geological specialists, the AWG also included some Earth System scientists and, because of the unprecedented importance of human factors, archeologists, historians, and a legal scholar. After much unpaid evidence-gathering and intense debate, the consensus grew that human activity had indeed abruptly altered the trajectory of the Earth System and etched a durable mark on the planet's crust. According to a 2019 press release by the AWG, "Many of these changes will persist for millennia or longer, and are altering the trajectory of the Earth System, some with permanent effect. They are being reflected in a distinctive body of geological strata now accumulating, with potential to be preserved into the far future." The Anthropocene's beginning, they announced, "would be optimally placed in the mid-20th century, coinciding with the array of geological proxy signals preserved within recently accumulated strata and resulting from the 'Great Acceleration' of population growth, industrialization and globalization" ("Working Group" 2019; see also Zalasiewicz et al. 2019b).

As all this shows, although the Anthropocene is fundamentally a geological concept, its context, origins, and impacts cannot be understood solely through the discipline of geology, or even through the sciences alone. The box labeled "Human Activities" in the Bretherton Diagram needs to be opened and its contents analyzed. Chapter 6 takes on this challenge, exploring the *anthropos* of the Anthropocene from the perspectives of paleoanthropology, archeology, anthropology, and history, followed by a discussion in chapter 7 of the economics and politics of planetary limits. We close by showing that having many ways of knowing helps us address the unprecedented existential crisis in which humanity now finds itself. In short, the central argument of our multidisciplinary approach is that reality, even the encompassing reality of the Anthropocene, dictates no single comprehensive planetary story; instead, there are many ways of looking back and, we hope, more than one way of moving forward.

Here in this book, even stretching ourselves thin, we do not cover all the modes of understanding that might be brought to bear on the Anthropocene. For instance, we say little about the visual arts or music, about religion or ethics, about psychology or poetry – or, indeed, about pathways in sedimentology, engineering, and geophysics – that might profitably be followed. These exclusions should not be taken as dismissals but as invitations. There is, and always will be, much more to say. The web of scientific and humanistic knowledge brought together here reveals that the Anthropocene gestated over many centuries, and even millennia, via a complex array of factors with no single smoking gun. When the twentieth-century forces of human population growth, globalization, and economic development, with its increasing disparities of wealth and power, combined to push the Earth System beyond Holocene norms, they struck a match to a long-primed powder keg. Our understanding of the Anthropocene is not reductive, but aims to be as rich, complex, and tension-filled as the human forces and physical forcings that produced it.

For us, creating this multidisciplinary portrait of the Anthropocene has been a fascinating and rewarding adventure. Putting together two British geologists with one American intellectual historian of Japan was an experiment that might have gone very wrong. It could have resulted, like oil and water, in a stand-off of mutual incomprehension. Alternatively, there could (with different personalities) have been pyrotechnic explosions. But this didn't happen either. We three share a deeply congruent understanding of the central challenge facing our world today, despite our differences in training and interests. What we hold in common is a desire to understand Earth and our human circumstances, a respect for evidence, and a keen sense of the urgency and importance of communicating what the Anthropocene means. How Polity Press knew all this when it orchestrated our collaboration is a happy mystery.

As you'll see in the chapters that follow, speaking in multidisciplinary tongues is not – and, we argue, should not be – a soothing, oceanic experience of seamless translation. Different disciplines use words differently. Take the word "Earth" for instance. For scientists, Earth is a planet in our solar system and should always be capitalized; for humanists and social scientists, the "earth" may refer to the world inhabited by human beings, our societies, or the spaces we move through, the landscape with its creatures. When Hamlet comments to his friend, "There are more things in heaven and earth, Horatio, than are dreamt of in your philosophy," he is not making an observation about the upper atmosphere of the third planet from the Sun. To take another example, both historians and geologists are concerned with dividing time into units of study and worrying about how one moment relates to the next. Yet the words "revolution," "age," and "epoch" take on a completely different valence in history than they do in geology. Between the Ediacaran Period and the subsequent Cambrian Period, there was, according to geologists, a "revolution." But few historians would use this term for an event longer than a century, let alone one that had a duration of 30 million years. Even calling this an "event," in philosopher Hans Gadamer's sense, would be problematic, given the time horizon. Arguments, too, are constructed differently. When we speak of debates within anthropology, history, and other social sciences and humanities, we commonly quote the language of others, because meaning lies in the specificity of their words and the resonance of their phrases with the phrases of other writers. Since value lies at the heart of humanistic enterprises, persuasive arguments often rely on precise and compelling word choice rather than on physical evidence and experimentation. In the sciences, the work of others is acknowledged in the references usually without extensive quotation.

But what is perhaps most striking are the convergences among us. All three of us approach categories and concepts as provisional means of organizing evidence in response to particular questions. For instance, the time intervals on the Geological Time Scale, including the proposed Anthropocene, are tools for thinking about how the Earth changes and why. So too in the social sciences and humanities, concepts such as "origin," "culture," and "economic system" serve as a means for understanding continuity and change in human societies. Evidence is crucial, whether it comes from rocks, artifacts, or archives, but the categories and concepts that organize the evidence are not inherent in the evidence itself. They are crafted through conversations and debates within and across disciplines, in society more broadly, and across the generations. Sometimes, one of the lucky few will have a flash of insight that helps make sense of the evidence with a new compelling conceptual tool such as the "Anthropocene." We hope our unlikely combination of human forces and different fields provides a fuller picture of our changing world that, largely by accident, we collectively have pushed on a new course.

Acknowledgments

In various and manifold ways, the following people generously helped in the creation of this book. We owe them our thanks: Gareth Austin, Ian Baucom, Dominick Boyer, Kate Brown, Dipesh Chakrabarty, Liz Chatterjee, Lorraine Daston, Fabian Drixler, Thomas Hylland Eriksen, Debjani Ganguly, Marta Gasparin, Amitav Ghosh, Kyle Harper, Gabrielle Hecht, Cymene Howe, Debra Javeline, Fredrik Albritton Jonsson, Bruno Latour, Tim Lenton, Tobias Menely, Anne-Sophie Milon, John Palmesino, Buhm Soon Park, Prasannan Parthasarathi, Ken Pomeranz, Jürgen Renn, Ann-Sofi Rönnskog, Christoph Rosol, Adrian Rushton, Bernd Scherer, Julie Schor, Roy Scranton, Emily Sekine, Lisa Sideris, John Sitter, Dan Smail, Rob Weller, Andy Yang, and the many colleagues who are members of the Anthropocene Working Group, including Jacques Grinevald, Peter Haff, Martin Head, Colin Summerhayes, Colin Waters, and Davor Vidas. We owe special gratitude to Stephen M. Zavestoski for his close reading of the manuscript, and to Leigh Mueller for her scrupulous and patient editorial work. To the many others who have supported this work, directly and indirectly, please forgive your absent-minded friends for failing to add you to this list. Please know that you too have our thanks.

Julia Thomas also wishes to thank the University of Notre Dame's Liu Institute for Asia and Asian Studies, the Kroc Institute, and the Institute for Scholarship in the Liberal Arts for their support.

1

The Multidisciplinary Anthropocene

Alexander von Humboldt (1769–1859), the great Prussian polymath, exemplifies the mix of scientific and humanistic knowledge required to comprehend the Anthropocene in all its complexity. An intrepid explorer, venturing across Siberia and traveling through South America, Humboldt gathered information on species occurrence, air temperature, ocean salinity, and much else. His goal was to integrate this information into global patterns. Only by uncovering these larger patterns could phenomena such as climate, ocean circulation, earthquakes, volcanism, and geomagnetism be understood – or so he argued. To achieve this global perspective, he mined travelers' accounts, interviewed indigenous people, and collected sailors' anecdotes, ultimately organizing a worldwide network of correspondents providing data. But his interests were also humanistic and political. He was intrigued by cultural differences, fascinated by the variety of ideas and customs, just as he was by the variety of plants and animals. Humboldt even argued that all the diverse peoples of the world were a single species, with no peoples or cultures a priori superior to or dominant over others. Ahead of his time, Humboldt "was a passionate and vocal opponent of imperialism, colonialism, and slavery" (Jackson 2019, p. 1075). On the one hand, he compiled measurements and descriptions of nature that were valuable for their accuracy and their systemic interrelatedness. On the other hand, he appreciated the rich, often incommensurate, ideas about society, gods, and time that give human lives meaning. In short, he wanted both data and stories. His model of genuine, wide-ranging, and generous multidisciplinarity serves today as the best approach to the Anthropocene.

The Anthropocene was born multidisciplinary. Early on, many types of scientists, along with social scientists, humanists, art critics, artists, journalists, and activists, sensed that something outlandish was happening, and then, in their various ways, went to work to try to figure out how and why the planet was changing. From all these perspectives, Earth, which had once seemed boundless and bounteous, began to seem girdled, befouled, and, above all, strange. As subsequent chapters show, progenitors of the idea that human activities have abruptly altered the planetary system include people as different from one another as eighteenth-century French naturalist Georges-Louis Leclerc (the comte de Buffon) (1707–88), nineteenth-century art critic John Ruskin (1819–1900), and Russian scientist Vladimir Vernadsky (1863–1945). More recently, science journalist Andrew Revkin, archeologist Matt Edgeworth, historian of science Naomi Oreskes, activist Greta Thunberg, and historian John McNeill, among many others, have drawn attention to Earth's radical transformation. In journalist Bill McKibben's view, we no longer live on Earth but on a different planet he calls "Eaarth" (McKibben 2010). While assessing the physical evidence of new, geologically significant strata and a shift in the Earth System is the job of geologists and, more broadly, Earth System scientists, the questions of how and why human activities propelled the planet on a dangerous trajectory concern everyone. Likewise, while the decision about adding the Anthropocene Epoch to the Geological Time Scale will be made within the geoscientific community, decisions about how to live in these harsher, unfamiliar conditions fall to us all. Our new Eaarth requires new forms of knowledge, drawing from the widest possible range of sources.

Most of us know something about the unprecedented conditions we face on our transformed planet. The US National Aeronautics and Space Administration (NASA) says that the level of carbon dioxide in the atmosphere is higher than at any time in at least the past 800,000 years – well before our species evolved – and it is causing the atmosphere to warm. Our strangely unfamiliar planet now has more than 193,000 human-made "inorganic crystalline compounds," which vastly outnumber Earth's ~5,000 natural minerals; more than 8.3 billion tonnes of plastics; amounts of fixed nitrogen roughly doubled since 60 years ago, with the nitrogen cycle perhaps more sharply impacted than in the last 2.5 billion years; novel kinds of nuclear radiation from bomb tests and power production; a biosphere undergoing rapid transformation; and much else. So, too, human societies are radically transformed. Our systems of communication, transportation, and manufacturing are global as never before. Never has the planet been so crowded with human beings. In 1900, there were around 1.5 billion of us; in the 1960s, around 3 billion; today, there are upwards of 7.8 billion. Our "anthropomass" (as Vaclav Smil calls it), combined with the mass of our domesticated animals comprise an astounding 97 percent of the total zoomass of terrestrial mammals, leaving wild mammals to make up a miserly 3 percent (Smil 2011, p. 617). Never before have most human beings lived in cities, especially in megacities such as Guangzhou, China, home to 25 million people. Needs multiply; desires grow; the capacity of Earth to renew resources shrinks. Extraordinary as each factor is on its own, the concept of the Anthropocene brings all of them – and others – together. It helps us see Earth as a single reverberating system, made up of feedback loops and tipping points that we cannot yet predict, and of thresholds we cross at our peril.

A Predicament, Not a Problem

No single way of knowing has a monopoly on understanding how and why some human activities coalesced to produce the Anthropocene in the mid twentieth century, or on the best responses to this unprecedented and unpredictable situation. Why is this the case? The reason is that the Anthropocene presents not a *problem*, but a *predicament*. The difference is important for our multidisciplinary project. A problem may be solved, sometimes using a single physical or conceptual tool produced by experts in the only appropriate field, but a predicament presents a challenging situation requiring resources of many kinds. We don't solve predicaments; instead, we persevere with more or less grace and decency.

Any hope of persevering with grace and decency on our transformed and increasingly inhospitable planet obliges us to draw on everything that might be useful in humanity's great storehouse of contentious wisdom. "The question," as historian Libby Robin notes, "is how people can take responsibility for and respond to their changed world. And the answer is not simply scientific and technological, but also social, cultural, political and ecological" (2008, p. 291). In the same vein, the historian Sverker Sörlin argues that one of the major problems is that "all relevant knowledge is not sufficiently considered as expertise." The contributions of the humanities and social sciences remain under-acknowledged, even though they should be central to "the sustainability endeavor, since their realm of expertise is precisely about value formation, ethics, concepts, decision-making, and other matters" that are essential to coping with immense global change (Sörlin 2013, p. 22). And social scientists and humanists are not the only people arguing that responding to the transformation of the Earth System requires more than scientific and technological understanding. Earth System scientist Will Steffen and colleagues point to the need for expansive change, including rapid "decarbonization of the global economy, enhancement of biosphere carbon sinks, behavioral changes, technological innovations, new governance arrangements, and transformed social values" (Steffen et al. 2016, p. 324). New economies, politics, and values are at least as important as science and technology.

From its beginning in 2009, the Anthropocene Working Group (AWG), set up to study the potential new geological time unit, included non-geologists among its members. This was an unusual move for a body of the International Commission on Stratigraphy. International governmental organizations, such as the UN's Intergovernmental Science-Policy Platform on Biodiversity and Ecosystem Services (IPBES), are also adopting this multidisciplinary approach (Vadrot et al. 2018). Recent academic initiatives around the world encourage geologists, Earth System scientists, historians, anthropologists, engineers, artists, and literary critics (among others) to talk and work with one another. These include The Anthropocene Project, a collaboration of the Haus der Kulturen der Welt cultural center in Berlin with the Max Planck Institute for the History of Science; the Center for Energy and the Environment in the Human Sciences at Rice University in Texas; the Integrated History and Future of People on Earth (IHOPE) in Sweden; the AURA project at Aarhus; the Vienna Anthropocene Network at Universität Wien; the Quotidian Anthropocene project; RIHN (the Research Institute for Humanity and Nature) in Kyoto; and the Center for Anthropocene Studies at KAIST in South Korea.

This volume also ventures beyond the sciences to some of the many disciplines concerned with humanity, the *anthropos* of the Anthropocene. Listening and learning across the frontiers of knowledge is far from easy. Each field has its own coherence, its own questions, protocols, genealogies of debate, and modes of argument. Even our citation styles differ. In an ideal world, navigating these differences might take the form imagined by paleobiologist Norman MacLeod, as meetings "of equals who possess complementary skills, data, and knowledge, who are open to the idea of having their views challenged constructively, and who can engage in the critical cut and thrust of robust debate because they are comfortable in their own intellectual skins" (2014, p. 1618). Creating such conversations is our aim too, not least because the stakes are so high. No one field can address all questions from all perspectives. No single group – be they geologists, anthropologists, geo-engineers, or anyone else – has all the answers.

Some have argued that the aim of multidisciplinary conversations is to dissolve disciplinary boundaries. E. O. Wilson (1998) calls this dissolution "consilience," and assumes that it is not only possible, but necessarily better than a multitude of perspectives and a democracy of effort. This book argues against consilience. Certainly, an interdisciplinary approach can work well when addressing some questions, but only those with one right answer. The hardest questions of politics, ethics, and aesthetics usually have more than one right answer. Not all approaches are compatible. Indeed, some are outright incommensurate due to considerations of scale, or because they represent fundamentally different forms of knowledge. Some fields produce verifiable information whereas others craft judgments (Thomas 2014; Kramnick 2017). The drawback of interdisciplinary consilience is that it ultimately gives priority to one perspective and a single style of analysis, with its circumscribed body of acceptable evidence. Only rarely do those seeking one unified story explain why the form of knowledge they have chosen is more valuable than other forms – why, for instance, we should always favor the worldview of rationalists over animists, or numbers over poetry. In the face of unprecedented challenges, we need the rigor of established disciplines to ensure expertise and to assess evidence, but we also need these disciplines to be self-reflective and to engage with work not just in adjacent fields but in distant ones. The goal is to create networks of knowledge, all focused on the reality of the Anthropocene but using their own lenses. The more this sort of multidisciplinary collaboration occurs, the more fruitful will be the debate on how we arrived at this crisis and how to navigate the tough choices ahead.

Stumbling Blocks of Scale, Causality, and Meaning

Yet even with the best will in the world, multidisciplinary conversations about the Anthropocene seem particularly difficult. Why is this so? Two factors seem central: the problem of scale and the issue of causality. A word about these two stumbling blocks is in order because scale and causality are central to all practices and disciplines, yet all approach them differently.

Let us begin with scale. In some ways, the Anthropocene is necessarily gargantuan. It is a "hyperobject," in literary critic Timothy

Morton's evocative term, meaning that it is "massively distributed in time and space relative to humans" (2013, p. 1). The anthropogenic forces now acting on the Earth System are redirecting the planet away from the glacial–interglacial cycles that have waxed and waned for the past 1 million years and more. Potentially, these forces could redirect Earth's trajectory beyond the cycles of the Quaternary Period (the past 2.6 million years). Evolutionary pathways are being abruptly altered as many species go extinct and the populations of others dwindle. Greenhouse gas (GHG) emissions have transformed the climate, not just for the next few centuries but for many millennia to come. The atmospheric changes have delayed the next Ice Age, previously forecast for 50,000 years from now, and possibly even the one after that, which was formerly "scheduled" for ~130,000 years in the future (Stager 2012, p. 11). Understanding the Anthropocene means traveling in hyper-time, going deep into the past and far into the future, while contending with a disjointed present.

Likewise, its spatial scale must be planetary; if it were happening only in East Dulwich, it wouldn't be happening. The Anthropocene is the transformation of the entire Earth System, not alterations to particular spots on Earth. Its significance lies in the scale, magnitude, and longevity of change to the Earth System, not the discovery of the "first traces of our species" (Zalasiewicz et al. 2015b, 201). Human beings started to develop a regional and highly diachronous influence on the Earth System thousands of years ago. With the European Industrial Revolution in the early nineteenth century, some societies became a more pronounced geological factor, but it was only from the mid twentieth century that the impact of accelerating population growth and industrialization became both global and near-synchronous (Zalasiewicz et al. 2015b).

Along with its enormous temporal and spatial scales, the Anthropocene is also a hyperobject in the sense that conceptualizing the Earth System is possible only through data collection of colossal proportions, and computer modeling (Edwards 2010). Without these tools, we would be blind to the magnitude of the Anthropocene, the Great Acceleration, and the overshoot of planetary boundaries. In the last few years, managing this immense amount of data has in itself become a problem of scale. Grappling with even one factor of the many that make up the Anthropocene requires the labor of thousands of scientists and extremely powerful computers. For instance, Jan Minx reported in 2018 that members of the International Panel on Climate Change (IPCC) had been struggling to prepare for the sixth Assessment Report, due in 2021, because of the sheer volume of scientific data; as of 2018, the relevant new literature since 2016 was somewhere between 270,000 and 330,000 publications. He called for machine reading and other techniques as the only way to corral and digest all this new information (Minx 2018). Notably, Minx's estimate includes only those papers that concern climate change and not those on such aspects as landscape transformation or biodiversity loss. Big data just keeps getting bigger. There is so much information that integrating it into a single planetary model becomes a steep challenge. Figuring out how the hyperobject of the Anthropocene – at odds with human scales of time and space, and our capacity to absorb information – can become "thinkable" in terms of human values, politics, and economies is an even steeper challenge.

And that's the rub. The scales of geological significance and the scales of social significance are not the same. Earth System scientists work on immense canvases of time and space; human communities suffer or celebrate the Earth's changes within varied local ecologies and cultural systems, measuring our lives in hours, days, and years. Connecting the Earth System with tonight's avocado salad, voting rights in Peru, next month's paycheck, or Aboriginal artwork means traveling up and down scales of time, space, and evidence. And yet, before the next decade is out, so as not to provoke dangerous tipping points and push Earth toward a "Hothouse state" (Steffen et al. 2018), Earth System scales and human scales must be calibrated together.

Two Types of Scale

Clarity requires distinguishing between two types of scale: one neatly integrated and nesting, and the other sprawling and tangential. The integrated scale permits us to slide fairly easily from "little" to "big." Constructing this type of scale showcases the similarities shared by each unit. We might think of this as the Russian doll view of scales, with little dolls fitting neatly inside the bigger ones, producing a monstrous, all-encompassing *babushka*. The second way to construct scales rejects neatly nesting units, and results in a messy web of connections and contrasts. Instead of looking only at the shared similarities, this approach accounts for differences as well; each unit shares some characteristics with neighboring units, but not all. The movement among units is uneasy, and startling new relations may be visible at different levels. In trying to capture the friction between orders of magnitude as well as their harmony, sprawling scales retain more of the world's complexity but lose the clarity provided by the encompassing *babushka*. The important point is that both types of scale can help us understand the transformation of the Earth System and its human entanglements. The first type of scale reveals the integration of the Earth System and its human components, while the other underscores the variety of quite different experiences of – and perspectives on – this phenomenon.

The first type of scale rests on proportional equivalences. For instance, quotidian time is measured with seconds fitting into minutes, hours, days, and weeks. All smaller units are neat subsets of larger units. Anthropologist Anna Tsing (2012) refers to this as "precision-nested scaling." Creating such coherence is far from easy, as historian of science Deborah Coen shows in her study of late Habsburg Empire climate science. Coen defines the aim of scaling as mediating "between different systems of measurement, formal and informal, designed to apply to different slices of the phenomenal world, in order to arrive at a common standard of proportionality" (Coen 2018, p. 16). Creating "a common standard of proportionality" highlights similarities while masking differences, so that the scale can be smoothed out from local occurrences to mega-units. Geologists might point to the Geological Time Scale, described in the preface, as an example of this type of scale in their discipline. Producing the GTS involved wresting fossils, ice cores, and other evidence into categories ranging from ages, epochs, periods, and eras, to eons. Although "epochs" (and all other units) vary as to how long they are, and even in the magnitude of change they represent, they provide a rough, pragmatic way to order time in increments. Much in the phenomenological world can, with effort, be made to fit into nesting scales.

Does this type of nested scale work for a multidisciplinary approach to the Anthropocene? Science journalist Christian Schwägerl argues that it does. The geological and social scales of significance can be and should be brought together: the "Anthropocene concept creates a single continuum that stretches from stones to human thought, from the most concrete and enduring phenomena to the most abstract and fleeting." Schwägerl stresses the way the Anthropocene overrides all kinds of dualisms, joining "the most short-term, seemingly ephemeral processes in human brains with the most long-term forces of geology," giving it, he argues, a "neurogeological" character (2013, p. 30). In Schwägerl's view, the Anthropocene places all of nature and all of humanity on one integrated scale. If a common standard could be devised across disciplines, then people working on the

Anthropocene might speak easily to one another, since they would all fundamentally be working on "the same thing." The threats would be similar at each level and locale; solutions could be scaled up and down.

This approach can work very well when dealing with some physical factors. For instance, the essence of interpreting the grand picture of Earth history entails putting a range of "proxy data" – chemical, magnetic, biological, astronomical, physical – onto interconnected scales of time and space in today's discipline of geological stratigraphy. It's a highly effective way to pick out patterns and relations, and to test hypotheses of causality: this approach can synthesize decades of diverse research results so that (for instance) the patterns of the Anthropocene can be discerned at a glance (Waters et al. 2016). But this approach is trickier when values and politics, art and economics, fashion and rituals are included. Putting a taste for marzipan, a commitment to democracy, or a dedication to monotheism on the same scale as the types of "proxy data" mentioned above requires developing a common standard of measurement and a shared view of knowledge. The difficulty of devising such a standard is an old conundrum in the philosophy of knowledge, now risen anew with the Anthropocene.

Some commentators, especially in the humanities and social sciences, work from the premise that no such common standard can be devised. No account of the world, no vision of knowledge, no single scale will ever be fully adequate to the world's complexity and all possible points of view. Tsing and others suggest that reality is instead best understood by embracing an archipelago of related, but not necessarily consistent, formulations of object, experience, meaning, and impact. They move among varying frameworks where each produces not just differences of magnitude, but incommensurable differences of type. Emphasizing the non-scalability of nature and humanity opens up the possibility that the reality that emerges from one perspective is at odds with the reality that emerges from another. It's like opening up a Russian doll to find a tiny golden frog inside who spits a helicopter in our faces.

Several fields are beginning to explore the second model of scaling. In physics, for instance, some have relinquished the search for a final "Theory of Everything" capable of explaining all the forces and phenomena of the universe through a single set of laws. Newtonian physics, once thought to be universally applicable, wilted in the face of later discoveries including dark energy, which seems to be accelerating the expansion of the universe when gravity should be consolidating it (Powell 2013). Concepts such as "eternal inflation" and "string theory" point to possible multiple universes, where time, dimensionality, and the strength of nuclear attraction in atoms have enormously different properties. In some of these universes, nuclear forces may be so much stronger than they are in ours that they create much denser lumps of matter; in others, they may be dramatically weaker. While our universe has three dimensions of space, others may have ten or even more (Lightman 2013, pp. 4–7). And there might perhaps be millions of these alternative, self-consistent worlds. As Stephen Hawking and Leonard Mlodinow explain, "For decades we [physicists] have striven to come up with an ultimate theory of everything – one complete and consistent set of fundamental laws of nature that explain every aspect of reality. It now appears that this quest may yield not a single theory but a family of interconnected theories" (2013, p. 91).

Anthropologists also explore the idea that phenomena resist incorporation on a single scale. They argue instead that social and natural phenomena emerge through a variety of practices only very loosely connected with one another. Take the ceremonial practice of "initiation" into adulthood sometimes portrayed as universal. Anthropologist Marilyn Strathern, working in Papua New Guinea, suggests that the practice of initiation "is no unitary phenomenon, and there appears to be as broad a gap between different initiatory practices as between the presence or absence of the practices themselves" (1991, p. xiv). In other words, a reality such as this important social ritual is best understood as a family of phenomena, often so disparate from one another that the category of "initiation" itself teeters on the edge of incoherence. Answers to questions about the importance and diffusion of an initiation practice – in other words, its scale – will be partial and dependent on deliberate efforts to construct meaning.

"Natural" phenomena also emerge through a variety of practices at different levels of magnitude and reification. Annemarie Mol (2002), author of *The Body Multiple*, looks at atherosclerosis, a disease of the arteries, in a Dutch hospital. She argues that this disease is not a single malady but a set of loosely connected disorders, which are not the same even if called by the same name. Approached by diverse specialists using a range of healing techniques, "atherosclerosis" emerges in practice as a set of conditions experienced and treated in many ways, rather than as one illness. Thinking about a practice like initiation, or a disease like atherosclerosis, as "more than one and less than many" and cohering only through "partial connections," as Strathern and Mol do, smashes the Russian doll. Those who work in this vein argue that, as we move among scales, we know *differently*, rather than more or less. There are both losses and gains to our understanding. Strathern argues, "scale switching not only creates a multiplier effect, it also creates information 'loss.'" Larger perspectives "in creating more also create less" (Strathern 1991, p. xv). This version of scaling, if applied to the Anthropocene, suggests that, depending on the level of analysis, the phenomenon takes on a different hue and valency.

Scales are vital tools for creating (and uncovering) order and patterns in natural and social worlds. They help us to produce knowledge, but, like any other form of representation, they are always provisional and in the service of particular questions. Even within formal geology as a whole, epochs are not consistent or equivalent in, for example, the amount of time they represent – they are simply useful subdivisions that geologists recognize within their common language. A nested scale helps us see Earth as a single, integrated system greatly impacted by human activities; sprawling scales point to the friction between experiences, perspectives, and values. Either may be helpful, depending on the issue at hand, but disciplines tend to have a preference for one or the other. This is why scale is such a stumbling block in multidisciplinary conversations. Figuring out how to navigate the challenge of scale – both integrated scales and sprawling scales – is a pressing imperative in Anthropocene discussions.

The Scales of Human Survival

For most people, the pressing question of the Anthropocene is human survival: can we make it through? This seemingly simple question is actually quite complicated, due to different scales of significance (Thomas 2015). The answer seems to be both "yes" and "no." On the largest scale, the Anthropocene threatens little. Our species, like any other, was always destined to go extinct. If we precipitate the Sixth Great Extinction, biodiversity may take as long as 30 million years to recover, but recover it will. The planet itself, regardless of humanity's disruptions, will continue in its orbit until the Sun undergoes dynamic change in about 5 billion years, blowing up into a fiery red giant. On these scales, we were never destined to endure forever.

On the smaller scale of the next several thousands of years, the disruptions of the Anthropocene loom large, though *Homo sapiens* as a species is unlikely to die out so soon. Paleoecologist Curt Stager argues that, on this scale, the species is here to stay and will be "fine," even in the case of extreme CO_2 levels reaching 2,000 ppm and an average global temperature rise of 9 to 16 °F (5 to 9 °C) (2012, p. 41). An informal survey conducted by philosopher Nick Bostrom (2002) revealed that, on this medium scale, academic risk experts give us an 80–90 percent chance of dodging ruination, defined as "the premature extinction of Earth-originating intelligent life or the permanent and drastic destruction of its potential for desirable future development." The bleakest view is that of cosmologist Martin Rees (2003), who only gives us a 50–50 chance of surviving to 2100, due to threats ranging from terrorism to environmental destruction. As *Homo sapiens*, then, we will likely persist well beyond the lifetimes of those alive today, though we might very well be limited to inhabiting the non-submerged land in the cooler mid to high latitudes of the transformed Earth.

But are we simply "a species?" Many would say no. At the more intimate scales of lifetimes and communities, humanity is threatened not as *Homo sapiens*, but as creative, contentious members of complex societies, some with a measure of liberal freedom, some with strong communitarian ties, and others existing under authoritarian forms of government. According to UN estimates, rising sea levels and desertification will create anywhere from 150 to 300 million refugees by 2050. A more recent study of the human climate niche suggests that those figures may be optimistic. Under the current business-as-usual scenario, and accounting for expected demographic developments, by 2070 the geographical position of the temperature niche in which humans have thrived will shift. Indeed, it will "shift more over the coming 50 years than it has since 6000 BP [before the present – 1950]" (Xu et al. 2020), stranding around 3.5 billion people in dangerously hot conditions and taking a deadly toll on the biosphere. Strong climate mitigation would reduce this theoretical number to about 1.5 billion for whom migration could be a matter of life or death. It is not implausible that this movement of people will spur aggressive nationalism and ruthless wars, a scenario explored by Naomi Oreskes and Eric Conway in their book *The collapse of Western civilization* (2014).

At this scale, the danger is far from equally shared, and issues of responsibility, justice, and value erupt urgently. Do we focus on short-term solutions like building sea walls, or long-term efforts to move coastal populations inland? Should our political activism address global capitalism, or local allotments for organic farming?

Do we help the current generation out of poverty by drilling for oil in places such as Uganda's nature reserves, even at the cost of future human impoverishment and the destruction of habitat for other species? Does nuclear energy's immediate reduction of CO_2 emissions outweigh the long-term problems of radioactive waste, rising cancer rates, and meltdowns? As we write, a coronavirus, COVID-19, its origin stimulated and its effects amplified by the emergent conditions of the Anthropocene, is killing many people, dislocating key aspects of the global economic system, generating political shockwaves – and also generating these wider questions over values and priorities.

As humanists and social scientists, policymakers and technologists, artists and philosophers address the Anthropocene in its many aspects, they work on different scales – different from that of Earth System scientists and different from those of one another. As historian Gabrielle Hecht argues, each of these scales has "epistemological, political, and ethical consequences" (2018, p. 115). In other words, depending on how "humanity" is framed, the Anthropocene may – or may not – be a threat. Riding up and down the scales of the Anthropocene can be bumpy and disorienting, making multidisciplinary conversations difficult. We are not always talking about the same thing, or talking about it in the same way.

Forcings versus Forces

The second stumbling block in multidisciplinary conversations is the question of causality. Almost all fields are interested in how the past affects the present, but they speak about causality in different ways. Very helpfully, literary critic Ian Baucom has distilled these differences into "forcings" and "forces." In science, a "forcing" is a perturbation in a system. The word does not suggest that there is will or intention behind the disruption. A forcing is not evaluated as good or evil. In other words, to say that CO_2 is the primary climate forcing is not to impugn this greenhouse gas with egregious intent. On the other hand, "the forces of history" include everything from Caesar deliberately crossing the Rubicon to the Black Death, from the majesty of the Assyrian Empire to Mount Tambora's eruption in 1815, from the rise of the multinational corporations to the seasonal patterns of monsoons. Historical forces that sculpt individual destinies and great empires are a mishmash of happenstance, inevitability, *and* intention. Humanists and social scientists called upon to analyze an event or a system ask who or what deserves credit or blame; in doing so, their purpose is not only to describe what happened but to judge its merit. That judgment then leads to critical reflection on contemporary values and institutions so that we might alter them. The tradition of critical thought, as Baucom observes, "has long understood its vocation as simultaneously descriptive and transformative: a method oriented to mapping the situation in which we find ourselves and to making something emancipatory of that situation" (Baucom 2020, p. 12).

"Forcings," with its neutral yet deterministic ring, is a word rarely used by humanists and social scientists, who are more comfortable with the language of "forces" when speaking of causation. For these humanists and social scientists, the great perplexity of the Anthropocene is how "the dynamics of *forces* and the operations of *forcings*" might be thought together, as Baucom argues (2020, p. 14). This task is extremely difficult. In one sense, as historian Dipesh Chakrabarty observes, the Anthropocene spells "the collapse of the age-old humanist distinction between natural history and human history" (2009, p. 201). Yet, in another, that distinction remains crucial since societies and individuals do not experience themselves as "species" but as moral and political actors (Chakrabarty 2018, p. 3). If the aim is both description and transformation, the tension between forcings and forces is irresolvable.

For Earth System scientists, this distinction is not an issue, because their foremost aim is accurate description. Natural and human factors can be framed together as "forcings" or "drivers." The US National Oceanic and Atmospheric Administration (NOAA) provides an example on their website of applying "drivers" to natural and human activities alike:

> Natural climate drivers include changes in the sun's energy output, regular changes in Earth's orbital cycle, and large volcanic eruptions that put light-reflecting particles into the upper atmosphere. Human-caused, or anthropogenic climate drivers include emissions of heat-trapping gases (also known as greenhouse gases) and changes in land use that make land reflect more or less sunlight energy. Since 1750, human-caused climate drivers have been increasing, and their effect dominates all natural climate drivers on Earth. (NOAA n.d.)

This passage does not even attempt to raise key social science and humanities questions about *why* "human-caused climate drivers" became more powerful and *who* benefitted, let alone *how* we might make something emancipatory of our condition. The different ways we talk about causality hamper the multidisciplinary discussions necessary to understand the Anthropocene.

To dramatize why causality is such a problem, let us compare the Anthropocene with two other geological transitions, the Holocene (with its designated lower boundary of ~11,700 years ago) and the Great Oxygenation Event (~2.4 to 2.1 billion years ago). When the glacial interval of the late Pleistocene gave way to the warmer conditions of the Holocene, *Homo sapiens* had been around for about 300,000 years. Though our species benefitted greatly from the warming Earth of the Holocene, our role in this geologically signif-icant drama was as neither "force" nor "forcing." Our species and other organisms were mere bystanders to the astronomical geometry producing the new epoch. As explained by paleontologist Anthony Barnosky and biologist Elizabeth Hadly, the Holocene arose because of the "complex interplay between three features of the Earth's orbit around the sun" (2016, p. 17). This orbit varies regularly and in three different aspects: how elliptical the Earth's orbit is; how much the axis of the planet tilts; and how much it wobbles as it rotates around its axis. Gradually, these three orbital features came into alignment so that Earth was positioned in just the right way to maximize the amount of sunlight striking the glaciers at critical seasons. When that happened, the planet crossed a warming threshold, glaciers retreated rapidly, animals and plants from southern latitudes moved north, and "new ecosystems assembled virtually everywhere." Then, about 11,000 years ago, "the global ecosystem stabilised into its interglacial new normal, where it has been right up until the last couple of centuries" (2016, p. 17).

This story of the Holocene's emergence is more complex in detail (see chapter 4), but it causes few interdisciplinary quarrels. Looking back at this phase of Earth System transformation, anthropologists and historians see that it created the conditions for the eventual emergence of agriculture and urbanization a few millennia later, but they rarely contest the geological unit. The Holocene was the result of forcings, not forces.

The Great Oxygenation Event (GOE), roughly between 2.4 and 2.1 billion years ago, offers a slightly more complex case. Oceanic cyanobacteria (a group of species commonly known as blue-green algae) learned the trick of oxygen-producing photosynthesis, possibly several hundred million years before the GOE (Smit and Mezger 2017). At first, the gas they exuded into Earth's surface environ-ments was largely captured in oxygen (O_2) sinks, and nothing much changed. Eventually, though, oxygen began to accumulate at the surface. Anaerobic life at the Earth's surface was forced to retreat underground or deep into the oceans to escape what, for them, was a lethal gas. Lynn Margulis and Dorion Sagan (1986) dramatically refer to this event as the "oxygen holocaust." Besides humans, cyano-bacteria are among the few major groups of living organisms to have engineered the Earth System into another state. A major difference is that, while humans have done so at lightning speed, cyanobacteria took billions of years to create the planet that ultimately gave life to our oxygen-breathing sort: the worms, spiders, mammals, and other multicellular species of our biosphere.

Where does the GOE leave us with the distinction between "forces" and "forcings?" Is it possible to speak of human beings as comparable to cyanobacteria in unwittingly transforming the planet? In some sense, yes, since neither *Homo sapiens* nor cyanobacteria intentionally set out to tip the Earth System into an altered state, and yet did so collectively. Researchers investigating the planetary trans-formation caused by blue-green algae do not blame them for evolving an oxygen-producing metabolism. Likewise, researchers investigating the deep history of *Homo sapiens* do not credit our distant ancestors with developing the cognitive fluidity or disease immunities that permitted our social organizations to grow strong and our numbers to skyrocket (Mithen 1996, 2007; Smail 2008). But evolving the mechanism responsible for making O_2, as did cyanobacteria, or abstract thinking and resistance to measles, as in our species, is quite different from deliberately inventing the steam engine, the Haber–Bosch process, antibiotics, and nuclear fission; it is also different from dreaming up concepts such as city-states, finance capital, and the weekend. Each individual blue-green alga became a little factory producing oxygen, but individual human bodies did not suddenly start to produce plutonium fallout, fuel ash particles, or plastics. The small amount of CO_2 each of us exhales is unproblematic. We are a species like cyanobacteria, and also unlike them.

The *anthropos* that created the Anthropocene is both the sum of our entire ecological history *and* the much more recent political, economic, technological, and social connections among us, mostly arranged to the benefit of a small minority. While the GOE was the result of an animate *forcing*, causality in the Anthropocene is a complex interplay of both systemic *forcings* and *forces* at different scales. It is this awkward combination that makes multidisciplinary dialogue both necessary and difficult.

Conclusion

We are at a critical stage in our understanding of the Anthropocene. Like Humboldt, we must seek every possible vantage point, scientific *and* cultural, to understand what is happening on our planet. How we shape the conversation now will mold future options. Scientists within the geological and Earth System science communities are ever more confident of the reality of the phenomenon emerging in the data. Likewise, humanists and social scientists are beginning to take this new reality seriously as the major political, economic, and existential challenge of our time. These two communities are now coming together with shared urgency and mutual curiosity, taking on board perspectives not supplied by their own research. Just as scientists recognize the limits of their expertise on questions concerning what it *means* politically, economically, and culturally for *Homo sapiens* to have transformed the planet, so too the humanities and social sciences understand that the definition, measurement, and periodization of the Anthropocene *as a geological unit* are the work of geologists. If our approach to the Anthropocene is structured only around scientific findings and technological options, it will be inadequate. So too will any response to the Anthropocene that is purely cultural without being rooted in scientific understanding.

In *The great derangement*, Amitav Ghosh calls the Anthropocene "unthinkable" if we rely on the intellectual armature of modernity, which neatly separated disciplines, siloed knowledge, and insisted that human choices were unconstrained by planetary limits (2016). It is time – past time in Ghosh's estimation – to try to think the unthinkable. Issues of scale and questions of causality will haunt our collaborative efforts as we take on this task. Yet only a generous multidisciplinary effort can make meaning out of the fact that the *anthropos* has transformed the chemical composition of the air and water, melted polar ice caps, delayed the next Ice Age, reconfigured ecologies globally, stripped the land of much of its fertile topsoil, and impacted 95 percent of the planet's habitable land surface. Only a multidisciplinary approach can find ways to create just, mutualistic societies that not only limit their demands on planetary resources, but actually stabilize the Earth System, producing cleaner air and water and enhancing biodiversity. While our joint efforts are very unlikely to produce a "grand integration" of all disciplines and worldviews, we can hope to cultivate global networks of data and stories, just as Humboldt once did. Confronting the Anthropocene is both a scientific and humanistic enterprise.

2
The Geological Context of the Anthropocene

Our planet is 4.54 billion years old, about a third of the age of the cosmos. This span of time is quite ungraspable. Even geologists, working with such near-eternity each day, can only navigate it with the help of a formal (indeed bureaucratic) construct, the Geological Time Scale (GTS), whereby the units – given names like Cambrian and Carboniferous, Permian and Pleistocene – are typically millions of years long. So how can a unit be proposed for the GTS that so far has a duration approximating to just one average human lifetime? This question, which reveals much about both the human and the planetary condition, is central to this book. To understand its full import, we need to range through both human and Earth history, to see how they intertwine.

The lineage of humans (those species in the genus *Homo*) occupies a little less than 3 million years (Villmoare et al. 2015), less than one-thousandth of our planet's enormous time-span. Within that sliver of time, our own species, *Homo sapiens*, is some 300,000 years old (Richter et al. 2017), but only began to have any kind of larger influence (beyond that of one of a number of more or less obscure, closely related hominin species) some 50,000 years ago, as forests began to be torched, and species of large mammal began to be hunted to extinction. Only in the last 10,000 years, as the latest of many retreats of ice and warmings of climate took place, did humans begin to settle, farm, and build villages, which grew into towns and cities, then nation-states and empires which quarreled and made alliances, and rose and fell against the backcloth of a relatively stable Earth that – no matter what scars of war or waste were inflicted – could be relied on to heal, to bounce back to support the dreams and ambitions of the next generation, and of the next empire. This epoch, called the Holocene, was a sweet spot for humanity. Writing, the world's major religions, and much of what some people call "civilization" then emerged.

In the last few centuries, though, a new phenomenon has appeared. At first gradual, it has become precipitous. In the last 70 years, climate, sea level, biological productivity and other major underpinning frameworks that support life on Earth have been set on a new trajectory. These vital frameworks will not bounce back, this time, to continue to provide a predictably stable and supportive backdrop for the lives of future human generations. This new phase of Earth history has been termed the Anthropocene. It is both a planetary phenomenon and one that affects, and is affected by, humans and the societies and structures that they build.

Our Time Within Geology

This chapter will explore the patterns and traditions of geology. Using this framework underscores the truly long-term consequences of human actions. It also makes sense because the man who launched the Anthropocene as a concept in 2000, Paul Crutzen, explicitly framed it in geological terms as an epoch (though he himself was an atmospheric chemist, a Nobel Laureate for his role in unpicking the mechanisms of human-driven destruction of the ozone layer) (Crutzen and Stoermer 2000).

There are solid technical reasons for this perspective, too. Most of the materials with which humans have built the structures that characterize the Anthropocene – megacities, aeroplanes, oil platforms – have come from rock structures within the Earth, and hence are the province of geology. Then there is the kind of planetary history needed to understand the import of the Anthropocene. In recent decades, advances in the geological analysis of rock strata have permitted us to develop a subtle, complex, and increasingly well time-calibrated Earth history. Reconstruction of such factors as the scale and rate of ancient climate change (along with estimates of past levels of greenhouse gases), the rise and fall of sea level, and the pattern of biological extinctions through time builds a picture of deep Earth history. Reconstructing the events that took place before consistent human observations and records means hammering out virtually all necessary information from rock strata. The multimillion-year canvas of planetary history so depicted extends to the present, when scientists can also make detailed real-time observations (e.g. by satellites) of a wide range of planetary processes. Keying geologically recent processes into the ancient record is possible through examining the most recent strata, such as sediment layers now accumulating on the floors of lakes and on seabeds, and the many clues that they contain. The overlap of the two forms of study, fusing observations of processes active today and deductions from ancient strata, is a good deal of what gives the Anthropocene concept its veracity and power.

We will also be talking within the framework of Earth System science, the scientific discipline within which the concept of the Anthropocene arose. Earth System science considers the whole planet – via its main components of the lithosphere and mantle (essentially, the solid Earth, down to its core), hydrosphere (and its frozen equivalent, the cryosphere), atmosphere, biosphere, and technosphere (see chapter 5) – as a single system (Lenton 2016). The behavior and properties of the Earth, in this view, are not simply the sum of its many components, but are *emergent* from their interaction, to set the conditions for fundamental properties such as climate. Earth System science is a relatively new, highly interdisciplinary approach. Its roots lie in the Gaia hypothesis proposed by James Lovelock and Lynn Margulis in the late 1960s and early 1970s, which suggested that the biosphere, via various feedback mechanisms, regulated Earth's conditions to maintain habitability. The Gaia hypothesis is controversial because non-biological planetary feedbacks have been recognized as well. Nevertheless, geology and Earth System science together have proved highly complementary in analyzing the Anthropocene from a planetary perspective.

There are several kinds of Earth System change, operating on different timescales, ranging from years to billions of years. These planetary changes include singular, essentially irreversible step changes in the evolution of the atmosphere, hydrosphere, lithosphere, and biosphere, and also times when the Earth changed repeatedly within fixed limits, as during the many, almost metronomically regular, glacial–interglacial cycles of the Ice Ages. There were also long periods of approximate stasis, and the ten millennia or so prior to the Industrial Revolution provide an example (albeit one of the briefer examples) of such planetary stability. Developing an understanding of these past states helps us to assess the impact of humans on the present Earth System.

The Earth in Middle Age

The Earth in its middle age has continuously sustained life for billions of years, via natural processes that have been fine-tuning their complex interactions and feedbacks over this timescale. The enormity of this history was only recently grasped by humans.

The year 1787 was transformative as regards understanding the great age of the Earth. That year, James Hutton (1726–97) observed the rock succession at Jedburgh in southern Scotland. There, he saw grey strata up-ended so they were vertical and, resting sharply on top of these, flat-lying red strata. Hutton had no way of dating the rock strata, but he surmised that the break in the succession, termed by geologists an unconformity, must represent a vast amount of time. In this time, the lower grey rocks were formed, then crumpled into a mountain belt, then eroded away, for the red strata to be deposited on top of their truncated remains. We now know that this process took more than 60 million years. There was no way Hutton could have known this figure, but through this deduction he intuited the immensity of time on Earth.

Later, in the middle of the nineteenth century, another Scotsman, William Thomson (1824–1907), who became Lord Kelvin, tried to calculate the real age of the Earth. Thomson thought that the Earth was originally molten, and he worked out how long it would take to cool. His calculations suggested the Earth was between 20 and 400 million years old. This estimate – especially the lower part of the range that Kelvin favored – became problematic for geologists, who, like Hutton, saw a history preserved in the rocks that seemed too crowded to cram into a few tens of millions of years. Kelvin was unaware that the Earth's interior is kept hot by radioactive materials, and it was not until the discovery of radioactive decay in the late nineteenth and twentieth centuries that the much greater age of the Earth could be properly established.

That age, 4.54 billion years (plus or minus some 50 million years), we now know through precisely dating the oldest materials found on Earth, via measuring their natural radioactivity. These materials, paradoxically, are later arrivals, in the form of meteorites, which represent debris left over when the planets of our solar system were forming. The Earth itself has been too active and transformative a planet to preserve anything quite so old – the oldest fragment we so far have of Earth itself is a zircon crystal from Australia, just a tenth of a millimeter across, some 4,404 million years old.

By combining the true age of the Earth with astronomical calculations of how long it will be before the Sun burns through its hydrogen
fuel, both Earth and Sun are shown to be about halfway through
their 10-billion-year lifetimes. The Earth, therefore, is a planet in
middle age. It is a rocky planet in the "Goldilocks zone" around the
Sun, a zone that has allowed liquid water to persist at its surface for
billions of years, a medium which allowed a complex biosphere to
evolve and persist. That biosphere is now powered primarily by the
energy of sunlight – and as one by-product has formed an oxygen-
rich atmosphere. These different components of the Earth System
– rock, air, water, and life – are intimately interrelated, and they have
co-evolved to produce the Earth we now live on.

The Earth has changed enormously over its long history, so much
so that it is almost like a succession of very different planets. With
each state, the composition of the planet's atmosphere, the configu-
ration of continents and oceans, the structure of the biosphere, and
the chemistry of the oceans varies profoundly. These changes are
brought about by physical, chemical, and biological causes, often
mutually interacting and bringing into play cascades of further
change. Sometimes, stabilizing mechanisms emerge as well. Now, as
the Anthropocene is beginning, it is worth examining this succession
of states, not least because the conditions on Earth in the near future
might well resemble some ancient planetary conditions.

Earth's Mobile Anatomy

At present, Earth's atmosphere is 78 percent nitrogen, about 21
percent oxygen, 0.9 percent argon, with traces of other gases such
as carbon dioxide, methane, water vapour, and ozone. Although
the atmosphere extends for about 480 km (300 miles) above the
Earth's surface, most of these gases are concentrated within the
lowest 16 km. Earth's atmosphere is radically different from that
of its sister planet Venus, where the atmosphere, some 90 times as
dense as Earth's, is composed mostly of carbon dioxide. Venus's
atmosphere is so loaded with this greenhouse gas that it is a hadean
world with surface temperatures around 400 °C (752 °F). On Earth,
by contrast, the large quantity of free oxygen in its atmosphere is a
telltale signature, detectable by the spectroscopic telescopes of alien
civilizations tens of light years away. It would tell those aliens that
the Earth has widespread liquid water at its surface, a weathering
cycle of nutrients to maintain life, a surface environment suitable

for photosynthesis, and organisms that store carbon in some combination of living bodies, skeletons, deep-sea sediments and soils. To
the aliens, that would certainly spark interest, for we now know such
a combination to be an extreme rarity among planets.

Just over 70 percent of the surface of the Earth is ocean-covered,
and from space our blue planet appears to be replete with water. But
the average depth of the oceans is just 4 km, and, when compared to
the diameter of the Earth, at 6,371 km, this is a thin skin – thinner in
relative terms than that of an apple. Water is just 0.05 percent of the
mass of the Earth, though it sustains all life on this planet. Earth's
oceans have persisted for 4,000 million years since their delivery to
our planet's surface by some combination of volcanic exhalations
and asteroid strikes. The chemicals dissolved within them, like silica,
calcium, and carbonate, are vital to the functioning of organisms,
such as tiny marine algae, which are the lungs of the ocean, responsible for generating much of its oxygen.

The chemicals in the sea are introduced from hot springs and
volcanoes at the seabed, and brought in by rivers from the weathering of rocks on land by air and water. Given how easily the weather
eventually breaks down even the highest mountains, one might ask why
all the rocks that ever formed on the land have not been completely
weathered back into the sea. This answer lies in the relationship
between water and the rock cycle, which runs deep into the interior
of the Earth, helping to sustain the process of plate tectonics.
The Earth's tectonic plates, 100 or more kilometers thick and up to
thousands of kilometers across, move relative to each other across the
Earth's surface about as fast as human fingernails grow, lubricated by
the water soaked into the Earth's crust from the oceans, and driven
by moving currents of rock in the hotter, more pliable mantle that
lies below the lithosphere. This process – unique, as far as we know,
to the Earth – drives the formation of mountains, by crumpling,
and so thickening, the crust where tectonic plates collide. From the
mountains flow the continuous supply of essential chemicals for
life, to be washed into the oceans. There is no such process on the
Moon or Mars, where the internal heat was dissipated long ago, and
where plate tectonics and a hydrological cycle do not operate. On
Earth, plate tectonics has operated in its current pattern for the last
3 billion years or so. Before that, the Earth seems to have had some
other fundamental mechanism of planetary heat release (the primary
"function" of plate tectonics) and a different crustal structure,
perhaps one in which continents and ocean basins were less clearly
defined than they are today.

Even within the Earth's core, there are processes that are vital to the maintenance of life, water, and an atmosphere at the surface. The core is composed mainly of iron, which is presently liquid between 2,890 and 5,150 km depth, and solid at yet greater depths, and is progressively solidifying. The core of the early Earth is thought to have been entirely liquid. Currents of dense molten metal in the outer core generate the Earth's magnetic field. This magnetosphere protects the Earth from the solar wind that would otherwise blow its oceans and atmosphere away. There would be no life at the surface of Earth without this protecting veil of magnetic force lines.

Living conditions also depend on planet-wide chemical cycles. Calcium and carbonate are weathered from rocks on the land by the action of rain and taken by rivers to the sea. There, once seawater becomes oversaturated in these chemicals, they precipitate to the sea floor as limestone, a process which in the last half-billion years has been mediated by organisms as diverse as algae, corals, and snails, which build their skeletons from calcium carbonate. This limestone formation, together with the burial of organic matter (the dead remains of once-living organisms) in strata, prevents carbon from accumulating in large quantities as carbon dioxide in the atmosphere. Thus, Earth avoids the hadean state of Venus. Other complex cycles involve phosphate, sulfur, potassium, nitrogen, and silica, and none of these would function without the interactions of water, air, rock, and life. Without the rock cycle, driven by plate tectonics, there would also be little or no formation of sediment, and therefore no building of enormous thicknesses of strata that continually refashion the Earth's surface. On the surface of the Moon, by contrast, the eyes of the "man in the moon" (the Sea of Rains and the Sea of Tranquility), visible from the northern hemisphere, are giant lava flows frozen in time from more than 3 billion years ago.

Long-Lived Changes in the Earth State

Changes to the Earth System can be transient, such as a warming of climate triggered by extra carbon dioxide released from unusually powerful volcanic outbursts, before climate is re-stabilized as excess levels of this greenhouse gas are removed from the atmosphere, over many millennia, by reaction with rocks at the Earth's surface. The *effects* of such transient warming can be permanent, though, if that warming phase causes extinctions that make biological evolution take a different course. Other Earth System changes can take our planet into a different state more or less permanently, with yet more profound consequences for the biosphere. The Anthropocene has already, in its brief existence, re-set the course of Earth's biological evolution, as we will see. And, just perhaps, it might bring with it a new long-lived state of the Earth System. To see how profoundly a planetary surface can be refashioned, one can examine how the Earth became oxygenated, between 2 and 3 billion years ago.

At present, oxygen is a major component of the Earth's atmosphere. It plays a vital role in the metabolism of most organisms. (One might think of it as turbo-charging these organisms by comparison with metabolisms – of sulfur bacteria, for example – that do not use *free* oxygen, O_2.) Oxygen is a major constituent, by mass, of the biosphere. It is also the main constituent of the Earth's crust and mantle, making up most of the material of silica (SiO_2) and silicate minerals, and of water (H_2O). But, free oxygen in a planetary atmosphere is a rarity, because it is soon used up in reacting with rocks (oxidizing them – i.e. causing them to rust) and with organic matter (oxidizing it to produce carbon dioxide gas). Earth would not be oxygen-rich unless free oxygen were continually replenished. Today, the amount of oxygen in the atmosphere is controlled by its daily production via photosynthesis, minus that which is used up in respiration. Longer-term, biogeochemical cycles involve, say, burying carbon deep in sedimentary rocks where it cannot react with atmospheric oxygen.

On the early Earth, before oxygen-producing photosynthesis evolved, Earth's atmosphere lacked oxygen. The original atmosphere, mostly formed through volcanoes degassing the interior of the planet, was probably rich in carbon dioxide and water vapor, probably with other volcanically emitted gases such as sulfur dioxide, hydrogen sulfide, nitrogen, argon, methane, helium, and hydrogen. When an oxygen-bearing atmosphere began to evolve, this change turned out to be essentially irreversible over billions of years, and transformed the Earth System.

The Oxygen Transformation

On the early Earth, soils would have formed as soon as there were continental areas that could be weathered, an atmosphere had formed, and water was widespread at the surface. The earliest record of soils, as fossilized traces of microbial mats on land, is from some 3.22 billion years ago (Homann et al. 2018). From about 3 billion years ago, there is widespread evidence of water flowing on the land, the action of rivers, and abundant microbial life (most evident on the sea floors of those days). The ancient rivers of that time (known as the Archean Eon) included kinds of sediment grain not found in river sands today, such as fool's gold (iron pyrite, FeS_2) and pitchblende (uranium ore, UO_2); both of these are unstable in the presence of free oxygen and soon oxidize to other minerals. Their presence in these ancient river deposits indicates that Earth's early atmosphere did not contain free oxygen. Fossilized soils termed a "paleosol" also preserved in rocks of this age suggest life on land (Crowe et al. 2013) – which was entirely microbial – that evolved in and was adapted to an anoxic world.

The Nsuze paleosol of South Africa, one such ancient soil that is dated to about 2.96 billion years ago, captures the beginnings of change to this planetary state. The soil formed on top of an ancient volcanic lava flow and was in turn buried under sediments that formed in rivers and seas. Much of this ancient soil was eroded away, but the part that remains contains chemical patterns that indicate the actions of microbes using free oxygen, and of the weathering of the lava flow beneath an oxygenated atmosphere. The levels of oxygen required to change the chemistry of the Nsuze soil are greater than can be produced by non-biological processes, and they suggest the presence of bacteria that were generating oxygen from photosynthesis.

At first, before 2.5 billion years ago, oxygen accumulated very slowly, in very small amounts in local "oxygen oases." Then, when it began to accumulate in the atmosphere, it was absorbed in oxidizing minerals like pyrite and pitchblende at the surface of the land. Once these oxygen "sinks" became saturated, free oxygen began to accumulate in the atmosphere and oceans. Large quantities of oxygen may be deduced from rock strata from about 2.4 billion years ago, perhaps reaching about one-tenth of their present atmospheric values (though there are widely diverging ideas about the level of oxygen at this time: Och and Shields-Zhou 2012). This interval of time (from 2.4 to 2.1 billion years ago), when significant amounts of free oxygen accumulated for the first time in the atmosphere, is the Great Oxygenation Event (GOE) that we first introduced in chapter 1. As one initial side-effect, the GOE changed global climate, creating an icehouse world (see below), as the strong greenhouse gas methane (CH_4) in the atmosphere was oxidized and converted to the weaker greenhouse gas carbon dioxide.

Oxygenic photosynthesis turned out to be irreversible. This process takes globally available materials of sunlight, water, and carbon dioxide, and uses these to generate carbohydrates as a store of chemical energy. The organisms that developed this ability had a big advantage over earlier organisms. Then, after the origins of oxygenic photosynthesis, other bacteria learned to use the by-product of this process, oxygen, for more efficient aerobic respiration (Soo et al. 2017). Thus, oxygen became a globally available – and increasingly biologically exploited – commodity at the Earth's surface. Metabolic pathways using oxygen generally yield more energy than those using anaerobic mechanisms, and so increased the available energy to the biosphere. It is likely that the complex bodies of animals could not have evolved without this mode of respiration, and thus the GOE had a long-term impact on the evolution of the biosphere, billions of years after it took place. This does not mean that anaerobic mechanisms of respiration vanished completely. Anaerobic respiration continued to exist and evolve, and some living organisms have the ability to use both aerobic and anaerobic metabolic pathways. Anaerobic mechanisms remain of critical importance to the cycling of nitrogen, iron, sulfur, and carbon through the biosphere.

Nitrogen, for example, is an element whose surface chemistry is profoundly changing in the Anthropocene (see chapter 3), modifying patterns that were established during the GOE (Canfield et al. 2010). In soils, plants assimilate nitrogen in the form of nitrate (NO_3), either absorbed from the soil or fixed by the bacterial process of nitrification. Nitrogen can be recycled back to the atmosphere through decomposition of nitrogen-rich plant tissues (by bacteria and fungi) that yield ammonia (NH_3), through bacterial nitrification processes that convert this back to NO_3, and then through the anaerobic respiration of denitrifying bacteria back to gaseous N_2. Humans now intervene by increasing – through brute chemistry on a massive scale – the nitrate input to plants. In a typical Anthropocene conjunction, this intervention perturbs a cycle that is more than 2 billion years old and feeds about 50 percent of the Earth's current human population, while also causing the loss of certain plant species, the depletion of soil nutrients, and, as runoff from fields, contaminated drinking water and the death of fish and other aquatic organisms (Galloway et al. 2013). These massive nitrate inputs also have economic, social, and political consequences as companies and communities, individual farmers, and international bodies deal with these outcomes – good as well as bad. As this example shows, the complexity of the Earth System is such that changing one factor reverberates throughout, affecting nearly everything.

Though forms of anaerobic metabolism like those of denitrifying bacteria have continued to thrive and evolve, the GOE curtailed the realms of obligate anaerobes – i.e. those microbes that are poisoned by the presence of oxygen. It confined these dominant forms of the first billion years of the biosphere to a much-reduced range of habitats – for instance, deeply buried in sediments. For obligate anaerobes, the evolution of an oxygenated atmosphere might be viewed as a catastrophe. These then made up most of life, and evidence has been unearthed of a crash in the Earth's biomass of at least 80 percent, and perhaps up to 99.5 percent, in the wake of the GOE (Hodgskiss et al. 2019) – the best part of a billion years after the time of the Nsuze soil, and of that first whiff of oxygen.

For about 1 billion years after the GOE, levels of atmospheric oxygen seem not to have exceeded around one-tenth of their present levels. In the oceans, too, dissolved oxygen was present in the surface waters, but probably not in the deep oceans, which appear to have remained essentially anoxic. The interval following the GOE is sometimes referred to by geologists as the "boring billion" and has been characterized as showing little indication of major climate change, or of major biological innovation. This may have been due to the sulfide-rich chemistry of the oceans, which limited the nutrients available to life. Nevertheless, despite these possibly widespread starvation conditions, near the beginning of this interval the fossil record shows the appearance of organisms that may be eukaryotes (see below), i.e. those that possess cells with complex membrane-bound organelles and a nucleus. They are the type of cells that make up the bodies of all animals, fungi, and vascular plants, and their evolution was probably another knock-on effect from the availability of free oxygen.

A further rise in oxygen occurred during the interval between 850 and 500 million years ago, and this is called the Neoproterozoic Oxygenation Event. This occurred a little before the widespread appearance of animals in the fossil record, between 550 and 540 million years ago. The elevation of oxygen levels to perhaps one-fifth of total atmospheric composition probably enabled the complex metabolisms of animals. Without such a high oxygen level, it is also unlikely that vascular plants could have evolved on the land from about 470 million years ago. High levels of oxygen have subsequently persisted on Earth, as is evident from the fossil record of fire, which extends back 350 million years to the beginnings of large-scale forests. The presence of fossilized burnt vegetation throughout this long interval indicates that atmospheric oxygen levels never dipped below 17 percent.

The (overall) progressive oxygenation of the Earth's surface has, therefore, been an extraordinarily protracted process, extending over more than half our planet's history. It included some major thresholds, but these affected the terrestrial and ocean domains to different extents and at different times. The GOE, itself in detail stretching from 2.4 to 2.1 billion years ago, for instance, was a phenomenon of the atmosphere and of land surfaces – and is one of the features that geologists use to distinguish the Proterozoic Eon from the Archean Eon. Afterwards, the bulk of the oceans, then, remained anoxic for more than a billion years. The Anthropocene conditions of today, wrought by technology-amplified biology – if they are sustained – may have similarly profound far-reaching effects to the GOE (Frank et al. 2018) in transforming the energy and material flows of a planet, though this potential transformation has been initiated in a matter of centuries, rather than the hundreds of millions of years of the GOE. The changes of the Anthropocene are not (yet) as fundamental as planetary oxygenation, but they have occurred *far* more abruptly, affecting both the terrestrial and oceanic realms simultaneously, considered in geological terms. There are other changes in deep geological time – some also wrought by biological organisms – that can be compared with the impact of the Anthropocene.

Changing Climates, and Prelude to an Earth System Revolution

The "boring billion" years of the Proterozoic Eon were ended by a decidedly un-boring event, technically known as the Cryogenian Period – and in the vernacular as "Snowball Earth." Between 720 and 635 million years ago, in two major phases, the Earth developed a carapace of ice covering most or all of its surface (there has been a long-running debate between the "most" and "all" camps), from pole to the equator and from land to ocean, which, at the height of the freeze, would have made the Earth more resemble one of Jupiter's or Saturn's icy moons than the welcoming globe of land and water we now know. A supremely hostile environment for life, one might think. But there are indications that the Cryogenian Period, counter-intuitively, was a driver, rather than barrier, to the development of complex multicellular life.

Strata from the narrow interval of climate warming – little more than 10 million years – between the two pulses of global glaciation

contain fossilized organic chemical biomarkers that suggest the
appearance of marine algae that, in that brief time, "broke the
incumbency" of the bacteria that had dominated global ecosystems
for billions of years (Brocks et al. 2017). Growth of the algae was
stimulated, they suggested, by a flood of nutrients into the sea,
scraped from the landscape by the glaciers of the first phase of the
Cryogenian. Sponges – simple animals – may also have appeared. If
this is correct, another of Earth's revolutions was triggered by extreme
physico-chemical conditions at the planet's surface, generating more
complex ecosystems that in turn triggered another revolution, this
time of eon-changing scale.

Before those larger eon-scale changes arose, geologists recognize an
Ediacaran Period (635–541 million years ago) abruptly following the
Cryogenian. The boundary between boulder-rich strata representing
glacial conditions and limestone strata representing a warmer Earth
is knife-sharp in places, suggesting that the collapse of the glaciers
was extremely rapid, perhaps catastrophically so. It is one of Earth
history's many examples of the crossing of a tipping point, where
an initial change (likely the beginning of ice melt, as levels of the
greenhouse gas carbon dioxide built up in the atmosphere, sourced
from volcanic emissions) was amplified and then made irreversible
by positive feedbacks (notably the increased heat absorption by
the Earth, as the strongly heat-reflective ice began to retreat in a
process that accelerated as ice was lost and more heat was absorbed
at the ocean surface). By such means, one kind of planet can rapidly
transform into another – a process which certainly has resonance for
the Anthropocene.

This transformation was used as the basis for setting up the
Ediacaran Period, a decision only agreed and ratified in 2004 (Knoll
et al. 2006). This late recognition reflects the difficulty of reconstructing Earth history – even for such a dramatic transformation
– in Precambrian rocks (those forming before 541 million years
ago), in which fossils (the usual time markers for geological strata)
are scarce. Deciphering this ancient history needed the use of other
forms of evidence instead of fossils, such as geochemical patterns
in the rocks, numerical ("absolute") dates of the rock strata derived
by analyzing their natural radioactivity, and so on. Even then, the
decision to define this new geological time period was, in a certain
sense, a leap of faith. This was the first geological boundary within
the ancient rocks of the Precambrian to be defined by means of a
carefully selected marker level within strata, which technically has
the cumbersome name of a Global Boundary Stratotype Section and

Point (GSSP), and, more colloquially, is known as a "golden spike." And while, at the place chosen for this boundary, in the Ediacara Hills of Australia, the boundary level selected is a knife-sharp change in the strata from glacially formed deposits to warm-water limestones, it was then still not quite certain that this transition was of the same age all around the world. Evidence gathered subsequently suggests that the collapse of glacial conditions did take place more or less synchronously (as far as can currently be established) across the Earth, and so the Ediacara Hills "golden spike" does represent a global change that can be traced (or correlated, as geologists say) in strata around the world, helping validate the Ediacaran as a useful formal period of time. Identification of the apparently rapid environmental change between the Cryogenian and the Ediacaran serves as a primary example of why geologists seek to identify and correlate synchronous events, permitting recognition of cause and effect between different components of the Earth System, and enabling a precise understanding of the Earth's evolution. A similar logic holds for the geological definition of the Anthropocene.

The Ediacaran Period itself was – barring one interval of glaciation midway through it – a relatively stable time. The strata sporadically include fossils that represent the "Ediacara Biota" – enigmatic organisms, some frond-like, others of varying shapes that cannot be firmly linked with any known animal or plant. Only recently, one of these, *Dickinsonia*, a curious segmented oval impression in these rocks, was shown to be a possible animal (a major advance in understanding) as traces of cholesterol, still detectable after more than 500 million years, were found on some exceptionally well-preserved specimens. Most of the Ediacaran organisms, for all their impressive shapes, were largely immobile, living attached to the sea floor and presumably taking in nutrients from the seawater that bathed them. Nevertheless, they were a prelude to a revolution yet to come.

The Animal Revolution

In a 30 million-year interval, starting some 550 million years ago, the world transformed – at least in the oceans – from its Precambrian state, one barely recognizable to us, to one that we would find familiar, with complex, highly active, animal-rich ecosystems. It represents a major evolutionary step change in the development of the biosphere, which is sometimes called the "Cambrian explosion" of life. It is associated with the appearance in the fossil record of animals that are bilaterally symmetrical, and have a recognizable head, and a gut and anus. This had a profound impact on the biosphere, for example producing a large standing biomass of marine animals, a substantial increase in the overall range of body types, and a significant increase in the size range of organisms. Some Cambrian apex predators, such as the nightmarish *Anomalocaris*, were formidable, their segmented bodies reaching a meter long, and bearing a pair of long, grasping appendages at the front. The animals affected the Earth System more widely – for instance, in changing the texture and chemistry of seawater (through the activities of myriad filter-feeders such as sponges, cleaning the water of oxygen-consuming organic detritus) and in burrowing deeply through the bottom sediments (ripping through the microbial mats of the seabed and altering the cycling of chemical elements between seawater and sea floor). The emergence of animal skeletons at that time, too, for both offense and defense, precipitated a biological arms race that has driven evolution until this day.

The 30-million-year span of this revolution (the duration makes its description by the geologist Preston Cloud as the "Cambrian eruption" more apt than that of an explosion) had several stages, which means that the task of defining a geological time boundary between the Ediacaran Period and the subsequent Cambrian Period was not straightforward. Some 550 million years ago, burrows started occurring in sedimentary deposits, marking the development of muscular animals with a head- and tail-end. A few million years later, organisms with mineralized skeletons emerged, at least in part as protection against predators. About 541 million years ago, a particularly distinctive "corkscrewing" kind of burrow, called *Treptichnus pedum*, represents the action of mobile worms, while, some 526 million years ago, a suite of small shelly fossils are the fragments of the skeletons of animals, many of which are still enigmatic. Around 5 million years later, the signature fossil of Cambrian times, the trilobite, began its long reign.

With this wealth of events, over such a long interval (Williams et al. 2014), which one should be used to mark the geological time boundary? The key question for the working group of the International Commission on Stratigraphy (ICS) pondering this problem was which one of these events was most likely to be practically effective, for working geologists, *as a time boundary*? The key factor is presumed synchroneity, rather than the presumed importance of any event to Earth history (all the events noted above were important to Earth history). Worldwide synchroneity of a geological marker will thus make for most precise *correlateability*, crucial to a functional time framework. Using this criterion, the best option at the time of boundary selection (in 1992) was decided to be the earliest appearance of the distinctive animal burrow *Treptichnus pedum* in strata, with the GSSP or "golden spike" being selected within a rock cliff at Fortune Head, in Newfoundland. It is an important boundary: it marks not only the beginning of the Cambrian Period, but also simultaneously of the Paleozoic Era which contains the Cambrian and five other periods, and also of the Phanerozoic Eon, within which we are still living.

A couple of decades later, the decision over this key boundary looked to some geologists to be the worse for wear. The *Treptichnus pedum* burrows turned out to appear in some different parts of the world at different times – and even at the GSSP section in Newfoundland, they were later found several meters below (i.e. in older strata) what had been presumed to be their earliest, boundary-defining occurrence (although, by the rules of the ICS, the boundary still remained as the one originally defined). It was suggested (Babcock et al. 2014) that the whole question of the Ediacaran–Cambrian boundary be re-opened, with the possibility that the boundary level be shifted, potentially to anywhere within that 30-million-year span. (Such an alteration can be made, as such formal geological time boundaries are not immutable, though they are required to remain stable for at least ten years.) If the Ediacaran–Cambrian boundary were altered, it would not mean that that interval of planetary history be fundamentally reinterpreted, or somehow be seen in a different light; it simply means that a rung of the time framework within which that history is assessed may become placed at a different level, so as to allow more effective analysis and communication. These considerations also – of practicality, and of the possibility of change of selected boundary level in the future, as more discoveries come to light – apply to the Anthropocene as well, as they apply indeed to all formal geological time intervals. The GTS is meant to be stable, but not to the point at which increasingly non-optimal solutions become petrified within it.

The Eon of Today: Biological Aspects

The Phanerozoic Eon, still continuing today, began about 541 million years ago. It comprises a little less than 12 percent of Earth time – and yet to many people (including most geologists), it represents the "normal" geology of familiarly fossil-rich strata, with trilobites and corals, mollusks, and (occasionally) dinosaurs. The fossils are not just there as an eloquent statement of abundant, evolving life. They are still the standard time-keepers for strata that allow a minutely detailed Earth history to be built, to a far greater extent than for the mostly paleontologically barren rocks of the Precambrian. The outlines of this history had already been worked out by the end of the nineteenth century, using fossil evidence, well before the numerical ages of those time divisions were established; today, this history has been elaborated and finely calibrated.

The Phanerozoic, and its formal subdivision within the Geological Time Scale, provides the real practical context for the Anthropocene as a geological unit. The GTS is more formally represented by the International Chronostratigraphic Chart of the ICS, which, in neatly arranged color-coded columns, shows all the main time units. (See preface, figure 1.) The Phanerozoic comprises only about an eighth of Earth's time-span – but it takes up about four-fifths of the column length of the GTS. This is because that history has been so much more finely divided, not only into periods – those periods are divided into epochs and those in turn into ages, representing a depth of under-standing that is simply not yet possible for the Precambrian. What kind of history, then, does the Phanerozoic represent, and how are those changes translated into formal time divisions?

The development of complex animal-rich ecosystems in the Phanerozoic was a major evolutionary step change in the devel-opment of the biosphere. These animal-rich ecosystems, from the Cambrian to the present day, were characterized by rapid species turnover, and, at times, subject to mass extinction events. Such extinction pulses happened when attributes that confer ecosystem resilience, such as species richness, and functional diversity and redundancy, were overwhelmed by environmental pressures of some kind, with resulting ecosystem collapse and massive species loss.

Since the Cambrian explosion of life, there have been five mass extinctions of life on Earth, characterized by the more or less sudden loss of 70 percent or more of species. But, despite these losses, no animal phylum (a very major group) has yet gone extinct. This too is an important statement, because it means that extinction events, though catastrophic, are in some sense redeemable. Biodiversity and ecosystems repair themselves over time, and ecologies such as reef systems, that are decimated by mass extinctions, can also reinvent themselves over time. Repair, though, typically takes millions or tens of millions of years for a complex species-rich ecosystem to emerge – albeit one populated by very different species from before.

Of the five mass extinctions in the Phanerozoic, four are used by geologists as the basis for major, era- or period-level boundaries, marking the ends of the Ordovician, Permian, Triassic, and Cretaceous periods (with the end-Permian and end-Cretaceous events simultaneously seeing the end of the Paleozoic and Mesozoic eras). The other mass extinction event, in late Devonian times, was a complex multi-phase event, extending over as much as 25 million years, though the last pulse occurred at approximately where the boundary of the Devonian with the succeeding period, the Carboniferous, is placed. The use of these catastrophic events is not so much to symbolize major global transformations but is more practical: the ending of one biological dynasty and the beginning of another means that their fossilized remains clearly fingerprint the strata. Mesozoic marine strata, for instance, can be recognized – even by a beginner – by the wealth of fossilized ammonites and belemnites they contain. These distinctive mollusk families (and many other fossil species, large and small) abruptly disappeared in the violent aftermath of the asteroid impact that, 66 million years ago, terminated the Cretaceous Period (and Mesozoic Era), and are replaced by other kinds of fossils in strata of the succeeding Paleogene, the first period of the Cenozoic Era that we still live in.

The end-Cretaceous event was one of the few truly abrupt major changes in Earth history. (Anthropocene changes to date are almost as abrupt, though it is not yet certain – the next few decades and centuries will be crucial here – whether they will be as major and far-reaching.) It is therefore logical that the consequent geological time boundary is tied to the bottom of the thin but worldwide debris layer, rich in the element iridium and in tiny frozen rock-melt spherules that resulted from the impact. The other four mass extinction events, driven by intrinsic changes in the Earth's environment, were more protracted, spanning many thousands to some millions of years, giving rise to the same kind of difficult decision-making process in defining the associated boundaries as happened in defining the beginning of the Cambrian Period.

The "Big Five" mass extinctions and their recovery intervals help define large-scale time units. Between these, there were more minor mass extinction events and their converse, bursts of evolutionary radiation of different organism groups. Such events commonly provide boundary markers for finer-scale divisions of the Geological Time Scale, such as epochs and ages.

Other biospheric changes have a less direct relationship with the Geological Time Scale. From about 470 million years ago, in the

Ordovician Period, a complex terrestrial plant biosphere began to evolve, with spores of mosses being washed into marine sediments as a record of the transformation – literally the greening – of the land (Wellman and Gray 2002). Later, the first vascular plants evolved to colonize the land during the Silurian Period, and the first large-scale forests formed about 365 million years ago during the Late Devonian Period. As these forests developed and spread in the succeeding Carboniferous Period, terrestrial plants were on their way to forming the largest standing biomass on the planet, currently weighing in at 450 billion tonnes of carbon (Bar-On et al. 2018). The burgeoning plants engineered environments for animals (first arthropods and later vertebrates) to colonize the land, and produced major changes in the weathering of rocks and soil, modifying wider chemical cycles such as that of carbon. These changes developed progressively across three geological periods, but do not provide the boundary marker for any of them (though this phenomenon is recognized through the name of the Carboniferous Period, from the burial of its swamp forests to become coal seams).

That this enormously significant event does not overtly provide a geological time boundary is not as surprising as it at first seems. The development of a terrestrial biosphere was slow, patchy, poorly preserved (as it is harder to fossilize organisms on land than in the sea), and took place in different patterns on different continents (as it is easier to isolate a land mass than a part of the ocean). All of this means that there are fewer specific events in this land-based history that can be used as global time markers. Nevertheless, the *globally synchronous* time markers established in marine strata for that long-time interval are indispensable to analyzing the course of biosphere development on land, even given the difficulty of correlating between the terrestrial and marine realms.

Many of the forces acting on, and driving change in, the biosphere are driven in one way or another by climate. Even in the asteroid impact that terminated the Mesozoic Era, and the massive volcanic outbursts that had previously brought the Paleozoic to a close, many of the biological consequences were driven by climatic consequences of these physically driven changes, either by sudden freezes as sun-blocking dust or ash was thrown into the air, or rapid spikes in global warming as the atmosphere was quickly loaded with greenhouse gases (or both in quick succession). Moving closer to the geological present, climate change of a (generally) more ordered kind becomes ever more important in defining the units of the Geological Time Scale, particularly as the latest of Earth's Ice Ages has developed.

The Eon of Today: Climatic Aspects

The geological record shows widespread evidence of changes in the global climate that take place on the scale of tens of millions to just a few years. We discuss the climate system in more detail in chapter 4, but here note how patterns of past climate change have helped shape the Geological Time Scale, to help consider how contemporary climate change might relate to the Anthropocene.

Today, the vast body of ice covering the southern polar continent of Antarctica exceeds 4 kilometers thick in places, and extends across more than 5,000 kilometers. Only the tips of Patagonian-sized mountains appear above its surface, while entire high-relief regions, like the Gamburtsev Mountains, are completely submerged beneath it, detected only by geophysical surveys that remotely penetrate the ice. It was not always so. In the Cretaceous Period, more than 66 million years ago, Antarctica had forests and even dinosaurs. The Earth was then in a greenhouse state, and it did not have permanent polar ice sheets.

This greenhouse state persisted across the Cretaceous–Paleogene boundary, and its asteroid-impact-driven mass extinction. The beginning of the subsequent (and present) icehouse, 33.6 million years ago, is precisely timed because the rapid (in ~200,000 years) growth of the Antarctic ice sheet can be clearly detected in chemical signatures preserved in the fossilized calcium carbonate skeletons of marine unicellular organisms called foraminifera. The shells of these organisms react to changes in the chemistry of seawater as ice sheets grow and melt, and also to the temperature of the water. Ice sheets advanced in the Antarctic as global carbon dioxide levels dropped. This event, a tipping point in the Earth System, is now represented in the GTS by the beginning of the Oligocene Epoch within the Cenozoic Era.

Much later, ice grew in the northern polar region too. About 3 million years ago, the closure of the Central American Isthmus between North and South America, and the continuing narrowing of the Indonesian Seaway between the Pacific and Indian oceans, deflected warm surface ocean water into the north Atlantic and Pacific oceans, respectively. There, the moisture that accumulated in the atmosphere, above a warmer sea, fell as snow across North America in what has been called a "snow gun" effect (Haug et al. 2005). As the snow built up to form a major ice sheet on the North American continent, feedback effects (such as reflecting the Sun's heat and light by what was, in effect, the construction of a gigantic ice mirror) cooled the hemisphere as a whole, extending the reach of the ice, which grew thicker on Greenland and northern mountainous areas. Climate changed more widely across the world, too – spreading wind-blown dust across central Europe and Asia as the cooler climate also became more arid, and creating savannah regions in Africa at the expense of rainforest. As one (then) minor consequence, a cluster of hominin species (representatives of our genus *Homo*, and the closely related *Australopithecus*) thrived on the newly opened landscape, and began to walk across it on two legs.

This development of a global, bipolar glaciation from the one that, over 30 million years, had been unipolar and centered on Antarctica, is reflected in the definition of the Quaternary Period (which we still live in) of the Cenozoic Era. This definition has had a curious history, with some resonance for the Anthropocene. In earlier studies, which were largely Europe-based, the first major cooling of these bipolar Ice Ages had seemed to come with the arrival of cold-water mollusk species into the Mediterranean about 1.8 million years ago, and the boundary was placed at that level. As time passed, though, evidence from around the world suggested the major threshold in fact took place at around 2.6 million years ago. Sharp debate took place between those who wanted the boundary retained where originally placed, citing the need for stability of the timescale, and those who wanted the boundary moved to the older level, a level that could be more easily recognized and more comfortably used in practice by many geologists working on Ice Age strata. After considerable debate (and, indeed, the temporary disappearance of the Quaternary as a whole), the boundary was moved to be at 2.6 million years (Gibbard and Head 2010), to the satisfaction of most (but not all) of the geological community.

Deciding where exactly to place the boundary was not straight-forward, though, as the threshold into the bipolar world was not abrupt, but took several hundred thousand years. At this scale, the main climate pattern of the Quaternary (indeed of late Cenozoic time in general, extending back over millions of years) is rhythmic and predictable glacial and warm (interglacial) phases, driven by changes in the Earth's orbit and spin (see chapter 4). Modulation of this astronomical "pacemaker of the Ice Ages" into a pattern with slightly deeper lows (and raised highs) was only gradual, when seen at this scale (Lisiecki and Raymo 2005). There are no particularly signif-icant species extinctions or appearances (at least of the common and widely used kinds of fossils used for dating strata) that offered use as a "primary marker" for the beginning of the Quaternary, either. So, instead, the boundary and its "golden spike" were based on an event of almost no environmental or climatic significance – one of the geologically occasional "flips" in the Earth's magnetic field, in which north pole becomes south, and south becomes north. The resultant, almost instantaneous geomagnetic change can be widely traced in strata (both marine and terrestrial) as changes in the alignment of magnetic particles – it is an effective practical marker for a geological time division which is otherwise characterized by a new climatic state of the Earth.

The Quaternary is marked by over 100 major transitions from glacial to interglacial climate (the boundary is set within the 104th transition from the present – though note that an interglacial state is still set within an overall icehouse world, *just with less ice than a glacial*). All but one of these are placed within the epoch that makes up the great bulk of Quaternary time – the Pleistocene. The Quaternary is thus marked by climate change – though, *highly* significantly for the Anthropocene, it has been a level of change that, so far, has occurred as an oscillation within fixed limits, and which the biosphere has adapted to. The Quaternary, for all of this febrility of climate, did not see any marked rise in species extinction rates, at least until human impact became significant some 50,000 years ago.

The latest of the interglacial phases is separated off as the Holocene Epoch, and marks an interval, now nearly 12 millennia long, of considerable stability of climate and sea level. The transition from the last glacial pulse of the Pleistocene Epoch was protracted, with carbon dioxide levels and sea level changing from "glacial" to "interglacial" levels over more than 10 millennia, and including some abrupt millennial-scale climate reversals, particularly in the northern hemisphere (and offset in a kind of climate "seesaw" pattern from more muted climate changes in the southern hemisphere). The Pleistocene–Holocene boundary has nevertheless been precisely placed, at a level, 11,700 years ago, within the last steep major northern hemisphere warming in climate toward interglacial conditions, though sea level was to keep rising for another 5 millennia, as the polar ice masses slowly melted before stabilizing.

The Holocene is three orders of magnitude shorter than the next-shortest epoch (the Pleistocene), but makes good sense geologically: its extensive sedimentary deposits make up the deltas, coastal plains, and river floors upon which much of humanity lives. The Holocene's relatively benign and relatively stable conditions allowed many human beings to develop agriculture, and the settlements that eventually gave rise to complex, literate urban societies. Only during the Holocene did some groups of people begin to build villages, then towns and cities, and progressively over millennia transform forest and savannah into farmland; transport species such as dogs, cats, pigs, and rats across the world; and develop many warring empires. Holocene deposits are locally rich in archeological remains, and this human imprint is one of the key characteristics of this epoch, which is, formally, still the one that we live in. Nevertheless, despite these emerging and intensifying human impacts, up until now the Holocene timescale has still been classified on the basis of geology. A recent subdivision into three sub-epochs (of which we now live in the latest one, termed the Meghalayan, which began 4,200 years BP, or around 2250 BCE) has been based on two brief and temporary "climate blips," each lasting a few centuries, rather than on any markers from the emerging human record.

In the past few centuries, and especially in the last century, human impacts have greatly increased, to the point that they are, in the words of an article that has already become a classic, "overwhelming the great forces of Nature" (Steffen et al. 2007). The magnitude of these human impacts seems, in the minds of many scholars, to justify a new epoch of the Geological Time Scale: the one called the Anthropocene. We will describe this new planetary situation, and the growth of this concept and its significance, in the chapters that follow.

3

The Anthropocene as a Geological Time Unit and the Great Acceleration

Discovering an Ancient Earth

Although the Anthropocene is a recent phenomenon, it is best understood in the context of deep geological time, a time far longer than the human historical record. Natural philosophers Nicolas Steno (1638–86) and Robert Hooke (1635–1703) were among the first to recognize fossils as relics of some prehistoric world (Rudwick 2016). A wider realization of the scale of geological time came only in the late eighteenth century, with two key figures, Georges-Louis Leclerc, the comte de Buffon, and the Scottish farmer and natural philosopher James Hutton. All of these thinkers drew on ideas that we now classify separately as "scientific" and "humanistic," but in their time this multidisciplinary understanding called "natural philosophy" was the norm. In other words, the modern vision of deep geological time emerged through both physical and philosophical investigations of Earth and the place of humanity within it. In many ways, this vision is one to which, in the Anthropocene, we now seek to return.

Buffon was one of the leading figures of the Enlightenment in pre-Revolutionary France, rivaling such figures as Voltaire (1694–1778) and Diderot (1713–84). Best known for his contributions to biological thinking, Buffon founded his reputation upon his encyclopedic, 36-volume *Histoire naturelle*, published through much of his working lifetime. Late in life, though, in 1778, he published a book, *Les Époques de la nature* (Buffon 2018), short and vividly written (too vividly written for some of his peers, one of whom chided him for writing for "chambermaids ... and lackeys"), which may claim to be the first scientifically based Earth history.

The Earth, Buffon said, evolved from a molten ball of material, that cooled, solidified, acquired oceans through the condensation of water vapor, formed sedimentary strata through the weathering and reworking of primary crystalline rock, went through a phase of spectacular volcanic outbursts, and acquired its pattern of continents through the foundering of the ocean basins. Different forms of life appeared and disappeared – Buffon was quite clear that the ammonites and belemnites he collected around his country estate represented animals that no longer lived on Earth. He proposed seven epochs of Earth history representing these various phases of planetary activity – and only in the last of these did humans appear and, late in *their* history, begin to change climate by cutting down forests for farmland and building cities, and to change the nature of living organisms by the domestication of plants and animals.

To build this Earth history, Buffon had to smash the biblical timescale of 6,000 years. The cooling to the present, calculated experimentally from how long it took iron balls to cool from red heat, he said, needed at least 75,000 years – and in *Les Époques* he hinted that the great thicknesses of strata that he saw probably required even longer spans of time (his private notes mooted figures of up to 3 million years). Even his published timescale was a provocation to the religious establishment, he knew, so he wrote a "First discourse" to the book arguing that his "purely theoretical" ideas could not impact the "unchanging verities" of the Bible. This diplomacy more or less worked: there was some grumbling amongst the clerics, but Buffon's carefully chosen words spared him serious persecution.

Buffon's timescale was long, with humans as a late addition, but it was still finite, comprising one cycle. The Earth's present mountains, to Buffon, represented the eroded remains of the wrinkles that formed on the globe's surface as it cooled and contracted. A few years later, James Hutton inferred a vastly larger timescale for the Earth, which he took to be essentially infinite, involving repeated cycles of destruction and renewal of the Earth's surface. His key evidence, discovered as he explored the landscapes of southern Scotland, came from the remains he found there of vastly more ancient landscapes (see chapter 2). He saw Earth history as a succession of such cycles "with no vestige of a beginning, or prospect of an end" (Hutton 1899 [1795]).

Building the Geological Time Scale

The Geological Time Scale was built upon this new realization of an ancient and changing Earth. Crucially to understanding of the Anthropocene, it was not so much built by an elaboration of Buffon's epochs – units of historical time, albeit inferred from geological evidence – but upon successive units of *strata* which represented geological time and events even before the age of the Earth had been ascertained. An Italian mining engineer, Giovanni Arduino (1714–95), in 1759 described, in a couple of letters to an academic colleague, a practical classification of rocks in the Italian Alps, from "Primary" crystalline rocks of the mountains, to the "Secondary" hardened strata that overlay these rocks, to "Tertiary" softer strata of the foothills, and a "fourth Order" of recent sedimentary deposits that was to become the Quaternary.

Arduino's classification evolved into the GTS we use today, in which specific rock units were used as a basis for the time units: the limestones of the Jura Mountains became the basis of the Jurassic; a rock succession including thick coal layers became the Carboniferous; the distinctive chalk strata of western Europe formed the Cretaceous, and so on. The emphasis on strata gave rise to a "dual nomen-clature" of rock and time units that is unique to geology. Thus, there is both a Jurassic *System* (the strata worldwide that are of Jurassic age: a physical unit that can be walked across, hammered, sampled, measured) and an exactly parallel Jurassic *Period* (the time interval that those rocks represent – an intangible unit of long-vanished time, in which dinosaurs lived and died and volcanoes erupted). Given that virtually all of Earth history can *only* be inferred from evidence in the rocks, this "dual nomenclature," with its emphasis on the rock record, is regarded by many geologists as central to Earth's timescale.

This arrangement turned out to provide an effective common language to navigate the enormous span of Earth history: Earth time turned out to be not quite endless, as Hutton had surmised, but to be enormous nonetheless, at 4.54 billion years. Our own species, *Homo sapiens*, appeared extremely late within this history – some 300,000 years ago, within the Pleistocene Epoch that makes up most of the 2.6-million-year-long Quaternary Period (the only unit to formally survive from Arduino's original classification) – while settled human civilization began in, and slowly spread during, the Holocene Epoch, which began 11,700 years ago, as the glaciers underwent their latest of many retreats.

Such is the context for any formal consideration of the Anthropocene as a potential geological time unit. Following Buffon, in the nineteenth and twentieth centuries, there were sporadic suggestions that humans were changing the Earth's geology. Most did not stem from the geological community within which the GTS was evolving. So, for most of that time, most geologists – if they were indeed aware of these suggestions – regarded them as fringe ideas.

Antecedents of the Anthropocene Concept

Ideas that humans have altered the Earth date from at least the seventeenth century. Thinkers such as René Descartes (1596–1650) and Francis Bacon (1561–1626) preceded the insights of Buffon and Hutton, in suggesting that humans had developed a dominance over nature, though these suggestions lacked the context of a deep Earth history. The historian of science Jacques Grinevald has studied these early roots of the Anthropocene concept (Grinevald 2007; Grinevald et al. 2019) and demonstrated their sometimes tenuous relation to the modern concept (Hamilton and Grinevald 2015).

In the mid to late nineteenth century, the neologism "Anthropozoic" appeared, coined to "assert human sovereignty over the world by divine decree" (Hansen 2013). It was used by the Welsh theologian and geologist Thomas Jenkyn (1854a, b; see Lewis and Maslin 2015), then by the Dublin geology professor and reverend, Samuel Haughton (1865), and later by the Italian priest and geologist Antonio Stoppani in his *Corso di geologia* (1873). Stoppani pronounced humanity to be a new force that was "unknown in ancient worlds," and that not only was changing the present but would change the future too.

Other terms appeared, variously synonymous with the Anthropozoic. The US geologist Joseph Le Conte in the 1870s coined the term "Psychozoic" as the "Age of Man" as an alternative to the widely used geological time term "Recent" (proposed by the hugely influential British geologist Charles Lyell for post-glacial time, and eventually replaced by the Holocene [Gervais 1867–9]). There was the Russian Anthropogene, too (sometimes transcribed Anthropocene), though this was in effect a synonym of the Quaternary Period, the time of the Ice Ages, without the implications of human dominance over geology that were present in the Anthropozoic and the Psychozoic.

From further away from geology came the related term "noösphere," a "sphere of human thought," a concept that arose in early 1920s Paris between the philosopher/priest and paleontologist Pierre Teilhard de Chardin, the philosopher and mathematician Édouard Le Roy, and the Russian scientist Vladimir Vernadsky. There were the beginnings, too, of cataloguing of material human impacts, made in environmental and geographical terms by George Perkins Marsh (1864, 1874), widely regarded as the "father of American conservation," and later via the more geologically oriented analysis of Robert Sherlock (1922), who assembled impressive data on the mass of minerals extracted, coal burnt, and earth and rock moved by humans.

This was a wide array of ways of suggesting that humans had brought something new and powerful to this planet, spanning a range that went from more or less straightforward geology to more abstract formulations, some with a religious slant. Meanwhile, progress in geology was showing ever more clearly the billion-year scale of Earth history, which demonstrably included extraordinary geographic changes and successions of biological dynasties – some that terminated catastrophically. Against such a backcloth, human importance appeared to recede, to a geologist, almost to vanishing point. Edward Wilber Berry (1925) expressed a common attitude among twentieth-century geologists when, talking about the Psychozoic, he said the idea of human productions being of geological magnitude was a "false assumption ... altogether wrong in principle" and "a surviving or atavistic principle from the holocentric philosophy of the Middle Ages."

Ideas that human activity *could* be significant, even on such an enormous stage of time and process, emerged only fitfully in the immediate post-World War II years. Studies of the ocean and atmosphere, of biogeochemical cycles, and of the biological fabric of our planet, provided the keys to finally recognizing the nature and scale of human impact – even as that impact was intensifying and developing new forms of perturbation. The emerging environmental movement was significant here – for example, the influential study *The limits to growth* by the Club of Rome (discussed in chapter 7). The International Geosphere–Biosphere Programme (IGBP) of the late twentieth century had a key role. In this large, highly multidisciplinary program, the science of an integrated "Earth System" was developed, with analysis of emerging global environmental issues such as climate change, acid rain, habitat destruction, and biodiversity loss.

Realization came that some of these changes, albeit brought about within a geological eyeblink, would have consequences that would persist for many thousands, and even millions, of years. In 1992, the science journalist Andrew Revkin, in a book on global warming, suggested that the world had entered a geological interval he called the "Anthrocene." The biologist Andrew Samways, in 1999, coined the term "Homogenocene" to highlight the unprecedented scale and transglobal nature of species invasions, while the fisheries biologist Daniel Pauly (2010) suggested the term "Myxocene," an age of jellyfish and slime, to reflect human-driven changes to the oceans.

Paul Crutzen's Intervention

All these terms could be justified by the evidence presented, but none had the impact that Paul Crutzen's improvisation of the term "Anthropocene" at an International Geosphere–Biosphere Programme meeting in Mexico had in 2000. Becoming irritated by constant reference to various forms of global change in the Holocene, he broke into the discussion to say that we were no longer in the Holocene, but in the ... (there followed a pause as Crutzen tried to put together his thoughts) ... the Anthropocene. This on-the-spot invention became a topic of discussion at the meeting. Later, Crutzen researched it, discovered that the lake ecologist Eugene Stoermer had independently invented the term, simply to use among his colleagues and students. He contacted Stoermer (though the two men never met) and they jointly published the term in the *IGBP Newsletter*. The term attained much wider circulation when Crutzen published it in a vivid one-page article in *Nature* in 2002. Crutzen was an atmospheric chemist, not a geologist, but his rationale, of altered chemistry of air and oceans, and a massively perturbed biosphere, was combined with the overt suggestion that the Holocene had terminated, making the Anthropocene a new geological epoch, the beginning of which he placed at the Industrial Revolution.

"Anthropocene" won out over "Anthrocene" not because the added syllable makes any difference, but because of the reach of the people who coined the terms. Andrew Revkin is a highly scientifically literate, even visionary, journalist, but Paul Crutzen was then the world's most-cited scientist, working within a large and influential community: simply, he was the right person in the right time and place to launch such a new term in a way that would quickly embed it into common use. "The Anthropocene" very quickly became used by the IGBP / Earth System science community (e.g. Meybeck 2003; Steffen et al. 2004) in a matter-of-fact way, as if it was a standard term. Few of the scientists of that community would have been aware of – or, perhaps, cared about – the complex bureaucratic procedures that geological stratigraphers used to assess and verify formal terms within the GTS.

Geological Analysis

Geological stratigraphers took a little while to realize that Crutzen's improvisation was emerging in the literature with sufficient force to be more than a passing fashion. Discussions started at the Geological Society of London's Stratigraphy Commission in May 2006. This is a national body, and therefore has no formal authority over international nomenclature – that being the prerogative of the International Commission on Stratigraphy and its various subcommissions and working groups. Nevertheless, it could consider the matter, and express a collective opinion. In 2008, it published a discussion paper in the journal *GSA Today* (Zalasiewicz et al. 2008), authored by 21 out of its 22 members, who were stratigraphers chosen for their technical expertise, representing academia, industry, and national institutes. In this preliminary geological study, it was mooted that the Anthropocene might be considered as a potential unit of the GTS.

The wording was characteristically cautious, partly because this assessment *was* very preliminary, and partly because the GTS is in many ways the backbone of geology, the device by which 4.54 billion years of crowded history, and an enormous – and enormously complex – rock record, can be deciphered. It is meant to be stable, to form part of the common language of geologists across different countries, and between different generations. Additions and revisions to it are carried out only slowly and grudgingly, based on overwhelming evidence – and overwhelming support from the geologists involved in the decision-making, with supermajority (over 60 percent) votes in favor being needed at each level of consideration. Decisions are not taken quickly – the processes involved can take several decades. Indeed, quite a number of long-used units of the GTS have yet to be formally defined and ratified. The base of the Cretaceous System – and simultaneously the beginning of the Cretaceous Period – still remains unformalized, for instance, not because of any doubt regarding the use and integrity of the Cretaceous as a geological time unit, but because of the technical complexity and duration of the formalization process. There are also some widely used *informal* time terms, such as "the Precambrian" and "the Tertiary," useful because their nature and limits are clearly understood by scientists. Few other fields operate with the slow, formalized deliberateness of geology – in the sphere of geological time nomenclature, at least – an important context for the Anthropocene.

The geological assessment differed from that of Crutzen and his colleagues in another way. The Earth System scientists, in proposing the Anthropocene Epoch, talked of change in environmental parameters – of new chemical components of the air, or species made extinct or translocated to new terrains. The geologists, by contrast, were looking for evidence of global change petrified within the rock itself. This makes sense for almost all of Earth history, where the only guide to that history is in the rock archive: as fossilized animals and plants, chemical patterns, mineral assemblages, stratal textures. From the totality of this geological *proxy* evidence, the history of ancient climate, geography, biosphere sickness and health, volcanic eruptions, and many other events on Earth has been worked out. With each successive study, this history becomes more clearly elucidated. There is no other way to reach into our planet's long past.

Therefore, geologists are less concerned with the historical events themselves – which have long vanished, and can only be reconstructed as models or narratives, the veracity of which is only as good as the evidence. Rather, they focus on the evidence base, the rock strata (i.e. fossilized sediment layers) and all that they contain. These strata form the chronostratigraphic timescale, parallel to the geochronological one (Zalasiewicz et al. 2013). Thus, the geologists' main focus is on a putative Anthropocene Series, comprising all of the material sediment layers deposited during the time of the Anthropocene Epoch. This crucial evidence base allows comparison between recent times (when humans have made systematic observations) and ancient times (where only the rocks have recorded the events).

For each ancient epoch, the layers of strata were deposited long ago, and there is a record of its beginning (the oldest layers, which lie upon the strata of a yet older epoch) and its end (its youngest layers, which are in turn overlain by the strata of a younger epoch). For the epoch of the present – which is still formally the Holocene – there is a succession of sediment layers already deposited over the past 11,700 years, there are sediment layers that are being laid down right now, and there are sediment layers that are still to form, in the future, for however long the epoch is deemed to last. If the Anthropocene is to be formalized as an epoch, then the youngest layers of what is now considered the Holocene will be transferred into the Anthropocene, which from then will represent the strata now forming and the strata still to come.

A surprising range of processes can be recorded in rock strata. The stratospheric, ozone-destroying chlorofluorocarbons on which Paul Crutzen made a good part of his considerable reputation, for instance, can leave faint traces in polar ice, detectable after ~1950 CE. Carbon dioxide and methane are also preserved in bubbles in polar ice strata, and the additional, human component of carbon dioxide in the air has a distinctive isotopic composition, inherited from burnt fossil fuels. These isotopic patterns are in turn absorbed within the skeletons of ocean plankton and corals and in tree rings. Some kinds of evidence are known to be biased. The fossil record that represents biosphere history is dominated by skeleton-bearing organisms, while fossils of soft-bodied organisms such as jellyfish are rare. Nevertheless, despite these gaps and biases, the stratal record is packed with information about both the shallow past and the deep geological past (and new kinds of proxies keep being discovered to further enrich the geohistorical narratives).

The preliminary assessment by the Geological Society of London led to an invitation from the Subcommission on Quaternary Stratigraphy, one of the component bodies of the International Commission on Stratigraphy, to set up an international working group to examine, formally, whether the Anthropocene might become part of the GTS (more technically, of the International Chronostratigraphic Chart). As one of the members of that working group was later to note, the process, compared with examination of any other geological time unit, was in essence upside down (Barnosky 2014). All the other units – the Jurassic, and Cambrian, and Pleistocene and Holocene, were based on long study of the strata, from which the units of geological "time-rock" of chronostratigraphy (representing in effect distinct dynasties of Earth history) emerged. In the case of the Anthropocene, the concept emerged with little consideration of the rock record, and a major task of the working group was to build on – and test (to the point of destruction, if necessary) – the geological evidence sketched out by the Stratigraphy Commission.

Another innovation was the composition of the Anthropocene Working Group. Previously, such working groups were composed almost entirely of geology-based specialists such as paleontologists, geochemists, and experts in rock dating methods. In the Anthropocene, in which human and environmental histories overlap with – and are often inextricably intertwined with – geological history, a range of additional expertise was needed. So archeologists, geographers, Earth System scientists, historians, oceanographers, and other specialists were invited to collaborate with the geological stratigraphers. There is even an international lawyer, helping to explore the utility of a formalized Anthropocene for wider communities – a question that simply does not arise for other units of the GTS.

The major questions to resolve were straightforward. Would the geological reality of the Anthropocene stand up to scrutiny? There was no guarantee that it would, and if the characteristics of the Anthropocene on closer examination turned out to grade insensibly into those of the Holocene, then the Anthropocene might be better suited as a general informal metaphor of human impact on Earth. Part of the resolution of this question hinged on how clearly this potential geological time unit could be characterized, defined, and traced. In particular, the boundaries of geological time units must aim to be both clear and *synchronous* across the planet. This insistence on synchroneity in part results from the diachronous, or time-transgressive, nature of so many geological phenomena (a classic example being a stratum of beach sand that can be of different ages in different places, the beach having migrated across the landscape as sea level changed).

Hence, the boundaries of many other kinds of geological units are more or less diachronous. This is particularly the case with lithostratigraphic (i.e. "rock") units, as in one representing such an ancient beach stratum. It is even the case with fossil-based biozones (termed biostratigraphic units). Such biozones are widely used as age indicators for rocks but, as the fossil species upon which these units are based took time to migrate across the world from where they first evolved, biozonal boundaries are rarely *precisely* synchronous. The synchronous time boundaries afforded by chronostratigraphy/ geochronology therefore provide a framework to allow such complex geological histories to be clearly charted in time and across space, with maximum precision and clarity. Geology requires synchronously bounded time units, but this is not true for other fields. For instance, archeology (discussed in chapter 6) has created time units such as the Mesolithic, Neolithic, and Bronze Age, which mark human cultural levels: the time boundaries of these units are understood to be different in different regions.

Synchroneity of chronostratigraphic boundary markers trumps the degree of significance of Earth System change. For example, the Ordovician–Silurian boundary marks one of the great upheavals of our planet, with a brief fierce glacial pulse linked with marked sea-level changes, two closely spaced pulses of mass extinction, and a profound episode of ocean anoxia. Yet the chosen boundary was not placed at any of these momentous events that propelled change from the Ordovician world into the Silurian one, but was placed a little later than any of them, at the appearance of a species of fossil zooplankton – an environmentally trivial event but, crucially, one that was thought to provide the best time marker worldwide (Zalasiewicz and Williams 2013). This precondition of synchroneity sets rigorous constraints upon the viability of the Anthropocene in geology that are irrelevant in other disciplines such as archeology, ecology, and history.

Another major question was the hierarchical level of the Anthropocene. Should it be set at a relatively high-rank level such as that of a period/system (to imply the Quaternary has terminated, as suggested by Bacon and Swindles [2016]), or even an era/erathem? Or should it be a subdivision of the Holocene, as an age/stage? Factors here include the perceived magnitude of the change, and also impacts on the architecture of the GTS as a whole. Currently, most members of the Anthropocene Working Group judge "epoch" to be an appropriate and conservative designation (Zalasiewicz et al. 2017a). The changes associated with the Anthropocene are considered sufficiently far reaching to produce an Earth System state distinct from that of the Holocene, with geologically long-term consequences. It is some measure of the scale of human impact.

When Did the Anthropocene Begin?

The beginning, or base, of the Anthropocene soon became a major issue. Crutzen's (2002) suggestion of the Industrial Revolution at *circa* 1800 seemed at first eminently reasonable. This approximated to the European beginning of major industrialization and fossil-fuel use, and roughly coincided with the start of what was to become a steep upturn in atmospheric carbon dioxide levels. But, crucially for geologists, there was no obvious sharp, globally synchronous geological marker at or very near that level. And, as wider interest in the Anthropocene grew, other suggestions appeared. They ranged across a broad spectrum.

Scholars who focused on the history of how human civilization grew and interacted with the environment emphasized the significant human footprint – from hunting, deforestation, farming – going back well into the Holocene and even into the Pleistocene (as discussed in chapter 6). Although much of this change was gradual, regional, and highly time-transgressive, some inferred changes were global. The beginning of a very slight, sustained rise in carbon dioxide some 7,000 years ago (and of methane some 5,000 years ago) has been ascribed to early farming (Ruddiman 2003, 2013). This remains controversial (see chapter 4). Nevertheless, the total range of evidence of early human impact is impressive, and has been used to support an "early Anthropocene," said to start "thousands of years ago."

A little later, metal pollution signals associated with late Bronze Age (c.3000 BP) or Roman (c.2000 BP) lead smelting (Wagreich and Draganits 2018), and soil levels associated with European cultivation over the past 2,000 years since Roman times (Certini and Scalenghe 2011), were considered as possible bases for a boundary. Or the "Columbian Exchange" of people and biota associated with the discovery of the New World was seen as a critical factor in global change, with a boundary being suggested at 1610 CE, marked by a brief dip in atmospheric carbon dioxide levels suggested to reflect forest regrowth after the colonization-related population collapse (in effect, genocide) of North American indigenous peoples (Lewis and Maslin 2015).

Should the Anthropocene be a formal geological unit at all? Some geologists noted that the global changes due to human impact have not yet reached their peak, suggesting that it would be more prudent to postpone any decision on the Anthropocene until a clear picture can be gained of how it will evolve (e.g. Wolff 2014). Or were Anthropocene strata simply too thin and insignificant to justify a new formal geological time unit? Or was the term more one of human history than geological history, or was it based on the future rather than the present? Or did it reflect a desire to make a political statement more than to do science (e.g. Autin and Holbrook 2012; Gibbard and Walker 2014; Finney and Edwards 2016)? All these alternatives and critiques needed engaging with.

The Great Acceleration and its Geological Legacy

Given these highly disparate views, what were the possibilities of defining the Anthropocene functionally and robustly in geological terms? To have an effective chronostratigraphic boundary, it needed to be widely traceable within recent strata, strata sufficiently substantial and distinctive for representing a new geological time unit in objective, rather than subjective (or politically motivated), terms (Waters et al. 2016; Zalasiewicz et al. 2017b).

There is a trade-off here. The longer the time span that might be allotted to the Anthropocene, the greater its physical representation by strata. But if the time span is too long, this would eat into the Holocene Epoch, a long-established unit. Some of the "early Anthropocene" suggestions in effect replace the Holocene as a name to emphasize early human impact. Such name-changing is unrealistic as a formal geological proposal, given how well entrenched the Holocene is as a unit, with its own large and highly active community of scholars, and its wide acceptance within geology generally. In geological terms, any formal Anthropocene would also have to fit in with, and not overly disrupt, the recently ratified tripartite subdivision of the Holocene into formal ages, whose boundaries are placed around 8,200 and 4,200 years ago, correlating with perceptible but transient global climate events (Walker et al. 2012, 2018). These careful distinctions also have important ramifications for non-geologists asking questions about how to conceptualize the impact of human forces on the planet.

Most of the boundaries suggested for the Anthropocene are not easily or widely traceable as synchronous levels within strata. The Industrial Revolution in Europe, seemingly an obvious threshold of modern times (Crutzen 2002; Zalasiewicz et al. 2008), spread only fitfully around the globe over the course of two centuries, propelled by processes linked to imperialism, colonialization, industrialization, and postcolonial development. Its associated upturn in carbon dioxide values is rather too gradual to use as an effective marker. Nor do there seem to be any obvious non-anthropogenic boundary markers (which would serve just as well in functional terms) around that time; the eruption of the Indonesian Tambora volcano in 1815 was powerful enough to spread an ash layer over large parts of the northern hemisphere – but not globally.

The concept of the Great Acceleration arose from the work of the International Geosphere–Biosphere Programme, then led by the Australian Earth System scientist Will Steffen. An enormous amount of data relating to both human socioeconomic and Earth System trends from 1750 CE onward was synthesized into 24 graphs – 12 of human factors (including population, economic growth, communication, and resource use) and 12 of Earth System factors (including greenhouse gases, biosphere degradation, and nitrogen emissions); these were published by Steffen et al. (2004) and later updated (Steffen et al. 2015a). The scientists involved knew that these factors had all been increasing since the British Industrial Revolution, but nevertheless were taken aback by the sharpness of the upturn in most of them from the mid twentieth century onward, though historians such as John McNeill (2000; see also McNeill and Engelke 2016) had already noted this phenomenon. The term "Great Acceleration" was coined for this phenomenon at a Dahlem meeting in 2005 (Steffen et al. 2015a), and published two years later (Steffen et al. 2007), then being interpreted as a "second phase" of the Anthropocene, following Europe's imperialist ventures extracting resources from around the world and its Industrial Revolution.

The suspicion that the Great Acceleration might provide an effective *geological* beginning for the Anthropocene came from comparing the ecological/geographic/socioeconomic processes catalogued in the graphs with their stratal imprints (Waters et al. 2016; Zalasiewicz et al. 2017c). This was mostly meta-analysis, reinterpreting and collating studies that had been carried out for other primary purposes, though some primary studies of Anthropocene stratigraphic trends had also been made (e.g. Swindles et al. 2015). The types of stratigraphic effects can be classed into physical (lithostratigraphy), chemical (as chemostratigraphy), and biological (biostratigraphy) stratal signatures.

Physical Deposits of the Anthropocene

Lithostratigraphy is the formal classification of bodies of rock, based on their physical properties, with the rock *formation* being the most commonly used category. The boundaries of lithostratigraphic units commonly cut across time planes – as with the beach deposits noted above – though some are much more nearly synchronous, such as an individual layer of ash from a single volcanic eruption, deposited across a wide landscape in a matter of hours. This is not to say that geologists necessarily disregard such small differences in time. The fearsome volcanic phenomenon known as a pyroclastic density current can move across a landscape as fast as an express train, draping it in incandescent ash. But, even within these almost-but-not-quite instantaneous deposits, volcanologists have identified "entrachrons" – mineral or chemical traces that mark successive positions within the advancing current, and which may be only a matter of *minutes* apart.

It is a myth, therefore, that geologists only think in terms of millions of years. They work to the limits of the maximum time resolution available in any particular situation. For instance, a very fine time distinction was drawn in placing the boundary between the Cretaceous and Paleogene periods, based on the worldwide layer of iridium-rich debris produced by a colossal asteroid impact. The site chosen for the "golden spike," or GSSP, placed at the bottom of the debris layer, is in Tunisia, several thousand kilometers from the impact site in Mexico. Therefore, in places between Tunisia and Mexico, the debris layer would have arrived a few hours earlier – and hence would have been latest Cretaceous rather than earliest Paleogene in age: a tiny but inconvenient technical difference. Therefore, the scientific team involved in formalization specified that the Cretaceous world ended, and the Paleogene one began, at the moment of impact, thus placing *all* of the impact deposits in the new time interval. This solution is a little irregular, but ingenious and effective in practice.

In proposing any definition of the Anthropocene, then, small amounts of time can matter (just as they can matter, where the evidence allows, in ancient deposits), and physical bodies of sediment can, depending on their situation, be either near-synchronous or highly diachronous, and so can run either near-parallel with or highly obliquely to any suggested time boundary.

These sedimentary bodies are made up of minerals (chemical compounds, typically crystalline, with a more or less fixed composition), in turn forming rocks (assemblages of one or more minerals). These are only rarely a factor in defining ancient geological time units, because genuinely new forms of mineral and rock have, for the most part, appeared only rarely in Earth history. The same rocks and minerals tend to repeat time and again, and only occasionally have novelties appeared that might help identify and define geological time intervals. The most striking example occurred between 2.4 and 2.1 billion years ago with the evolution of microbial photosynthesis that yielded free oxygen to the atmosphere (see chapter 2). The Earth's surface began, for the first time, to rust, and a suite of new oxide and hydroxide minerals appeared. Until recently, this was the last major (if protracted) step in mineral innovation on our planet (Hazen et al. 2008, 2017), after which some 5,000 different minerals were present on Earth, most very rare.

Subsequently, new rock types and rock textures have appeared (or disappeared) from time to time, usually reflecting more or less major changes in the Earth System. For example, the evolution and diversification of muscular multicellular animals associated with the beginning of the Cambrian Period (and, simultaneously, of the

Paleozoic Era and Phanerozoic Eon) led to the widespread appearance of bioturbated sedimentary rocks – that is, rocks representing sediments which have been churned over by animal burrowing. Bioturbated strata, absent from the enormous length of Precambrian times, are one of the signature features of the Phanerozoic Eon. Other examples include the appearance of significant coal deposits in the Carboniferous Period, reflecting the spread of vegetation onto land, and the evolution of common calcium carbonate-secreting oceanic plankton in the Mesozoic Era that, by the mass accumulation of their tiny skeletons on the sea floor, give rise to such distinctive rocks as the chalk that gives its name to the Cretaceous.

In the relationship of minerals, rocks, and strata to the Anthropocene, an issue of classification and terminology appears. Human-made crystalline inorganic chemical compounds are, by recent amendment (Nickel and Grice 1998), formally *excluded* from classification as minerals, according to the rules of the International Mineralogical Association. The official list does include 208 more or less human-made or human-mediated minerals that were approved before the exclusion ruling, but how many more distinct anthropogenic inorganic crystalline compounds (i.e. minerals in all but formal name) might there be beyond those? Given that these anthropogenic compounds might serve as useful markers of Anthropocene strata, this question of classification matters.

The human addition (whether formal or informal), via the laboratories of materials scientists, dwarfs the figure from the natural world. Hazen et al. (2017) quoted the Inorganic Crystal Structure Database, hosted at the Leibniz Institute, Karlsruhe, that then included more than 180,000 inorganic crystalline compounds (that is, human-made "mineral" types). The figure is now, as we write, 193,000. Human ingenuity and technology now synthesize more new mineral species *each year* than formed on Earth through 4.54 billion years. Hazen et al. (2017) describe the Anthropocene as a time of "unparalleled inorganic compound diversification," and note, too, the unprecedented redistribution of natural minerals by humans in mining, manufacture, and trade.

Nearly all of these "human-made minerals" have been synthesized since 1950 (http://icsd.fiz-karlsruhe.de), in ever-more sophisticated chemical laboratories, simultaneously reflecting and being part of the "Great Acceleration" patterns. Many of these new "minerals" are present in tiny quantities, but some are manufactured in large amounts. Plastics are novel mineral-like substances, first synthesized in the early twentieth century but only produced in globally significant amounts since the mid twentieth century, with global annual production climbing from about 1 million tonnes/year in ~1950 to more than 300 million tonnes/year now. More than 9 billion tonnes have been produced, of which more than 6 billion tonnes have now been discarded as waste (Geyer et al. 2017). Easily transported by wind and water and resistant to decay, plastics have become part of Earth's geological cycle, and now contaminate sediments almost ubiquitously, even on remote beaches and the deep ocean floor (Zalasiewicz et al. 2016a).

There are geologically novel and distinctive anthropogenic rock types, too, including various kinds of ceramic and brick – the most abundant being concrete. Although made since Roman times, the growth of concrete on a planetary scale is also a post-World War II phenomenon, responsible for perhaps 99 percent of the half-trillion tonnes made to date – equivalent to a kilo for every square meter of Earth's surface, both land and sea (Waters and Zalasiewicz 2017). These distinctive mineral and rock types are components of Anthropocene strata which, like all strata, may be classified by means of lithostratigraphy, using their physical characteristics as a basis.

The term "Anthropocene strata" in this sense involves intersections of time and material objects specific to the discipline of geology, and unfamiliar outside of that discipline. The "Anthropocene," if considered as a chronostratigraphic unit, is defined in terms of *time*, as we discussed above. Its beginning, when traced within strata, is by definition synchronous around the Earth. Anthropocene strata do not necessarily have to be formed or influenced by humans – nor are all anthropogenic strata part of the Anthropocene. They will include wind-blown desert sands of the Sahara, with no perceptible human influence, as well as truly anthropogenic mine-waste and urban "artificial ground." A rubble layer beneath London may have fragments of Roman tile near its base and date from over 1,000 years ago, medieval pottery in its middle part, and abundant post-World War II concrete fragments and plastic debris in its upper part. These are all anthropogenic – but only the last of these would be Anthropocene in chronostratigraphic age. This whole unit, across its long time span, might be termed part of the *archeosphere*, to distinguish it from the "natural" deposits beneath (Edgeworth 2014). Within the entire rubble layer (which might be classified as a single lithostratigraphic unit), a time boundary would be sought, to allow classification of different parts of it into two geological time units – of the Holocene and Anthropocene, respectively – using whatever evidence can be found (Terrington et al. 2018).

This kind of situation is the norm for any age of strata, right back to the Precambrian, in which great care is taken to separate what used to be called the "holy trinity" of rocks, time and fossils (which these days includes a host of other phenomena, including chemical and magnetic patterns). One might say it is a way of keeping geology honest. Anthropocene strata, thus, need to be considered in both their anthropogenic and non-anthropogenic forms, these being end members of a continuum, rather than wholly distinct categories.

Not all more or less directly human-formed deposits are traditionally considered as "geology." Geological maps have long included a category of "artificial deposits" – the layers of reworked soil and rock and rubble that underlie urban areas. But the buildings above are not usually regarded as being "geology," even though they are mostly made from eminently geological ingredients such as sand, gravel and mud – and will sooner or later revert to them. Similarly, an active road surface is not generally considered as a geological unit – but the built embankment it rests upon *is* so considered. Of course, this is an artificial distinction, similar to the classification of minerals discussed above. A human-made city, in reality, is analogous to, say, a termite nest or a coral reef, as a biologically mediated modification of the Earth's surface.

The Anthropocene – so far – as a geological time interval is minuscule: some 70 years, or roughly one average human lifespan. Nevertheless, the Anthropocene deposits formed in that geological eyeblink of time are by no means proportionately trivial. The total mass of material reworked, transported, and discarded by humans on Earth roughly approximates to some 30 trillion tonnes, of which urban areas make up about a third (Zalasiewicz et al. 2016b). This is equivalent to about 50 kilos for each square meter of our planet's surface, or a worldwide rubble layer a few tens of centimeters thick. The great bulk of that has formed in the Anthropocene. Clearly, there are large variations: artificial deposits reach tens of meters thick under many cities, in landfill sites, and around quarrying/mining areas, but are negligible in remote areas. Nevertheless, the averaged thickness considerably exceeds any long-term geological background rate of global erosion and sedimentation, reflecting the considerable part of the extraordinary outpouring of energy over the last century (see below) being directed toward reshaping the landscape in various ways: the bulldozer is arguably an even more potent symbol of the Anthropocene than is the family automobile.

Extending underground is "anthroturbation": pipes, tunnels, metro systems, mineshafts, boreholes, and other subterranean extensions of human activity (Zalasiewicz et al. 2014a; Williams et al. 2019). The name derives from the comparison with bioturbation, the churning through of sediment by burrowing organisms. The human equivalent is analogous, though carried out on a much greater scale, extending kilometers down into the ground. These underground structures, being well out of the reach of erosion, are likely to be preserved for many millions of years.

Anthropogenic deposits of Anthropocene age rest side by side with naturally deposited sediments of the same age, laid down on land surfaces and river and lake beds, on the sea floor, and – for these are considered geological strata too – in the snow and ice layers of the polar regions. These sediments are part of the Anthropocene just as much as are the anthropogenic deposits, demonstrably so when they contain even tiny amounts of time markers such as plastic fragments. These natural sediments deposited in Anthropocene time will commonly be thinner than the anthropogenic deposits, often being measured in centimeters or decimeters (or millimeters, on the abyssal ocean floor). Although thin, they may contain complete, continuous sedimentary records of the Anthropocene, particularly where the deposits show annual layering, as on some lake floors. Paradoxically, the mostly complete and fine-resolved archives in geology commonly accumulate in remote locations distant from where most perturbation took place: this seems to hold true for the Anthropocene, too (Waters et al. 2018a).

Chemical Signals of the Anthropocene

Earth's habitability is predicated on natural global cycles of key chemical elements such as carbon, nitrogen, and phosphorus, as they move between their natural stores, which include rock, soil, water, air, and living organisms. Many of these cycles are now impacted by human activities.

Carbon

Carbon is originally released from deep in the Earth via volcanic eruptions, as carbon dioxide. Once in the atmosphere, part of the carbon dioxide is extracted via photosynthesis in plants, which use it to grow their tissues. Those plants (and the animals that eat them), in both respiring and dying/decaying, re-release the carbon as further carbon dioxide. Incompletely decayed remains of these organisms, though, can smuggle large amounts of carbon into soils and sediments, or dissolve it in seawater. Carbon can be fossilized in rocks, too, as coal, oil, and gas, or as the "carbonate" part of calcium carbonate in limestones. Once so trapped, it can stay underground for many millions of years, until re-released in some episode of volcanism or mountain building. The interconnected carbon stores, and the pathways between them, are critical to maintaining life on Earth.

Today, the amounts of carbon in each of these global stores, and how they change from year to year, can be estimated from direct scientific measurements. How and where the Earth's carbon was distributed in earlier times, before such scientific measurements began, can be inferred from clues in rock strata.

The extraordinary outburst of fossil-fuel burning since the Industrial Revolution is set to disrupt a long-established climate pattern (chapter 4). The climate effects will be felt for millennia, but it has already left a chemical signal in strata as a result of the roughly one-third (and rising) increase in atmospheric carbon dioxide levels over pre-industrial levels.

The signal involves a change in the isotopic composition of carbon at the Earth's surface – that is, in the ratio between the most common isotope carbon-12 (or ^{12}C, with six protons and six neutrons) and a heavier stable (that is non-radioactive) isotope ^{13}C, which has an extra neutron. Fossil fuels are enriched in ^{12}C, and burning them has therefore enriched the entire surface carbon cycle in this component. This enrichment is then taken in by plants using carbon dioxide for photosynthesis, and by organisms that build skeletons from calcium carbonate, such as corals. The resultant signal (Waters et al. 2016) is known as the "Suess effect" after the geochemist Hans Suess, who recognized its significance. It is now widely recognizable in sediment layers that contain calcium carbonate shells, in tree rings, and in other comparable stratigraphic archives, as a "carbon isotope anomaly" similar to – but considerably sharper than – similar anomalies that are used by geologists to characterize and date ancient strata, such as that associated with the Paleocene–Eocene epoch boundary (see chapter 4).

Another imprint is a direct by-product of the burning process: fly ash, which comprises the particles that make up industrial smoke, which subsequently settle onto the ground or onto the surface of a lake or sea, where they sink to form part of the sediment layers. The particles are made of either melted rock impurities ("inorganic ash spheres") or unburnt carbon ("spherical carbonaceous particles").

They are tiny – just a few tens of microns across – but the carbon-based ones in particular are decay-resistant and so highly fossilizable (similar particles have been found in soot present in the end-Cretaceous boundary layer, ascribed to firestorms generated by the asteroid impact). Fly ash particles appear in European lake sediments from the nineteenth century, and this became a near-global, and much stronger, signal from the mid twentieth century – to such an extent that fly ash was suggested as a primary defining marker for the Anthropocene (Rose 2015; Swindles et al. 2015).

Another carbon-based signal is from manufactured organic chemicals, including pesticides such as DDT, dieldrin, and aldrin, and also inadvertent industrial by-products such as dioxin. These have since spread widely, and may be detected in sediment layers on land and on the sea floor; this phenomenon, again, largely dates from the mid twentieth century (Muir and Rose 2007), being an effective identifier of this interval.

Nitrogen and Phosphorus

Two other major element cycles critical to the biosphere, of nitrogen and phosphorus, have also been strongly perturbed, largely through the "supercharging" of biological productivity to feed ever-increasing numbers of humans.

Nitrogen makes up the bulk of the atmosphere. But its atmospheric form, as the dinitrogen (N_2) molecule, is extremely stable and difficult to convert to biologically active forms within molecules such as amino acids (the building blocks for proteins) and DNA. In nature, the dinitrogen molecule can be torn apart in lightning strikes, but most biologically active nitrogen is produced by nitrogen-fixing bacteria, which have special enzymes to convert nitrogen into ammonia (NH_3), which is then converted by the bacteria and higher plants (and the animals that eat them) into other nitrogen-containing compounds.

This tortuous process is a bottleneck, or "limiting factor," in biological production. As agriculture became intensive in the eighteenth and nineteenth centuries, to feed a growing human population, extra nitrogen was sought from sources such as saltpeter (sodium nitrate) deposits in Chile, or guano (accumulations of seabird excreta) along Pacific coastlines, or via the recycling of human excreta (as "night soil") on fields. In the early twentieth century, these laborious activities were largely rendered redundant by exploiting the abundant nitrogen in the atmosphere via the energy-intensive

Haber–Bosch process in the early twentieth century, synthesizing ammonia directly as a basis for fertilizers (and for munitions, too). Production expanded enormously from the mid twentieth century, to roughly double the amount of reactive nitrogen at the Earth's surface – proportionately, an even greater change than has taken place for the carbon cycle. This single process is now said to be responsible for feeding about half of the world's current human population. The expansion of nitrogen exploitation can be tracked in strata as a geological signal of the Anthropocene because of the way it has changed the proportions of the two stable isotopes ^{14}N and ^{15}N in many lake deposits (Holtgrieve et al. 2011; Wolfe et al. 2013), the main change being, once more, around the mid twentieth century.

Phosphorus is another biologically crucial element, being (as calcium phosphate) the stuff of our bones and teeth, and also an ingredient of adenosine triphosphate, the molecule that regulates energy transfer in our metabolism. Agricultural phosphate accompanies nitrogen in guano, and in the nineteenth century was also obtained from bones – from slaughterhouses, from the bones of dead soldiers gathered from battlefields (in this once-thriving trade, millions of cadavers a year were collected by gangs of workers to import into Britain), from dinosaur bones and fossilized excreta ("coprolites"), and, in one instance, from a cache of some 180,000 mummified ancient Egyptian cats, also ground up to spread on English fields. This vital element is now mined from phosphate-rich rocks, so that its surface concentration, like that of reactive nitrogen, has also roughly doubled (Filippelli 2002).

Together with nitrogen, phosphorus affects wider biological productivity as it escapes from farmland into the wider environment. Fertilizer overspill into rivers and then the sea has led, since the 1960s, to hundreds of "dead zones" in shallow seas, covering hundreds of thousands of square kilometers in total (Breitburg et al. 2018). These develop in summer as plankton blooms grow, die and then sink and decay on the sea floor, using up oxygen and causing mass deaths of sea floor organisms. The resulting biological changes can be preserved into the fossil record.

Other Elements, Including Radionuclides

Many other surface element concentrations have been altered by humans (Sen and Peuckner-Ehrenbrink 2012) within new "anthro-biogeochemical" cycles (Galuszka and Wagreich 2019). The mining of metals (in effect, highly selective erosion by humans) is one large source of this perturbation. Of the metals, lead has a long history of mining, and far-traveled aerosols from Roman smelting produced detectable signals in distant peat bogs and ice sheets (Wagreich and Draganits 2018). Lead's subsequent industrial history can be tracked in these sedimentary archives, via total lead concentrations and also changes in isotope ratios – the latter recording the use, and then phasing out, of lead as an anti-knock agent in gasoline during the twentieth century.

The sharpest signal of the Anthropocene currently known reflects the production and environmental dispersal of artificial radionuclides of elements such as cesium, plutonium, and americium, through the detonation of atomic bombs and leaks from nuclear energy facilities. Production started with a race to develop a nuclear weapon during World War II, once such a devastating and potentially decisive weapon became technically feasible. The first successful test of a bomb (based on the nuclear fission of plutonium, an element exceedingly rare in nature, large quantities of which had been specially synthesized for the task) was at Alamogordo, in New Mexico, on July 16, 1945. On August 6, a "Trinity" atomic bomb was exploded over Hiroshima in Japan, and on August 9 another was exploded over Nagasaki, the two bombs killing over 100,000 people. These are still the only two uses of nuclear weapons in warfare, although the death-toll has mounted from above-ground nuclear bomb tests such as the 1954 "Lucky Dragon (Daigo Fukuryū Maru) Incident," and from nuclear energy plant meltdowns such as Chernobyl and Fukushima.

Despite the horrific casualties at Hiroshima and Nagasaki, the resulting radioactive fallout (and that from the Trinity test) was only locally distributed, and did not form a global geological marker. Nevertheless, this was a key historical moment, with a suggestion (Zalasiewicz et al. 2015a) that the first, Trinity, test explosion might mark a boundary for the Anthropocene, albeit one based on a time instant (as a Global Standard Stratigraphic Age, abbreviated as GSSA) rather than on the physically recognizable global marker of the more widely used Global Boundary Stratotype Section and Point (GSSP) (see chapter 2). This suggestion of a GSSA did not find wide support among the stratigraphic community (Zalasiewicz et al. 2017a), as it did not offer a globally traceable radionuclide layer. In the arms race triggered by the development of nuclear weapons, though, global radioactive markers were soon to appear.

The far more powerful hydrogen (fusion) bomb was first tested on November 1, 1952, by the USA on Elugelab Island, Eniwetok.

Equivalent to more than 10 million tonnes of TNT, it obliterated the island, the power of the eruption injecting radioactive debris (including that from the nuclear fission trigger for the bomb, with plutonium and other heavy radioactive elements) up into the stratosphere. From there it was spread by winds around the globe, drifting down to contaminate land and sea surfaces worldwide; the Soviet Union detonated its own H-bomb the following year.

This nuclear arms race – soon joined by a few other countries, including China, France, India, and the UK – saw over 2,000 nuclear weapons tests in the following years. Over 500 were atmospheric tests, spreading radioactive debris widely, the rest of the tests being underground, confining most of the radioactivity (Waters et al. 2015). After the Partial Test-Ban Treaty of 1963, atmospheric tests were sharply reduced and eventually ceased, and after the Comprehensive Test-Ban Treaty of 1996, most underground tests ceased too.

The history of the atmospheric tests can be read as a clear "bomb spike" of cesium, plutonium, and "extra" radiocarbon, widely traceable in sedimentary layers worldwide (Waters et al. 2015, 2018a). It may provide the basis of a formal definition of the Anthropocene.

The peaceful use of nuclear power has resulted in geological signals, too. There are some 450 nuclear power plants in existence today, which together generate about 14 percent of the world's electricity. The residue of spent nuclear fuel from power generation should, in most cases, not leave anything other than a very localized (and long-term inaccessible) signal, if contained within managed repositories. Where fuel has been released to the environment, though, through accidents such as at the Windscale, Cumbria, reprocessing plant in 1956, Chernobyl in 1986, and Fukushima in 2011, widespread distinctive signals resulted, each recognizable through their particular cocktail of radionuclides.

Biological Signals of the Anthropocene

Despite its short duration, the Anthropocene has already had an enormous impact on the Earth's biosphere, sufficient already to be traceable in the Earth's future fossil record. In a present-day context, and from any practical (and moral) perspective, the most important features of the Anthropocene are its effect on the life of this planet (see chapter 5), but here we focus more narrowly, on the "modern fossils" being left in sediment layers today, and the way they help characterize the Anthropocene.

In ancient strata, the appearance and extinction of fossil species provide unique time markers that can be exploited using the discipline of *biostratigraphy*, to navigate effectively through the last 541 million years of the Phanerozoic Eon. For this long time interval, fossils are still the best way to tell the geological age of rock strata.

At shorter timescales, things get more complicated. In the Quaternary Period of the last 2.6 million years, such age-dating does not work so simply because, in such a short time-span, there were relatively few species origins and extinctions. More commonly, the cross-country migrations of animals and plants, sometimes over thousands of miles, to follow the many warmings and coolings of Quaternary climate are used as time markers. Such "climatostratigraphy" forms a useful – though complex – means of paleontological dating.

Similar creativity needs to be applied to the Anthropocene, the brief duration of which contrasts with the large biological perturbations taking place. The most widely broadcast of these is the enhanced and accelerating rate of biological species extinctions (e.g. Ceballos et al. 2015), both terrestrial and marine. This phenomenon began well before the Holocene, with a wave of extinctions of large terrestrial mammals – including such well-known forms as the mammoth and woolly rhinoceros – that began some 50,000 years ago and peaked some 10,000 years ago. This "megafaunal extinction" has been linked with both the climate change of the Pleistocene–Holocene transition and the emergence of culturally modern humans, with their enhanced social (and, therefore, hunting) capabilities and weapons. Climate change may have played a part in the loss of megafauna, but none of the previous glacial–interglacial transitions of the Quaternary triggered such an extinction wave. The later and better-documented local extinctions were clearly linked to human arrival, as with the extinctions of the moas and other animals in New Zealand, shortly after humans arrived on these islands in the late thirteenth century. These rolling mammal and bird extinctions, linked to habitat loss and human predation, were protracted, highly time-transgressive, and may be regarded as part of the characterization of the late Pleistocene to Holocene interval.

Extinction rates have clearly accelerated more recently, though cataloguing the fate of the approximately 9 million species on Earth (Mora et al. 2011) is a difficult and time-consuming task, especially as most of these species are elusive and more obscure than the charismatic large mammals that for most people symbolize the biodiversity loss. Anthony Barnosky and his colleagues (2011) addressed the question of whether we are in a sixth major mass extinction in Earth history. Their answer is "not quite yet," as known extinction rates in most biological groups are still of the order of 1 percent of the species known. But they note that a far greater proportion – up to several tens of percent of species within some groups – are in low numbers, being endangered or critically endangered. They estimated that, at current rates of species decline in a "business-as-usual" scenario, and without factoring in the effects of climate change, the Earth would undergo a sixth extinction of end-Cretaceous scale (i.e. a loss of some 70 percent of species) within a few centuries.

Extinction is clearly a major part of the rapidly evolving Anthropocene picture, but its complexity in time and space makes it difficult to simply translate into the age-dating of strata. The appearance or disappearance of small, abundant, and (crucially) skeleton-bearing – and therefore fossilizable – organisms typically provides the basis for such age-dating, more technically known as biostratigraphic zonation. For the Anthropocene, another, related phenomenon may turn out to be more practically effective as a time marker: the species invasions (increasingly referred to as the arrival of *neobiota*) that are transforming the biology of many regions of the Earth (see chapter 5).

Species invasions have, like extinctions, been going on for thousands of years, as animals such as cats, dogs, pigs, and rats have accompanied humans on their migrations across Earth. Humans, of course, are the most successful invasive species of all. This process accelerated sharply with the globalization of trade, notably with the global transfer of ballast water and sediment in cargo ships, which spread many organisms around the world. There has also been an upsurge in intentional transplanting of species for both agriculture and horticulture. As a result, invasive species now make up a large proportion of biological assemblages in many parts of the world (McNeely 2001). Many invasive species, when they find new terrain in which they can outcompete native species, explode in numbers, to become so common that their remains can easily be found in the kind of standard sediment samples that paleontologists analyze.

Examples can be found among the "small fry" of the biological world: the zebra mussel (*Dreissena polymorpha*), the Asian clam (*Corbicula fluminea*), and the Pacific oyster (*Crassostrea gigas*) have all spread in the last century or so from their native regions to many parts of the world – the first two accidentally via lumber transport, and the last purposely transplanted as a food species. Such neobiota, only a few years after arrival, may come to dominate biological assemblages:

a recent sampling in the Thames showed that *D. polymorpha* and *C. fluminea* together made up 96 percent of the total mollusk shells recovered, with native species now a tiny minority (Himson et al. 2020). Tracing such incomers allows the Anthropocene to be recognized by its modern paleontological record.

Such paleontological characterization can result, too, from the re-engineering of both biological landscapes and animal and plant species by humans in modern agriculture. A very few species are selected to supply humans with the bulk of their food, their biology modified by selective breeding (and now by genetic engineering) and their numbers vastly amplified. The scale of this transformation is extraordinary: the scientist Vaclav Smil (2011) has estimated that the biomass of large land mammals, in pre-human times divided among some 350 species (Barnosky 2008: the number halving during the megafaunal extinctions), is now mostly divided between humans (about one-third) and domestic animals such as cows, pigs, and sheep (about two-thirds), with the biomass of all the remaining species of wild land mammals now representing a few percent of the total (Smil 2011).

The bones of butchered domestic animals, abundant in landfill sites, can thus provide another biostratigraphic signal. The most striking example is the domestic broiler chicken, now the most common bird in the world with a standing population of around 23 billion (turning over rapidly with its roughly 6-week lifespan), and a skeleton transformed in postwar times by the "Chicken of Tomorrow" breeding program to become a distinctive new Anthropocene morphospecies, which is now globally distributed (Bennett et al. 2018).

Formal Future of the Anthropocene

This extraordinary array of physical, chemical, and biological markers suggests that the Anthropocene – whether ultimately formalized on the GTS or not – has a coherence and reality in geological terms (Zalasiewicz et al. 2017a). This reality led the Anthropocene Working Group to decide to work toward a proposal to formalize the Anthropocene, by the standard means of locating and choosing a Global Boundary Stratotype Section and Point (GSSP), or "golden spike." This elaborate process has begun (Waters et al. 2018a), involving carrying out many analyses of candidates for the "golden spike" section, selecting the perceived best of these and then basing a formal proposal on it. This proposal must then be agreed by supermajority (over 60 percent) votes, successively, by the Anthropocene Working Group, the Subcommission on Quaternary Stratigraphy, and the International Commission on Stratigraphy – and finally there must be ratification by the International Union of Geological Sciences. The proposal can fall at any of these hurdles, and so eventual formal acceptance of the Anthropocene is by no means assured. In May 2019, the Anthropocene Working Group agreed by an 88 percent vote to pursue formalization of the Anthropocene. At the time of writing, they are in the midst of that process.

The new Earth System that the Anthropocene represents is evolving, and for at least many millennia will continue to evolve – even if human pressures cease tomorrow. Among the most important aspects in this ongoing evolution is climate, the theme that we pass to next.

4

The Anthropocene and Climate Change

Climate change – and the more specific topic of global warming – is one of the most important aspects of contemporary Earth System change, with huge significance for human society, indeed for all living organisms. The fundamentals of the science are widely agreed by the scientists researching this phenomenon, much as the fundamentals of Darwinian evolution are widely shared among working biologists. But the issue of climate change is divisive within society as a whole, not least because the central means by which we power our society – the burning of fossil fuels – is also the central factor driving climate change. Many other processes on which modern societies depend also emit greenhouse gases (carbon dioxide, methane, nitrous oxide, and fluorinated gases). Well-entrenched industrialized modes of agriculture and artificial fertilizer use, large-scale waste management, biomass burning including deforestation, industrial processes and refrigeration, and concrete manufacture add to the political and social resistance to curbing emissions.

The Anthropocene is sometimes held to be effectively synonymous with – or even merely to represent a repackaging of – the science of global warming. It is not that, and indeed in some respects global warming might be said to be – for now – a relatively minor, if rapidly growing, part of the array of phenomena that make up the Anthropocene. Nevertheless, climate change has been a fundamental driver of wider physical, chemical, and biological changes during Earth history, while human activities have had powerful effects on the factors that control climate. The resulting impacts will probably amplify over coming decades and centuries, and persist for many millennia. Climate change thus needs particular consideration within the overall trajectory of the Anthropocene.

Climate Control – the Planetary Context

Earth's surface is warmed by the heat and light we receive from the
Sun, the component of energy from the Earth's hot interior being
negligible. Part of the Sun's energy is simply reflected back to space
(by bouncing off clouds or the planetary surface), while part is
absorbed and then re-emitted as infra-red energy (infra-red because
the Earth is a relatively cool object, and does not glow at temperatures our eyes can see). How much of the Sun's radiation gets
reflected depends on the albedo – or reflectivity – of the planetary
surface: bright white materials such as ice reflect a lot of energy,
while darker surfaces such as the forested land and open sea reflect
less, and thus absorb more, energy. How much of the re-radiated
energy returns to outer space is controlled by levels of greenhouse
gases in the atmosphere, such as carbon dioxide, methane, and water
vapor, so called because they absorb infra-red energy and therefore
trap heat, a little like the panes of glass in a greenhouse. When the
British scientist John Tyndall discovered this property of greenhouse
gases (not possessed by the nitrogen or oxygen in the atmosphere),
he was astounded that a gas that was transparent to visible light could
nevertheless trap "invisible" radiant heat, and repeated his experi-
ments hundreds of times to make sure of his results. There are other
factors too, such as the amount and type of clouds and aerosols in
the air, which, depending on their type, may act to warm or cool the
planet. Overall, the Earth's surface temperature reflects the balance
of energy that is absorbed, and that which is reflected or re-radiated,
and surface albedo and levels of greenhouse gases play a large role
in this (IPCC 2013).

Our planet has maintained this radiation balance to stay within
a relatively narrow temperature range, so that liquid water exists at
the surface, accompanied by water vapor in the atmosphere, and, for
much of Earth history, significant amounts of ice in the polar regions
and at the tops of high mountains. It is a unique situation for our
solar system. Even though other bodies (notably moons of Jupiter
and Saturn, such as Europa and Titan) possess substantial water
oceans, these lie beneath a thick carapace of ice. Of other planetary
bodies, there is evidence suggesting that both Venus and Mars once
possessed surface oceans in their early history, but quickly lost them.

Venus lost its water to outer space through a runaway greenhouse
effect, and now maintains surface temperatures of around 400 °C
(752 °F) through a dense carbon dioxide atmosphere, while Mars

now has a frozen surface, with its remaining water as icecaps and buried permafrost. Earth's situation is all the more remarkable in that it has maintained its ocean-bearing, habitable state for something like 4 billion years, even while external conditions have changed substantially: for instance, the Sun's luminosity has risen by about 20 percent over that time. Therefore, our planet evidently has some kind of long-term thermostat to maintain a life-supporting climate.

A critical negative feedback mechanism for long-term control of Earth's climate is the adjustment of greenhouse gas levels by silicate weathering (Walker et al. 1981). As climate warms, a more powerful hydrological cycle (that is, globally more frequent rain) enhances reaction of carbon dioxide dissolved in rainwater with rock minerals, to produce dissolved carbonate ions that are then washed into the sea. This process draws carbon dioxide out of the atmosphere, leading to cooling. As climate cools, the carbon dioxide drawdown effect diminishes, allowing levels of this greenhouse gas to build up again, to produce warming.

This is a slow, long-term process (highly simplified in this description: for more detail see Summerhayes 2020), working on timescales of many millennia. Silicate weathering is probably the main factor that has ensured that the Earth has not boiled and not frozen. Within this broad control, other factors have modified climate over various timescales. Earth's history at scales of hundreds of millions of years shows somewhat irregular alternation between *greenhouse states* – such as those of the Mesozoic Era, with generally higher atmospheric carbon dioxide levels, little or no ice on Earth and high sea levels – and *icehouse* states – such as the one we currently live in, with significant and persistent polar ice. The alternation of these two states is probably controlled by the very slow-moving "tectonic weather" of our planet, leading to long-term variations in carbon dioxide outgassing from the Earth's mantle, and different continental configurations, which affect albedo, patterns of heat-transporting ocean currents, and variations in the rate of carbon dioxide removal from the atmosphere via the weathering of continental rocks (e.g. Jagoutz et al. 2016).

Shorter-term variations include regular climate oscillations within both greenhouse and icehouse states. They are more sharply expressed in icehouse times, being the alternations between glacial and interglacial phases that were long known and puzzled over by geologists. They are now known to be controlled by predictable astronomical variations in the Earth's orbit and spin, with intersecting "Milankovitch" periodicities of 400, 100, 40, and 20 millennia – these were named after the Serbian mathematician Milutin Milankovitch, who made detailed calculations of these astronomical variations in the early twentieth century, and suggested their role as drivers of glacial–interglacial change. The slight changes in the amount and seasonal balance of sunlight so produced are amplified by variations in atmospheric levels of greenhouse gases to produce marked differences in climate state. The pattern is well-nigh metronomic (Lisiecki and Raymo 2005), with theoretical, astronomical calculations of climate state showing a close match with the climate record deduced from continuous archives of ocean floor sediments and polar ice.

The polar ice layers provide crucial evidence. There are about a million years' worth of them on Antarctica, and something over 100,000 years' worth on Greenland. They contain myriad bubbles of "fossil air" that can be analyzed to show past levels of greenhouse gases, while the chemistry of the ice itself yields a record of temperature and much more (such as dust levels, traces of major volcanic eruptions, and so on).

These tell us that, over the past 800,000 years (as far back as this record has yet been analyzed: EPICA Community Members 2006), carbon dioxide levels in the atmosphere regularly oscillated, at timescales of tens of thousands of years, between about 180 parts per million (ppm) and 280 ppm; 180 ppm represents about 1,400 billion tonnes of carbon dioxide – at these levels, Earth's surface temperature dropped low enough to allow large ice sheets to grow in the northern hemisphere, and to enable Antarctica's ice to grow a little more extensive (Antarctica's ice sheet cannot grow too much bigger, as it soon runs out of land to grow on). As the Earth's orbit and spin subtly but regularly changed, so did amounts of sunlight hitting Earth, and this changed the patterns of currents of air and ocean water around the Earth. One of the results was the degassing, over several thousand years, of some 800 billion tonnes of carbon dioxide from the deep oceans (the oceans are a *huge* carbon store, and the 800 billion tonnes is a small fraction of this) into the air (Skinner et al. 2010). With the ensuing extra 100 ppm of this greenhouse gas, the Earth grew warmer, to temperatures something like today's, and the great ice sheets shrank back. As the Earth's orbit and spin changed again, carbon dioxide began to be absorbed by the oceans once more, and the ice advanced again.

This intricate planetary climate machine, with carbon pathways at its heart, has been working for millions of years. Its multi-millennial climate rhythmicity is further complicated by smaller-scale – but still profound – millennial-scale climate oscillations, present in glacial phases but muted in the more stable interglacial phases. The interplay of these millennial-scale fluctuations with the Milankovitch rhythms via natural feedbacks in the Earth System often led to abrupt climate change episodes at regional/hemispheric scales, as various tipping points were crossed.

Thus, in the transition from the last glacial phase to the present interglacial of the Holocene, the rise in atmospheric CO_2 levels started some 17,000 years ago, again by degassing of CO_2 dissolved within the deep ocean, and was largely complete by about 12,000 years ago. The accompanying climate transition was not a similarly more or less smooth rise, though, but was effected through large temperature jumps that could take place in just decades. These jumps separated multi-millennial plateaus of warmth or cold, the last of these being the long warm plateau of the Holocene itself. The "tipping points" between these states were more or less abrupt transitions in North Atlantic Ocean circulation that in effect switched the warmth-providing Gulf Stream on and off.

Thus, it is perfectly true that climate has always been changing, and at times dramatically. But, for the past few million years, it has always been changing along long-established and well-studied patterns, as part of what some scientists have called "limit cycles" (Steffen et al. 2015a), with well-defined maxima and minima of temperature and of atmospheric levels of carbon dioxide, the latter oscillating between limits of approximately 180 and ~260 ppm (+/–20 ppm in different interglacials) over at least the last 800,000 years. For the last 11,000 years or so, the Earth has been in the "warm" setting of the Holocene interglacial state, and in its natural state would be slowly declining toward a glacial state. Humans, however, have perturbed the picture.

The Human Factor

A typical pattern of interglacials over the past 800,000 years has been for atmospheric carbon dioxide to reach its highest level early in the interglacial. There followed a very slow decline by some 10–20 ppm over the course of the interglacial, over several millennia, this decline being a prelude to the downturn as the next glacial phase began.

As the paleoclimate scientist William Ruddiman has emphasized (2003, 2013), the Holocene trajectory has been different. The beginning followed the same path, with a high of 265 ppm being reached early, and then a decline to 260 ppm by 7,000 years ago. Then the pattern changed: atmospheric CO_2 levels began to rise, equally slowly, steadily climbing to 280 ppm just before the Industrial Revolution began in Britain around 1800. The trajectory of that other important greenhouse gas, methane, showed a similar departure, though with a different inflection point: a steady decline from 700 parts per billion (ppb) to 550 ppb about 5,000 years ago, much as in previous interglacials, before climbing back to 700 ppb by the end of pre-industrial times. Ruddiman argued that these changes in the trajectory of these greenhouse gases were effects of early farming and deforestation, he and his colleagues amassing an impressive range of evidence to demonstrate the wide extent of human occupation of the Earth in early to mid-Holocene times. It is a central plank of the idea, held by some, that the "Anthropocene began thousands of years ago" (cf. Ruddiman et al. 2015).

Ruddiman's thesis of atmospheric carbon dioxide change through early human impact is well researched and plausible, and the extra carbon dioxide drip-fed into the atmosphere may have sufficed to maintain Holocene warmth, preventing a slide back into glaciation (Ganopolski et al. 2016). It is the best established of such ideas of early human influence on climate, but has not gone uncontested, with evidence also amassed that the Holocene is not unique in its climate pattern, and that much of this extra carbon dioxide came from the oceans, not the land (Elsig et al. 2009; Zalasiewicz et al. 2019a, and references therein).

However interpreted, the observed slow and modest changes in greenhouse gas patterns through the Holocene might be regarded as a stabilizing factor of Holocene conditions, especially if they have indeed prevented the onset of the next glaciation. They contrast sharply, in scale and significance, with the changes that took place subsequently during the Industrial Revolution and Great Acceleration.

The Mark of Industry

Industry fueled by burning hydrocarbons has a history that stretches long before the modern Industrial Revolution, as is memorably – if not altogether accurately – depicted in the medieval blast furnaces of Japan central to Hayao Miyazaki's 1997 film *Princess Mononoke* (Miyazaki 2014). Coal mining took place in China in the third millennium BC, and coal was later exploited by the Romans. Nevertheless, as with many phenomena of the Anthropocene, the significance lies not in its origin, but in its scale. The First Industrial

Revolution centered in Britain saw the rise in the use of coal to power steam engines – the invention of a steam engine design by James Watt in 1784 being suggested by Paul Crutzen (2002) as the start of the Anthropocene – which in turn powered emerging patterns of growth in transport and manufacture.

The growth in the use of coal may be charted by production statistics (e.g. Price et al. 2011), or by the tracing of its combustion product, carbon dioxide, for past centuries from the ice-core record, and from 1958 by the systematic atmospheric measurements initiated by Charles Keeling. The two measures are not equivalent: a little more than half of the carbon dioxide emitted is absorbed by the oceans or by extra plant growth, while the rest stays in the atmosphere. Even that remaining part will eventually be absorbed, ultimately by silicate weathering, but without active human efforts to remove it, significant amounts will remain in the atmosphere for many thousands of years (Clark et al. 2016). The atmospheric proportion affects climate directly, while the extra carbon dioxide dissolved into the oceans is responsible for anthropogenic ocean acidification, with growing effects on marine life (Orr et al. 2005). The growth of methane (part released during fossil-fuel extraction, and part emitted from livestock, landfill, and land use changes) can be similarly tracked through time, including in ice cores (Waters et al. 2016), though methane has a much shorter lifespan in the atmosphere, on the order of decades.

The pattern of rise in carbon dioxide – the bottom line here, as it were – is clear. Between around 1000 and 1800, levels had stayed around 280 ppm, rarely fluctuating by more than 5 ppm. By 1900, levels had climbed to 295 ppm, an increase of 15 ppm in this century of spreading industrialization. By 1950, it had climbed to 310 ppm, this 15-ppm rise taking half a century. By 2000, it had reached 370 ppm, a further quadrupling of the rate of rise as the postwar "Great Acceleration" took hold (Steffen et al. 2015a; McNeill and Engelke 2016), averaging 1.2 ppm/year. By early 2020, CO_2 levels exceeded 412 ppm, the rate of rise this millennium averaging 2.2 ppm/year. The amount of rise from pre-industrial times – now greater than 130 ppm – exceeds the difference between standard glacial and interglacial states of the Quaternary. Levels are now higher than at any time in the Quaternary (Voosen 2017) and are probably near those of the Pliocene Epoch, a time when mean global surface temperature was a couple of degrees higher than today, and sea levels more than 10 meters higher. The rate of atmospheric carbon dioxide rise over the past century is more than 100 times faster than that which took place as the Pleistocene gave way to the Holocene. There is now an extra 1 trillion tonnes of human-made carbon dioxide in the atmosphere. This is the equivalent of a pure gas layer about a meter thick (and growing at a millimeter every fortnight) – or the mass equivalent of about 150,000 of Khufu's Giant Pyramids, hanging in the sky (Zalasiewicz et al. 2016b).

The rate of rise of methane over this time is proportionately greater and steeper. From about 800 ppb at the start of the Industrial Revolution, levels climbed above 1,800 ppb by 2016, and have begun to climb again after a five-year plateau in the early part of this millennium.

The Temperature Effect

The rise in greenhouse gases has formed a clear pattern, and the direct heating effect of the rise in carbon dioxide can be measured (e.g. Feldman et al. 2015). The extra heating from the carbon dioxide and other greenhouse gases that humans have added to the atmosphere since 1750 (minus the cooling effects of anthropogenic aerosols, etc.) is now about 1.6 watts per square meter. This is a small climate forcing compared with the roughly 240 watts/m^2 that the Earth receives on average from sunlight, but, summed over the total surface area, it is a large amount – about 0.8 petawatt (i.e. 0.8 x 10^{15} watts), of which some 0.3 petawatt is absorbed (the rest is lost to space). Around 15 times the current total global power consumption of the human world (see below) and continuously maintained, it can change global average surface temperature.

Most of this extra heat – some 90 percent – is going into the oceans, with estimates taken by different means (Resplandy et al. 2018; Zanna et al. 2019) indicating, over the past quarter-century, somewhere between 6 and 13 "extra" zettajoules (Zj) of energy entering the oceans each year (NB: a watt is a joule/second). One Zj is 10^{21} joules: for comparison, the *total* energy consumption by humans (of which approximately 7 percent is from the burning of fossil fuels) is about 0.5 Zj each year (McGlade and Ekins 2015). Hence, the long-term "secondary" ocean heating effect of burning fossil fuels, via the greenhouse effect, is far greater than is the energy we obtain by burning them. The extra heat going into the ocean has been compared to pouring, each second, a billion cups of tea (heated to boiling point) into the ocean (Laure Zanna and Jonathan Gregory, personal communication). Thus, make yourself a cup of tea, using fossil-fuel energy, and you are also in effect pouring more than a dozen cups of tea straight into the sea.

The ocean waters take something like 1,000 years to mix thoroughly, for this heat to equilibrate within them and with the atmosphere. For the foreseeable future, the Earth System's heat balance will be a moving target. On Earth, several factors other than carbon dioxide (including other greenhouse gases, the reflectivity of different land and sea surfaces, and so on) also influence climate, and so the pattern of global temperature change has not been straightforward.

Earth's surface-temperature history since Britain's Industrial Revolution has climbed overall, though irregularly. The nineteenth century was, more or less, the tail end of the "Little Ice Age" which had followed the relative warmth of the "Medieval Climate Anomaly." These two climate phases had significantly impacted human life (e.g. Fagan 2001; Parker 2013), though the difference between them in terms of global average temperature was less than 1 °C (1.8 °F) (IPCC 2013). Global temperatures decreased by about 0.5 °C in the late nineteenth century, then climbed by a similar amount to 1940, which began the start of a temperature plateau that lasted until the 1970s, when temperatures climbed by a little over 0.5 °C to the 2000s, stayed on a decade-long plateau, then from 2010 climbed by another 0.2 °C to levels that are now about 1 °C above the 1950–80 average. Of the warmest years on record, 16 have been in the last 17 years.

This overall, if staggered, climb is the essence of the much-discussed "hockey stick" pattern of global temperature published in 1999 by the US climate scientist Michael Mann (Mann et al. 2017). The original hockey stick is now known to be a simplification, not least as the warm and cold peaks of the Medieval Warm Period and the Little Ice Age were staggered in time and space. But its essence has held up well and been reinforced. The warming over the last century departs from this long-term heterogeneous pattern in being synchronous globally – and for 98 percent of the world, it was the warmest interval in the last two millennia (Neukom et al. 2019).

It is now widely agreed in the climate science community that the overall temperature rise is largely human-driven, principally through the rise in greenhouse gases (IPCC 2013; Oreskes 2004). Its irregular nature – which might be seen at a fine temporal scale too, with three- to seven-year-long rises and falls of one or two tenths of a degree C – reflects that other climate factors have modulated the steady increase in heating due to rising greenhouse gas levels.

Some of the factors here affected the overall radiative balance of the Earth. The 40-year "plateau" from around 1940 to 1980, even while greenhouse gas levels were rising, has been at least partly attributed to another effect of fossil-fuel burning – the release of industrial smoke particles and sulfate aerosols into the atmosphere to cause "global dimming," reducing the amount of sunlight reaching the Earth's surface. This balance is complicated, as some smoke particles – black carbon, for instance – trap heat rather than reflect it, but overall the effect was of cooling. This effect was subsequently diminished by the widespread adoption of particulate- and sulfur dioxide-trapping filters as many of the old smokestack factories were phased out in the late twentieth century. Major volcanic eruptions can demonstrably have similar, albeit short-lived, effects, as they eject ash and sulfate particles into the stratosphere: the eruptions of El Chichon in Mexico in 1983 and Mount Pinatubo in the Philippines in 1991 each cooled the Earth by about half a degree for two to three years.

Then there are those factors that redistribute heat within the Earth System. The "global average temperature" that is measured is effectively an average air temperature. The atmosphere stores much less heat than the oceans, and most of the extra heating caused by anthropogenic greenhouse gases is going into raising ocean temperature. Variations in ocean–atmosphere behavior modulate this ongoing heat transfer process. In El Niño years, when a pool of warm water spreads eastward across the Pacific, the balance goes toward heating the atmosphere, and in La Niña years, when this effect is suppressed, the effect is of atmospheric cooling. This fundamental, relatively short-term oscillation helps explain a good deal of the jagged nature of the temperature record. There are longer cycles too, such as the Atlantic Multidecadal Oscillation, and the Pacific Decadal Oscillation. Their interplay has been implicated in alternating between storing extra heat in the oceans, helping to account for the temperature "plateau" of the early part of this millennium, and then releasing heat so the atmosphere warmed more rapidly afterwards.

In a geological context, where is global temperature now? The pre-industrial Holocene was in many ways a standard interglacial, though proxy evidence in strata (such as fossil pollen assemblages) suggests that global average temperature was a degree or so below peak warmth reached in some previous interglacials – such as the last interglacial, about 125,000 years ago, and the third-before-last, some 400,000 years ago. Now that the mean surface temperature has risen a degree Celsius above pre-industrial levels, further warming will take it beyond the envelope of Quaternary interglacials into a new long-term climate state, as projected by Clark et al. (2016). The Earth of the present Anthropocene state is still (just) within interglacial temperature norms. The course of future climate change beyond these norms will in large part be determined by feedbacks in the Earth System, including choices made by human societies in the coming decades.

Enough further warming is already locked in for the world to come very close to the maximum 1.5 °C (2.7 °F) hotter that the Paris Climate Accord in 2016 chose as its aim. According to the IPCC in 2019, if all power plants, factories, vehicles, ships, and planes were replaced at the end of their useful lives with zero-carbon alternatives, there is still a 64 percent chance of staying under 1.5 °C. Most mitigation scenarios proposed by the IPCC also assume the development of large-scale use of CO_2 removal methods, but effective and affordable carbon drawdown technologies have proven elusive. Improved land stewardship to increase carbon storage and avoid greenhouse gas emissions has been proposed as both effective and cheap (Griscom et al. 2017).

Ancient and New Climate Feedbacks

Anthropocene climate is on a warming trajectory. An equilibrium state of ocean and air temperatures reflecting the new radiative balance brought about by increased levels of greenhouse gases is still many centuries into the future – not least as levels of greenhouse gases in the atmosphere are still increasing at geologically rapid rates. Only after they stabilize can the system begin to finally equilibrate, and then to adjust to slowly declining carbon dioxide levels as silicate weathering begins to take effect. The great uncertainty regarding the total amount of greenhouse gases that human societies will produce means that projections of future climate (e.g. IPCC 2013; Clark et al. 2016) take the form of different scenarios, each with different levels of greenhouse gas emissions and peak levels of carbon dioxide, resulting in differing degrees of ultimate warming.

In each of the scenarios, there are uncertainties as to the course and tempo of climate evolution, which will depend on the interaction of feedback effects in the Earth System that act to amplify warming (if they are positive feedbacks) or diminish it (if they are negative). These feedbacks act at different rates, from almost instantaneously to acting over many millennia. The negative feedbacks that will ultimately bring the current global warming to an end, of silicate weathering and carbon burial in sedimentary strata, work very slowly. But feedbacks amplifying global warming often work more rapidly, from the almost instantaneous effect of raised temperatures increasing evaporation rates and adding water vapor (an important greenhouse gas in its own right) into the atmosphere, to the melting of highly reflective sea ice over decades to reduce albedo and so allow the surface part of the ocean to absorb more heat.

Some feedbacks are uncertain: a changing climate will undoubtedly alter patterns of the Earth's cloud systems, but clouds can act either to warm the Earth or to cool it, according to their type and distribution, and so this factor remains difficult to predict. A widely predicted feedback is the emission of methane from methane clathrates (a waxy methane–water compound) currently buried in sea floor sediments and permafrost soils, and sensitive to decomposition and methane release in warming regimes. This feedback might provide powerful amplification, but its significance to a warming world remains poorly constrained, and its current contribution is difficult to disentangle from contemporary enhanced methane release from industry, agriculture, and land use change.

The geological past also holds examples of ancient global warming events that may act as useful comparisons with the present, ongoing event. One such "hyperthermal" event is the Paleocene–Eocene Thermal Maximum (PETM), which took place 55 million years ago, and another is the Toarcian event of the early Jurassic, some 183 million years ago (Cohen et al. 2007). Both took similar courses, as "spikes" of rapid global warming of around 5–8 °C (~9–14 °F) associated with large, geologically rapid natural emissions of greenhouse gases from the ground to the ocean/atmosphere system, the perturbation of the global carbon system being evident through changes in carbon isotope ratios preserved in the strata. Recovery in these cases took in the order of 100,000 years, through enhanced silicate weathering, and through increased burial of carbon in sediments as sea and lake floors became oxygen-deprived.

These ancient warming events hold clues to the rate and tempo of climate change. Detailed analysis of the Toarcian event shows the course of carbon release and of warming not to be smooth (as depicted in typical and necessarily simplified projections of global warming today, e.g. Clark et al. 2016), but to be stepped, in the form of several steep rises separated by plateaus, ascribed to modulation of carbon release by astronomical cycles (Kemp et al. 2005). The nature of the carbon released – especially the relative proportion of carbon dioxide to methane – has been much discussed. A common model is a two-stage process: an initial release of carbon dioxide producing some warming, which in turn triggers a massive methane release producing the bulk of the warming. However, a recent study of the PETM, exploiting geochemical evidence of how much the oceans acidified, suggested that very large carbon dioxide emissions – considerably larger than humans have so far produced, but emitted rather more slowly – from a pulse of volcanism as part of the North Atlantic Ocean opened were the main factor (Gutjahr et al. 2017).

These ancient examples may be used only cautiously as imperfect guides to the future. Today, there are some striking similarities, not least in the flooding of the Earth's surface with isotopically "light" carbon, that becomes preserved in strata as evidence of the event (see chapter 2). But there are also important differences. The ancient hyperthermal events typically took place in warm "greenhouse" phases of climate, when there was little or no ice on Earth – and, of course, the climate forcing that then took place had physico-chemical causes. In this ongoing climate event of the Anthropocene, the human climate feedbacks may well be the crucial ones.

Human Climate Feedbacks of the Anthropocene

A simple view of the relationship between science and policy might suggest that, after scientific research identifies a looming environmental problem, policymakers absorb that information, create the appropriate regulations, and design some means of overcoming the danger. Thus, science and policy work hand in glove to ameliorate problems. Sometimes the relationship does indeed work in this straightforward manner. Examples include the redesign of London's sewer system in the mid nineteenth century to eradicate cholera, England's Clean Air Act of 1956 which eliminated the deadly smog of that city, and, internationally, the Montreal Protocol that entered into force in 1989 to successfully phase out the production of the chlorofluorocarbons that had created the "ozone hole" in the stratosphere discovered by routine scientific observations only in 1985. In each case, the measures were forced through against the opposition of a variety of vested interests who had profited in one way or another from the original, environmentally damaging situation, on the grounds that the common good should take precedence. These are all examples of conscious efforts to respond to scientific evidence in order to stabilize systems supporting human health.

However, in the case of global warming, efforts at mitigation in response to the very clear science on this issue have not yet been effective, despite the high public profile and widely – if not universally – perceived urgency of the issue. The steady rise of carbon dioxide levels in the atmosphere (and, indeed, its acceleration) in just the past few years shows the current ineffectiveness of political and social measures to reduce greenhouse gas emissions. We investigate this general phenomenon in detail in chapter 7, but key factors in the resistance to change are the commitment to an economic system premised on growth, a deep-seated reluctance in many societies to put the common good first, and a pathological path dependency on fossil fuels, industrial agriculture, global shipping and travel, building materials such as concrete, and other greenhouse gas-emitting activities common to all modern societies.

Climate Consequences in the Anthropocene

Climate history is such an important part of geological history because of the range and profundity of climate-driven processes and effects in the Earth System. Intense climate change events lie at the heart of four of the five great mass extinctions in Earth history (the exception is the meteorite-impact-driven Cretaceous–Paleogene mass extinction, though even here severe, transient climate effects from the impact have been inferred: Bardeen et al. 2017), and climate patterns overall have been strong controls on patterns of erosion, sedimentation, and biological evolution. Contemporary climate change is treated so seriously because its impacts, just beginning, may become severe or catastrophic as the Anthropocene world evolves, under almost any trajectory other than that of determined and successful attempts to prevent carbon dioxide levels from rising above agreed ceilings. This is currently 450 ppm, a level considered to have a chance of limiting global mean surface temperature rise to less than 1.5 °C above pre-industrial levels. The potential characteristics of a warming world have been widely explored (e.g. Letcher 2016). Here, we limit ourselves to brief discussion of some features of particular significance to the Anthropocene Earth System (including its human component).

Among these features is, simply, higher temperatures, and the consequent physiological effects upon living organisms. As climate changes, the high latitudes experience most temperature change, with relatively limited temperature changes in the low latitudes. Nevertheless, even modest temperature rises in areas that are already hot can increase the incidence of lethally high combinations of temperature and humidity – 30 percent of humanity already lives in areas where the lethal threshold is exceeded for at least 20 days a year. Mora et al. (2017) suggested that this figure would rise to 48 percent by 2100 even in a regime of drastic reductions in carbon emissions, and 74 percent in a business-as-usual scenario. In this regime of increasing heat spikes, and the need to shelter from them, increased demand for energy-intensive air conditioning (Davis and Gertler 2015) will act as a positive feedback mechanism, making the climate yet warmer.

Increasing heat-death affects communities other than human ones. In the phenomenon of coral bleaching, heat-stressed coral organisms expel their symbiotic algae, turning a ghostly white and losing much of their nutrition, and dying in severe instances. It is a modern phenomenon, first reported in 1984 (Hughes et al. 2018). Since then, it has become more frequent and widespread as tropical and subtropical waters have become hotter (Heron et al. 2016), extending over thousands of kilometers in the greatest event so far, in 2016–17, and being recognized as an emergent phenomenon of the Anthropocene (Hughes et al. 2018), which threatens the very existence of the coral reef ecosystem, and all of the rich biodiversity – and the thriving human systems – that it supports.

Coral reefs are more or less immobile, at least as regards the kind of real-time change that the Anthropocene involves. Other biological systems can migrate, at least as far as geographic barriers – and now also the human-made barriers of urban areas and agricultural monocultures – will allow them to. One of the signatures of the emergent Anthropocene is the shifting of animal and plant ranges toward higher latitudes and higher topographies, with the 1 °C or so (1.8 °F plus) of warming that has been taking place since the mid twentieth century. This has affected both terrestrial and marine communities, the latter more acutely because marine organisms, having evolved in the more thermally buffered environment of the sea, have narrower temperature tolerances. For instance, over the past half-century, plankton communities of the northeast Atlantic have been moving northward at up to 200 km per decade, more than ten times faster than typical range change rates on land (Edwards 2016).

These biological changes are of planetary importance, and on a trajectory to become profound, but they and their significance are mainly hidden from human sight. Nevertheless, they are already involved in questions such as what biological conservation might mean in the developing Anthropocene (Corlett 2015): for instance, to what extent assisted migration – or even the welcoming, rather than extirpation, of some invasive species – might become an option in a world where much of the remaining native fauna and flora may soon find itself out of its comfort zone in its original Holocene range. One key factor here is that contemporary climate change involves going from an original state that is already very near peak interglacial warmth, and pushing it into a yet warmer state, of the kind that the Earth has not experienced for several million years. The many repeated climate oscillations between glacial and interglacial states of the Quaternary did not lead to enhanced extinction rates: the biosphere had adjusted to a pattern of modifications and migrations over these 2–3 million years. It is the departure from this envelope of conditions, combined with other anthropogenic pressures on the biosphere (see chapter 5), that is leading to rapid change.

There are other consequences of climate change that are currently trivial geologically, but are already of societal consequence, and are set to be profoundly important societally well before they become profound geologically. The most striking change in this category is sea-level rise.

The Sea Rises

The glacial–interglacial cycles of the Quaternary have been accompanied by repeated, geologically large-scale global sea-level oscillations as ice caps alternately grew and melted. In the last of these, as the Pleistocene gave way to the Holocene, sea level rose by some 130 meters, starting some 20,000 years ago, before stabilizing close to its current level 7,000 years ago. Since that time, sea level rose slowly by some 3 meters until about 4,000 years ago, after which it has crept up by less than a meter, but with no detectable century-scale individual pulses of sea-level rise of more than 15–20 cm, and no apparent sea-level response to minor climate fluctuations such as the Medieval Warm Period and Little Ice Age (Lambeck et al. 2014). During this time, human civilization developed and began to exten-sively colonize an apparently fixed and stable shoreline.

Over the past century, sea level has begun to depart from this stable state, as the world has warmed. In part, this is due to thermal expansion of the oceans, as the surface warmth has begun to spread to deeper layers of the ocean. And, in part, the oceans are being added to by water from melting ice, partly from the shrinkage and disappearing of mountain glaciers, and partly from the melting of polar ice.

As with most Anthropocene phenomena, this is an ongoing and accelerating process. The total amount of sea-level rise over the last century remains geologically trivial, at a little over 20 cm (approximately 8 inches). This is because the melting of ice lags behind the increase in global temperature, which itself lags behind the change in the radiative balance of the Earth brought about by the buildup of greenhouse gases in the atmosphere. Nevertheless, there is a detectable increase in the rate of sea-level rise, the rate for the early twenty-first century being around 3 mm/year from satellite altimeter data (accelerating from little more than 1 mm/year over much of the mid twentieth century), and simply extrapolating the current rate of acceleration would mean that sea level would rise by some 65 cm this century (Nerem et al. 2018).

The mechanism of polar ice melt – the important component – is partly due to extra heat at its surface where it meets the atmosphere; this kind of melting would take many millennia, though, given the thermal inertia of ice. Rather, melting at the bases of ice sheets, where warmer seawater is impinging, is increasingly recognized as crucial. As this process happens, the entire grounding line that separates land-based from floating ice can retreat inland, a trend that has been observed this millennium from satellite data (Konrad et al. 2018). As ice masses lift off their rocky floor and begin to float, the loss of frictional restraint can make the land-based ice surge toward the sea, where it breaks up as icebergs, which drift to lower latitudes and melt. The sudden breakup of floating ice shelves may ensue, as happened with collapse of the Larsen B ice shelf (with an area about the size of Wales) of the Antarctic Peninsula in 2002, and a section of the Larsen C ice shelf in 2017.

While the breakup of floating ice in itself does not add to sea-level rise (in the same way that melting a cube of ice floating in a gin and tonic does not make the glass seem fuller afterwards), the loss of its restraining effect on the land-based ice behind can, likewise, make that land ice flow more quickly into the sea, a process already observed. The record of sea-level rise from the ice sheet melting around the Pleistocene–Holocene transition shows that the sea level rose not smoothly but in fits and starts, with the most rapid phases of sea-level rise (exceeding 40 mm/year) reflecting episodes of ice sheet collapse (Blanchon and Shaw 1995). This kind of pattern of irregular rise may be expected over the coming centuries and millennia of the Anthropocene. The sensitivity of ice sheets to even minor rises in temperature can be seen in the last interglacial phase, 125,000 years ago, when, at global temperatures little (if at all) higher than today's, sea level rose to about 5 meters or more (about 16.5 feet) above its current level (Dutton and Lambeck 2012).

While 5 meters is geologically a very modest sea-level change, its impact on human society would be very large. This reflects the way that the coastline has adjusted to the stability of Holocene sea level, particularly with large deltas that stretch out as platforms at, or only just above, sea level, over many thousands of square kilometers. Humans have preferentially colonized these low-lying, fertile, and water-rich places – and in recent centuries have made them yet more low-lying by draining them and compacting their loose soils, and pumping groundwater and hydrocarbons out from beneath them (Syvitski et al. 2009). The resulting subsidence can be of several meters below densely populated coastal areas such as those around New Orleans, Jakarta, Shanghai, and other coastal cities.

Large parts of these heavily populated areas will be inundated, or made more prone to catastrophic flooding, with only a meter-scale rise in sea level, especially given that warmer oceans seem already to be producing more powerful and flood-inducing tropical cyclones (Trenberth et al. 2018). This scenario now seems considerably more likely than not over the next century or two. Navigating the resulting rebuilding and resettlement – and containing the manifold effects of marine erosion on inundated human infrastructure and waste sites – will probably be one of the greater and more challenging tasks of the evolving Anthropocene.

We are experiencing only the first stresses of the global heating. This unleashed force is so powerful that it will continue to impact our planet for many generations of human societies. Already, climate change is affecting the biosphere. As described in the next chapter, the intensifying heat, along with myriad other human influences, is rapidly altering our planet's living skin.

5

The Anthropocene and the Biosphere's Transformation

In the last few hundred years, human beings have modified the biosphere profoundly. Human-driven changes include extraordinary species translocations between all continents and all oceans, modification of a whole range of animal and plant species that we use for food – the populations of some, such as chickens and pigs, having grown gigantic – and changes to entire ecosystems. The position of humans as now (in effect) top predator, both on land and in the oceans, and humanity's appropriation of something like a third of total net primary productivity (that is, the total energy stored in the biomass of plants and other primary producers) on this planet is a unique state in Earth history. Here we examine the complexity of the biosphere and how it can be defined, the roots of human impacts on the biosphere and how they have developed over time, how they manifest at present, and what their possible future trajectories may be.

The Biosphere

A modern scientific understanding of the connections between life, air, water, and land began to emerge from the expeditions of nineteenth-century naturalists. At the turn of that century, Prussian naturalist Alexander von Humboldt (1769–1859) and French botanist Aimé Bonpland (1773–1858) traveled together through South America, making observations that demonstrated a clear relationship between plants, animals, and the environmental conditions that surrounded them. In the forests of Venezuela, the two men witnessed *"trees of stupendous height and size,"* and observed, as they descended from high ground, that the *"ferns diminish and the number of palm-trees increase,"* and that large-winged butterflies became more common (vol. I, ch. 1.8, translated by Thomasina Ross). By the close of the nineteenth century, organisms had been documented from environments as diverse as the deep oceans and the tops of mountains, and natural geographical constraints on the distributions of species had been widely recognized. By the time Austrian geologist Eduard Suess (1831–1914) first used the term "Biosphäre," in his book *The origin of the alps* (*Die Entstehung der Alpen*, 1875), the notion of a biosphere had already begun to take shape in the literature, and Suess conjured the specific term to express it. Suess's book was primarily concerned with the processes of mountain building, and the biosphere was mentioned only once, to denote the zone of organic life interacting between the upper sphere (of the atmosphere and hydrosphere) and the lithosphere. Suess used the term again, however, in his five-volume work *The face of the Earth* (*Das Antlitz der Erde*, 1885–1909), writing (in vol. II, 1888, p. 269) about a world divisible into two "chief groups," one formed by those organisms living directly under the influence of the sun, and one by those living in darkness. Suess saw evidence of complex interactions between environment and organisms deep in the fossil record of trilobites, an extinct group of marine animals that possessed an external skeleton, like that of a beetle, but impregnated with the mineral calcite. The trilobite head often displays magnificent eye-lenses built into the skeleton, but some trilobites lacked eyes and were blind, as they lived in marine environments beyond the influence of light. From other fossils, Suess was able to discern ancient animal communities living at different water depths in ancient seas (1888, p. 337).

Half a century after Suess, Russian scientist Vladimir Vernadsky formulated a concept of the biosphere that fully integrated its evolution with the atmosphere, hydrosphere, and lithosphere. *The biosphere*, published in 1926, outlined the complex relationships between plants and animals, and the way that chemicals flow into and out of biological matter. It explored the parameters within which life could flourish. Vernadsky's observations in this latter regard were prescient, being based on real physical constraints such as temperature, exposure to ultraviolet radiation, and availability of water. He predicted life could exist to 3.5 km depth in the continental crust and noted the presence of life in the upper regions of the troposphere. Subsequently, science has discovered microbes in the Earth's continental crust to 4 km depth, whilst 10 km above the surface of the Earth, in the upper troposphere, thousands of bacterial cells can be extracted from a cubic meter of air. Vernadsky viewed life as a geological process, and considered that life engineered the planet so as to make more parts of it become habitable over time. He noted that hundreds of minerals in the upper part of the Earth's crust, such as calcite and iron hydroxides, are continuously formed by the influence of life. Later, Vernadsky incorporated the concept of a noösphere (used differently from the noösphere of Teilhard de Chardin; see Levit 2002) into his biosphere, the noösphere being "the sphere of reason," and in this sense he viewed human reason as part of an "inevitable manifestation of a great natural process having lasted in a regular way for at least two billion years" (see Vernadsky 1997, p. 31). The biosphere, thus, is best defined as all life on Earth, and its interconnectedness with the atmosphere, hydrosphere, and lithosphere. Over time, the biosphere has modified all of these different components of the Earth System – in the process, engineering a greater range of environments for life. Plants have evolved to become the overwhelmingly dominant component of the biomass on the land, bacteria and protists in marine settings, and bacteria and archaea in deep subsurface environments. Animals, a small component of the overall biomass, have their greater component of mass in the sea, where they originated.

Biological transformations of the Earth System are evident in the geological record. The evolution of plant photosynthesis using water and carbon dioxide to produce carbohydrates to build plant tissue, with free oxygen released into the environment as a by-product, was transformative from 2.4 billion years ago (see chapters 1 and 2). Photosynthesis allowed the biosphere to become independent of more localized chemical sources of energy and to become the basis of food supply – the primary production – in the oceans. That free oxygen released accumulated to change the hydrosphere, atmosphere, and lithosphere – on land, making a whole new suite of minerals, including reddening the landscape through iron oxides. Much later in Earth's history, plants colonized the land from about 470 million years ago (Wellman and Gray 2002), growing to become the bulk of planetary biomass. Their root systems evolved to bind together sediments and stabilize riverbanks. Rivers began commonly to flow in meandering patterns across their floodplains for the first time, leaving a distinctive suite of sediments that, once changed to rock, would preserve the muds accumulating on these ancient riverbanks. Root-bound, these muddy sediments would make new space in which other organisms could live. Onto these ancient floodplains moved animals, their fossil traces being preserved in rocks from a little over 400 million years ago (Davies and Gibling 2010, 2013).

The complex interrelationships between organisms and their environment explored by Vernadsky can be witnessed even in the smallest of living ecosystems. In a small coastal rock pool, for example, connected to its wider marine ecosystem, there will be primary producer organisms, such as the algae or phytoplankton that source their energy from the sun by photosynthesis. There will be animals like limpets, snails, and tiny crustaceans that graze on the algae. Some animals in the rock pool – like crabs – will be predators on the snails. Others, like small shrimps, may scavenge the carcasses of dead animals, or they may remove dead skin or parasites from fish living in the rock pool, in a mutually beneficial (symbiotic) relationship. Microbial organisms, not visible to the naked eye, decompose the tissues of animal or plant carcasses, releasing components that can be recycled into new living matter: an integral process of the biosphere. All of these organisms will interact with the physical and chemical environment of the rock pool. Its crevices may provide small animals with respite from predators. Seaweed may serve the same function. There will be complex connections with the wider marine environment when the tide comes back in, bringing with it water, nutrients, oxygen, and other organisms. These interrelationships exist, whether in a rock pool, on the savannah of East Africa, or elsewhere.

For billions of years, the major controls on the distribution of organisms have been environmental: the availability of light, food and water, a surface temperature range amenable to life, and physical constraints of landscape and oceans that limit or allow migration. These patterns have resulted in characteristic assemblages of plants and animals in distinct climate zones, referred to as biomes. One can talk of a savannah-type biome, a tropical rainforest biome, or at high latitudes a tundra or polar desert-type biome. These biomes have been evolving for hundreds of millions of years. During the Carboniferous Period, for example (359 to 299 million years ago), tropical rainforests existed, inferred from the distribution of fossil plants, though the component species of those forests were very different from those living today. This natural pattern of biomes was virtually undisturbed by humans until just a few millennia ago, as were the patterns of organisms that resided within them. Thus, maize was still limited to Central America 10,000 years ago, and the red jungle fowl, the ancestor of domesticated chickens, occupied the rainforests of South and Southeast Asia, including what is now southern China, but nowhere else. Biomes can also be recognized in the oceans, but here their patterns are more dynamic, being influenced by ocean currents and their contained heat, nutrient supply, and primary production.

Now, human agency has become a primary control on the distribution of organisms. This new control has developed over several thousand years and has accelerated in the last century or so. One of the key processes here is a transplantation of species, on a scale unprecedented in Earth's history.

A Globally Homogenized Fauna and Flora

Eduard Suess's observations of fossils helped to discern patterns of ancient ecologies. He was also able to use fossils to map the position of ancient continents. He noted that a fossil fern called *Glossopteris* could be used to identify an ancient supercontinent that he named Gondwanaland. This giant landmass existed some 300 million years ago, connecting South America, Africa, India, Antarctica and Australia in the southern hemisphere. Suess surmised that, for a plant to be so widespread, these continents must have had a common connection. Geologists use the same kinds of patterns in the fossil record to track the movement of continents by plate tectonics. When continents converge, their complements of species converge. And when they are far apart, they diverge, as the environments of different landmasses move farther apart. When North and South America were bridged, some 3 million years ago, by tectonic uplift through the Isthmus of Panama, faunas and floras were exchanged. Armadillos and sloths went north, while cougars and sabre-toothed cats went south, this cross-transfer being preserved in the fossil record. These patterns show that the distribution of animals and plants on land and in the oceans has been strongly controlled by geography for hundreds of millions of years.

For a future geologist examining the patterns of organism distribution forming at present (in our twenty-first century), the pattern would be highly confusing. One might expect, for example, that the fauna and flora of New Zealand would be isolated from the influences of other places, a function of its geographical isolation in the southwest Pacific for tens of millions of years. But there are now nearly as many introduced plant species in New Zealand as there are indigenous plant species, and many of these are likely to endure and evolve to leave a lasting signal of their presence in fossilized leaves, pollen, and spores. In the oceans, too, ancient patterns of species distribution have broken down, as something of the order of 10,000 marine species have been translocated in the ballast tanks of shipping (Bax et al. 2003). Long-term patterns of geographically and climatically controlled biogeography are collapsing, and this, even before Paul Crutzen's improvisation of the Anthropocene, led to the suggestion of a "Homogenocene" (Samways 1999) reflecting the global homogenization of biota.

The process of humans moving organisms across the globe has developed over millennia and is intimately associated with domestication of animals and plants for food supply. The European rabbit (*Oryctolagus cuniculus*), for instance, has been translocated across the world. This species was taken into mainland Britain 2,000 years ago by humans, and later, in the eighteenth century, Europeans took it on the First Fleet to Australia, where it has become invasive to the extent of seriously degrading local ecosystems by overgrazing. To curb the numbers of rabbits in Australia, new non-indigenous organisms have been introduced, such as the myxomatosis virus from South America. Another widespread invasive species, the domestic cat (*Felis catus*), began its process of domestication and dispersal from the Near East 9,000 years ago. Its patterns of dispersal follow human routes of trade and connection (Ottoni et al. 2017). Cats kill over a billion birds and several billion mammals each year in the United States alone (Loss et al. 2013).

The species inventory of many ecosystems has been drastically changed by these migrations, and this is particularly evident in geographically remote areas that have been subject to human influence only recently. Such ecologies evolved in geographical isolation and are characterized by distinctive species with narrow ecological and geographical ranges.

Reconfigured Island Ecologies

The isolated islands of the Republic of Mauritius, also known as the Mascarene Islands, are an iconic symbol of the impact of introduced species on local fauna and flora. Lying in the Indian Ocean several hundred kilometers east of Madagascar, they are characterized by an indigenous biota in which over 50 percent of the flowering plants are only known there. The principal islands are Mauritius, some 855 kilometers east of Madagascar, and, a further 574 kilometers to its east, Rodrigues. Direct human impact on Mauritius is recent. Arab traders discovered the islands during the thirteenth century, and in 1598 Mauritius was claimed by the Dutch East India Company.

Black rats (*Rattus rattus*), possibly introduced from shipwrecks, appear to have impacted the island for longer than its occupation by humans. Subsequent periods of French and British colonial rule collectively introduced a fauna and flora that had geographically widespread origins.

Mauritius is most famous for the loss of the dodo (*Raphus cucullatus*), the last sighting of which was in 1662. This is the first species in human history to be documented as extinct. Ironically, the dodo was a columbine, a relative of pigeons and doves that are a widespread and numerically abundant group of birds. But, unlike its columbine relatives, the dodo was a flightless bird, probably evolving this strategy because of the abundance of food at ground level on the island, and because of the absence of predators prior to human influence. Its less famous relative, the Rodrigues solitaire (*Pezophaps solitaria*) adopted the same life strategy on Rodrigues Island, and suffered the same fate in the mid eighteenth century. Although the dodo was extinct less than a century after people occupied Mauritius, its demise appears to have been due to introduced animals such as rats, pigs, and deer, rather than to hunting by the small number of humans that occupied Mauritius in the seventeenth century.

The dodo is only a small part of the story of extinction on Mauritius, where something of the order of 80 native vertebrate species have been lost over the past 400 years, whilst some 100 non-native species have been introduced. Black rats had apparently arrived by 1598. Deliberately introduced animals include wild boar (*Sus scrofa*) and goats (*Capra hircus*) before 1648, used as a means of feeding passing sailors. Later, these were joined by brown rats (*Rattus norvegicus*) – which were accidentally introduced – and by the deliberate introduction of the giant African snail (*Lissachatina fulica*) and small Indian mongoose (*Herpestes auropunctatus*), for food and to control the rats, respectively; neither of these strategies achieved their intended goal. At the same time, many plants were introduced from as far afield as the Americas, including the mimosoid *Leucaena leucocephala*. As a result, all of the native forests of Mauritius have been invaded by foreign plants.

The pattern of introductions to Mauritius accelerated during the twentieth century. Of 22 insect species arriving during this time, 14 did so after 1975. Not all invasions are irreversible. The invasive oriental fruit fly (*Bactrocera dorsalis*), detected near the airport in 1996, was contained by 1997, and it was declared eradicated in 1999. And success was also achieved in preserving the Mauritius Kestrel, at one point reduced to a population of just 4 wild birds, and thereby being the rarest bird in the world in 1974. It is now known from about 400 mature birds in the wild, though this figure is half what it was a decade ago and the species is still endangered.

The patterns of species introduced to Mauritius have been well documented for the land, and they show that it is virtually impossible to return the terrestrial ecosystems of the island to a pre-human state. Mauritius's marine ecosystems have similarly been impacted, by species – such as the Pacific oyster (*Crassostrea gigas*) – that have a global signature of migration.

In some island settings, it is possible to observe the human impact on the landscape developing over centuries, as in the sedimentary succession of the ancient Hawaiian island of Kauai, preserved in the sinkhole at Mahaulepu. Here, sediments accumulating over the past millennium show the first instance of an introduced Pacific rat (*Rattus exulans*) sometime between 1039 and 1241 CE, as an indication of the arrival of Polynesians. Declines in numbers, and extirpation, of many indigenous species of snails recorded in the sinkhole succession first of all show the influence of Polynesian settlers, and latterly the influence of Europeans, with all indigenous snails going extinct in the nineteenth and twentieth centuries. From the mid twentieth century, the sinkhole preserves fossil evidence of the introduced giant African snail and of the cannibal snail of Central America (*Euglandina rosea*). Analysis of the sinkhole succession led David Burney and his colleagues to the conclusion that the diverse landscape of Kauai had been completely transformed by humans, resulting in the decline or disappearance of most native species, to be replaced by introduced ones (Burney et al. 2001). Mahaulepu demonstrates the evolution of the island's landscape over 1,000 years, from a natural biome, one established by geography and climate, to a pervasively human-influenced biome, one established by its interaction with humans.

Reconfigured Continental Ecologies

The reconfiguration of island faunas and floras in just a short interval of time is clear evidence of human impacts on the biosphere, but large landmasses are also subject to major species introductions and to concomitant ecosystem reconfiguration. Sub-Saharan Africa serves as a prime example of a continental area with mass introductions that are altering its natural ecologies. This is the birthplace of humanity, and home to the greatest surviving megafaunal diversity. But out on the savannah, things have changed, as invasive species disrupt long-evolved biological relationships.

Ant communities in Kenya, for example, have been reconfigured as a result of the introduction of the bigheaded ant (*Pheidole megacephala*), the native range of which may be Southern Africa or Madagascar. The bigheaded ant has impacted on four species of ant that live on the whistling thorn acacia (*Acacia drepanolobium*) (Riginos et al. 2015). The relationship between the plants and these ant species had coevolved to be mutualistic. The plant provides food and a place to live for the ants, and in return the ants vigorously defend the plant from herbivores. Three species of these ants belong to the genus *Crematogaster*, a widespread group characterized by a heart-shaped abdomen. They feed on the nectar produced by the acacia. A fourth species – *Tetraponera penzigi* – exists by farming fungus and actually destroys the nectaries of the plant to discourage other ant species from colonizing. The bigheaded ant crashed into this finely honed natural ecology. *Crematogaster* ants can face off the invaders individually, but they are overwhelmed and quickly despatched by the sheer numbers of bigheaded invaders. The *Tetraponera* ants fare better by a policy of discretion rather than valor, and can hide in swollen acacia thorns for up to a month. In areas where bigheaded ants have invaded, there is now an up to sevenfold increase in catastrophic damage to the acacia by elephants, as the plants now have no natural defenders. The wider implications of this change are not yet understood, though the mutualistic relationship of the indigenous ants and acacia trees may ecologically be a keystone feature of the savannah. The invasive bigheaded ants are just one part of the disruption to the region. At least 245 invasive plant species have been documented in the Serengeti–Mara savannah ecosystem of East Africa that covers part of Kenya and neighboring Tanzania (Witt et al. 2017). The invasive Latin American "famine weed" (*Parthenium hysterophorus*) is already displacing the natural vegetation that supports the annual migration of large mammals such as wildebeest and zebra (it is also invasive in Australia, Asia, and the Middle East). Other plants, such as the invasive prickly pear (*Opuntia stricta*), are dangerous to animals that eat them, causing infections when their spines get lodged in gums, tongues, and guts. These plants also impede the movement of large animals across the landscape.

The impact of introduced species on the indigenous wildlife of the African savannah is becoming severe. And it is clear that even those environmental settings that we consider pristine have been modified so much that the term "biomes" for them is becoming increasingly ill suited.

A Domesticated Landscape

The African savannah is changing in other ways. The concept of human-modified ecosystems has been given a strong focus by Erle Ellis at the University of Maryland, and Navin Ramankutty at McGill University in Canada. The pair developed the concept of "anthromes," or human biomes, and first presented this idea to the scientific community in 2008. Unlike biomes, which represent the interaction of species with nonhuman environmental parameters such as rainfall and temperature, anthromes are dependent on human population density and land use. Ellis and Ramankutty devised a number of different types of anthrome according to these interactions. At one end of their spectrum of human influence are "used" anthromes, dense settlements such as major cities, villages, croplands, and rangelands. Village anthromes, for example, represent dense rural populations where agriculture is intensive. Between the "used anthromes" and the "wildlands," are the "semi-natural" landscapes, the populated woodlands, remote woodlands, and inhabited barren lands.

Ellis and colleagues plotted the development of these anthromes – divided into 19 different types – through the past 300 years on a global map, excluding the Antarctic. The maps track the rapid anthropogenic influence on the landscape. In 1700, the terrestrial biosphere could be defined as just 5% "used," with many areas of the world – such as the Americas, North Africa, central Asia, Siberia, and Australia – still showing little human influence on the landscape. Even then, less than 50% of the landscape could be classed as wild, though much was still semi-natural. This pattern largely persisted through the eighteenth century, but by the beginning of the twentieth century large areas of North America, central Asia, and Australia had been incorporated into "used" anthromes. By 2000, the terrestrial biosphere was 40% used, and less than 25% wild, with those remaining wildernesses being largely limited to deserts and polar regions. The change is so profound that Ellis and his colleagues have noted that the world is no longer dominated by natural ecosystems with humans disturbing them, but rather is transformed by human systems with more or less modified natural ecosystems embedded within them. More recent estimates show 95% of the land, excluding Antarctica (some 127.22 million km^2), modified by humans (Kennedy et al. 2019), the 5% of unmodified lands being concentrated in remote regions of tundra and boreal forests.

This echoes past major changes preserved in the geological record. Earth's early biosphere, originating perhaps 4 billion years ago, before oxygen-generating photosynthesis had evolved, was later embedded within the oxygen-metabolizing biosphere that began to evolve about 2.4 billion years ago. Most of the surface of the Earth is now dominated by oxygen-metabolizing organisms, while the oxygen-avoiders retreated to environments such as the deeper, anoxic levels of subsurface sediments, where they still thrive. The microbial world of the Precambrian, too, became embedded within the complex trophic structures of the animal-dominated world that evolved from about 540 million years ago in the oceans, and the plant-dominated domain that spread across the land 470 million years ago.

Over the past 300 years, animal, plant, fungal, and microbial components of the biosphere have become deeply embedded in human anthromes. The savannah of East Africa was already a human-modified semi-natural landscape 300 years ago. Since then, it has become a mosaic of used and semi-natural landscapes, from rangelands to urban settlements. A swathe of western Europe – from Germany, running through the Low Countries and on into England – is effectively one huge urban and intensively agricultural anthrome, whilst South Asia and much of East Asia have become gigantic village anthromes into which vast cities, such as Mumbai and Shanghai, are integrated.

As humans, in the early twenty-first century, became a dominantly urban species for the first time, and as this process of urbanization is set to continue, humans have been inducing another marked change to the biosphere, through their appropriation of the energy of biomass, both living and fossil. A recent estimate (Bar-On et al. 2018) suggests that the biomass of the biosphere currently includes some 550 billion tonnes of carbon (including 450 billion tonnes in plants, 77 billion tonnes in bacteria and archaea, 12 billion tonnes in fungi, and 2 billion tonnes in animals). The figure for plants, it was estimated, is roughly half of that which existed before humans began modifying the biosphere for agriculture as civilization began. Although humans and their livestock now dominate mammal biomass (at about 160 million tonnes of carbon), this still remains a small component of the total animal biomass which is dominated by arthropods (at 1 billion tonnes), followed by fish (at 700 million tonnes; Bar-On et al. 2018). With these large biomass changes come winners and losers. Not all the winners, though, are to be envied.

A Domesticated Biosphere

Bear attacks on humans are responsible for fatalities most years in North America, often striking hikers, campers, and even cyclists. Several thousand miles away in India, it is tigers eating humans. Some, like the prodigious Champawat Tiger of Nepal in the early twentieth century, are reputed to have killed hundreds of people. In some regions of South Asia, including the densely forested areas of the Sundarbans that straddle the Indian–Bangladeshi border, fatal tiger attacks remain quite common. And in the oceans, for example along Australia's Gold Coast, it is shark attacks that are feared. All of these human tragedies invoke strong sympathy for the victims, together with a kind of primeval terror that wild animals may still attack and kill us. But for most of us, indeed billions of us, this is an inverted fear, because the numbers of wild animals that attack humans are dwindling, while the numbers of wild mammals in total are diminishing sharply. Wild tigers may number only 4,000, or roughly the equivalent of the human population of one small village. And the once vast geographical range of tigers, from the Black Sea to the island of Java, is now reduced to fragments of land. Shark populations have been decimated too. The boot is overwhelmingly on the human foot.

In contrast to the fewer than 4,000 wild tigers, there are about 23 billion chickens (*Gallus gallus domesticus*) alive (Bennett et al. 2018). This is more than ten times greater than the standing population of the most prolific wild bird, the African red-billed quelea (*Quelea quelea*), at a mere 1.5 billion. Moreover, the biomass of chickens, measured in tonnes of carbon, is 2.5 times greater than that of all wild birds (5 million tonnes in chickens, versus 2 million tonnes in wild birds). The domesticated chicken may be the most populous bird species in Earth history, exceeding the estimated 3 to 5 billion passenger pigeons of the nineteenth century. Some 63 billion domesticated chickens are consumed by humans each year, as the life expectancy of each is curtailed from the *circa* 15 years of the ancestral species, the red jungle fowl, to about 6 weeks. Chickens now live in ecologies (battery farms) that are wholly unlike those of their jungle ancestor, and their geographical range extends to all continents bar Antarctica, though even in that continent chicken meat is consumed by humans, in dehydrated meals given to Antarctic scientists camping deep-field. Archeological chicken bones from the Indus Valley of Pakistan show that domestication of this bird by humans began at least 4,000 years ago, and probably earlier in China. The expansion of the chicken population, the modification of their anatomy, their translocation to different regions of the Earth, and their spread into a wider range of ecologies, including artificial ecologies made by humans, mirrors those of other domesticated animal species, such as cattle, sheep, and pigs. Much of the change to chicken physiology and anatomy, though – including a roughly threefold increase in body mass – has taken place since the mid twentieth century: this is when this distinctive and abundant morphospecies (the kind of species recognized by paleontologists, defined on distinctive skeletal shape, as opposed to genetic make-up) appeared and became widespread and hyper-abundant.

This process of domestication of a wide range of wild animals and plants may have begun more than 20,000 years ago, and marks the origin of a wholesale reconfiguration of the biosphere for human consumption. Along the shore of the Sea of Galilee in Israel are the charred remains of seeds associated with a small hut settlement from 23,000 years ago (Snir et al. 2015). These fragments identify weeds that co-occur with cultivated crops, and the people at this site were already consuming wild emmer wheat, wild barley, and wild oats, which would later become major human foodstuffs. More remarkably, the huts are also associated with animals that would become characteristic of human towns and cities, such as the black rat.

Archeological and fossil plant evidence of greater human impact on the environment begins from about 11,000 years ago, in the interval of time immediately postdating the retreat of the great northern hemisphere ice sheets, and associated with an amelioration of climate. Several centers of agriculture developed, with the cultivation of maize in the Americas, wheat in the Fertile Crescent of the Middle East, and rice in East Asia. Animal domestication also began about this time, with dogs at multiple sites in Eurasia from about 30,000 years ago. Since the beginnings of domestication, our major food animals and plants have become global in their distribution, and colossal in numbers. As well as the 23 billion chickens, there are about 1 billion pigs (*Sus scrofus domesticus*), each weighing up to 350 kg, and mostly used by humans for food. Other domesticated animals in colossal numbers are the over 1 billion cows, with sheep and turkeys occurring in similar numbers.

Domesticated plants have accumulated to similar scale. Maize, a staple of the early civilizations of Mesoamerica, was domesticated about 7,000 years ago and spread through the rest of the Americas over several millennia. It extended to the Old World during the

Columbian exchange of the sixteenth and seventeenth centuries, and has become a global food exceeding over 1,000 million tonnes of production each year, greater than that of wheat and rice. China, remote from the origins of maize domestication, is now the second-largest producer in the world.

Uniquely for a terrestrial species, humans have also domesticated animals and plants in aquatic settings, from Scottish salmon to Atlantic oysters, and rates of domestication of marine plants and animals are rising. Fish aquaculture has ancient origins, and, like agriculture, developed independently at many sites around the world from Australia to Europe, to include the cultivation of fish, shellfish, arthropods such as lobsters, and seaweed. But aquaculture as a food source was trivial until the later twentieth century. By early in the twenty-first century, humans were removing 170 million tonnes of fish products from the oceans each year, of which a little over 40 percent was farmed. In tandem with the development of aquaculture is the impact of humans on the biota of "natural" marine ecosystems. Using carbon again as a measure of biomass, the exploitation of marine mammals, including whaling, is thought to have reduced mammal biomass from 20 million tonnes of carbon to just 4 million tonnes, whilst in the case of fish there has been a loss of 100 million tonnes of carbon (Bar-On et al. 2018). Humans have removed most top predators in the oceans, including by some estimates 90 percent of the largest predatory fish stocks, and at the same time are harvesting the majority of the continental shelf fish stocks, ranging down onto parts of the continental slope. Aquaculture, like agriculture, has also led to the wholesale translocation of organisms across the planet, accelerating the homogenization of the biosphere.

With these changes comes biodiversity loss.

Death of an Animal Phylum Foretold

Can the current Anthropocene biodiversity changes come to rival the major extinction events of the geological past? Extinction rates are now much higher than background levels (see chapter 3), and one example suggests the developing extinction event already threatens the deep-time fabric of life. Amongst the fossils of animals found in Cambrian rocks from about 520 million years ago is a loosely defined group called the lobopods, with long flexible bodies above many pairs of stubby legs. Fossilized Cambrian lobopods have been unearthed in places as far apart as western Canada and south

China. Some bear a strong resemblance, and are likely related to, living onychophorans, despite the chasm of time between them. The Onychophora, colloquially known as velvet worms, are a phylum of entirely land-living animals that have a worm-like body a few centimetres long bearing a few tens of pairs of stubby "lobopod" legs (Blaxter and Sunnucks 2011). Velvet worms are unobtrusive predators capturing their prey by squirting a sticky immobilizing fluid onto them. A recent assessment of their biodiversity recognized about 177 species from tropical and southern hemisphere localities (Oliveira et al. 2012), though more species may lurk undiscovered. Many velvet worm species have small ecological ranges, occupying habitats that are perpetually moist, such as rainforests. They are highly vulnerable to human activities such as deforestation. Those few species that have been evaluated by the International Union for Conservation of Nature's (IUCN) "Red List" have mostly been classified as near-threatened, vulnerable, endangered, or critically endangered, and, given their narrow ecological ranges, most are potentially vulnerable to extinction (Sosa-Bartuano et al. 2018), though some are actively conserved (Morera-Brenes et al. 2019).

Velvet worms may be barely known to the casual observer, but they represent an entire animal phylum – a unique, major branch of the tree of life. More "famous" animal phyla include the chordates (the group that includes fish, mammals, amphibians, reptiles, and birds), echinoderms (the group that includes starfish, brittle stars, sea lilies, and sea urchins), and mollusks (including snails, bivalves, squid, and octopuses). The Onychophora may have small species diversity, but it is a phylum with a deep geological history, probably beginning in the Cambrian. They have been part of the evolution of the biosphere and its environments over hundreds of millions of years.

Velvet worms have survived all five mass extinctions of the past 500 million years, though their fossil record is too poor to recognize the strategies they used to do this, largely because they became an exclusively terrestrial group. If humans are indeed making them vulnerable to extinction, a significant and irreversible loss to the biosphere is pending. If the biosphere loses a whole phylum, this would be, from an evolutionary sense, more final than the extinction of the dinosaurs, whose chordate relatives the birds, reptiles, mammals, amphibians, and fish live on in tens of thousands of species. The body plan of onychophorans would be extinguished forever. All that onychophorans might ever become in the future would be gone, and the Earth's animal disparity (the range of body plans in nature) would be irreparably reduced for the first time in over 500 million years. That, indeed, would be a very significant biological marker of human impact.

Human Consumption and the Biosphere

On the eastern outskirts of Nairobi lies the suburban settlement of Dandora, just a few kilometers to the north of the Nairobi National Park, where tourists flock to watch giraffes and ostriches graze freely on the African savannah. Dandora is the site of Nairobi's largest municipal dump, standing in stark contrast to the graceful savannah and resembling a hellish scene from a medieval painting by Hieronymus Bosch. It is one end-state for a human anthrome, which might be described as "almost totally used up." Here in microcosm is what happens to the Earth if humans do not recycle.

At Dandora, the plastic, glass, metal, and food waste from the city arrives daily in a line of trucks. The dumpsite has been accumulating for several decades, and is now large enough to be visible on satellite images. It has its own stratigraphy, with layers of waste that can be traced for tens of meters across the site. Its northern fringes are bounded by the Nairobi River, which erodes some of the waste and carries it downstream back into the city. The dumpsite is being partly recycled by the thousands of people who pick over its rubbish to make a living. There are neat piles of glass, tin cans, and bags of food that can be sold. The bags of food sell for 30 Kenyan shillings (30 US cents) to local pig farmers. Collecting this material is arduous, and some of the people are so poor that they eat the food waste they collect. Pigs, too, pick over the food waste at the dumpsite, escorted by a flock of scavenging, gaunt marabou storks. Dandora now has many parallel developments around the world. It is one of many living examples of how the human component of the biosphere is inefficient at recycling the things it needs to sustain itself over long time frames. Plastics, accumulating in vast quantities in the dumpsite, and in the global environment generally, are derived from the fossil fuels that help sustain this short-term phenomenon.

Growing Human Appropriation of Energy

Until very recently, and over very long geological timescales, the amount of energy stored by the Earth in the global biomass of plants, and in the fossilized remnants of plants preserved in rocks as oil, gas, and coal, has increased. This is evident simply from the observation of the amount of biomass contained in terrestrial vegetation, estimated to make up most of the roughly 1 trillion tonnes of carbon present in the total biosphere prior to human impact, and also by estimating the amount of coal, oil, and gas that has accumulated over the past 450 million years. However, humans have been utilizing the stored energy of the Earth's surface biosphere since the first hunter-gatherers collected vegetation on the African plains, and subsequently learned to use fire by burning plant biomass or animal dung as a means of obtaining heat, light, and protection. These early humans lived in approximate equilibrium with their local environment, not exceeding its ability to generate enough primary production to sustain the local ecology.

As humans began to develop agriculture, this led to a greater population (and biomass) of people and provided a surplus of food for specialist activities not related to food production. The human population was perhaps *circa* 1–10 million at 10,000 years BP, 200–400 million at 1 CE, and *circa* 1 billion people by 1800 CE. Together with the expansion of agriculture and domesticated animals across the land, this led to the increasing appropriation of production from the biosphere. This may have had a knock-on effect on the atmosphere, as William Ruddiman has argued, controversially (see Zalasiewicz et al. 2019a, and chapter 4 in the current volume), that increasing levels of atmospheric carbon dioxide from about 7,000 years ago, and of methane from 5,000 years ago, may be linked with the spread of agriculture: the rise in carbon dioxide caused by deforestation, whilst the rise in methane reflects rice cultivation in East Asia and the spread of livestock farming in Asia and Africa. From the seventeenth century onward, advances in farming facilitated increasing appropriation of primary production from the biosphere. These innovations included drainage and restoration systems, extensive mulberry dike and fishpond ecosystems for silk production in China, improved plow designs, mechanized farming from the early eighteenth century, breeding and genetic manipulation, and new fertilizers in the twentieth century.

The Haber–Bosch process for synthesizing ammonia, through its enhancement of food production, has enabled the recent, swift rise of the human population. The process is energy-intensive, though, being supported by use of fossil fuels. The widespread use of fossil energy to make processing of land (e.g. plowing and paddy construction) quicker and more efficient, to support a greater number of humans and their domesticated animals, to facilitate rapid national/international transfer of produce, and to enable more efficient harvesting of the sea and sea floor, has further amplified the impact of humans on both production and consumption in the biosphere. During the twentieth century, the appropriation of net primary productivity by humans roughly doubled, via a doubling of reactive nitrogen in the environment and the focusing of very large amounts of fossil energy on agricultural production. In 2014, humans extracted 225 million tonnes of fossil phosphates, projected to have risen to 258 million tonnes in 2018. Phosphates are a limited resource, and annual human addition to the phosphorus cycle considerably exceeds the amount of available phosphorus from natural recycling. The approximate human-caused halving of the biomass noted above has taken place despite this artificial nourishment, because forest (high biomass, but slow-growing) has been replaced by croplands and pasturelands (lower total biomass, but with a much more rapid turnover).

Nevertheless, overall human energy consumption remained relatively contained even as late as 1850. At that point, humans collectively used much less than 100 exajoules (EJ) of energy per year (1 EJ = 1,000,000,000,000,000,000 joules; by comparison, an old-fashioned 60-watt light bulb burns through 60 joules per second). Once humans developed technologies to extract fossilized energy, this pattern changed dramatically, particularly during the post-World War II "Great Acceleration," when some societies became voracious consumers of these new fuels. In the developed world, energy consumption has become truly colossal, overall energy consumption doubling in the past 40 years. In 2014, humans consumed the primary energy of 13,699 million tonnes of oil equivalent (or "mtoe"), or – to put it differently – some 572 EJ of energy (in 1973, it was "just" 6,100 mtoe). Humans currently harvest or destroy about 30 percent of the above-ground net primary production of plants, equating to a further 373 EJ of energy each year. These quantities are yet more striking if one includes estimates of near-future energy consumption. By the mid twenty-first century, when 60 percent of humans will live in urban areas, those of us in towns and cities may burn through 730 EJ of energy each year (Creutzig et al. 2014). Overall human energy consumption may then approach the harvestable energy of all above-ground vegetation on Earth, estimated at 1,241 EJ/year. This level of energy consumption is almost certainly unprecedented for a single species in 4 billion years of biological evolution on Earth (Williams et al. 2016). For any kind of sustainability, it is a prerequisite that humans develop interactions with nature that restore some kind of balance between the biomass stored from net primary production (from photosynthesis) and the energy released from that biomass via respiration. A new conceptual tool known as the "technosphere" may help us understand how to rebalance human energy use.

The Technosphere

The technosphere is a recent and controversial concept developed by geologist and engineer Peter Haff (2012, 2014, 2019; see also Zalasiewicz 2018). It offers a certain prism with which to view the collective and now tightly interconnected human modifications to and impacts on the Earth – one which is non-anthropocentric, and so usefully complements those many approaches to understanding the driving forces of the Anthropocene which focus on human and social qualities (explored in chapters 6–8). The technosphere as defined by Haff is a phenomenon akin to, and joining the ranks of, other planetary "spheres" such as the lithosphere, hydrosphere, atmosphere, and biosphere, all these being mutually interconnected. It encompasses all of the technological objects manufactured by humans, together with humans and their diverse cultures, including the professional and social systems by which we interact with technology: factories, schools, universities, trade unions, banks, political parties, the internet. The technosphere also includes the domestic animals that we raise in enormous numbers, and the crops that are grown to sustain both them and us, and the agricultural soils that are extensively modified from their natural state – plowed, drained, doused with fertilizers and pesticides – to carry out this task. The technosphere incorporates roads, railways, airports, mines and quarries, oil and gas fields, cities, engineered rivers, and reservoirs. It has generated extraordinary amounts of waste, from landfill accumulations to globally dispersed plastic trash to the pollution of air, soil, and water. A proto-technosphere of some kind has been present throughout human history, but for much of this time it took the form of isolated scattered patches of little planetary significance. It has now become a globally interconnected system: a new and important development on our planet, and one that is intimately connected to the biosphere.

This new system has introduced novel phenomena at a fundamental level. Solids transport on Earth in pre-human times was almost wholly driven by regional to global energy gradients, notably gravity, in the form of soil creep, avalanches, river flow, and submarine turbidity currents (Haff 2012), and also by energy gradients, such as those producing wind and tidal currents driving the movement of sand dunes. The pre-human biosphere could also move matter, usually diffusively over short distances (e.g. earthworms turning over soil), with more directed longer-range movement being of the biomass itself (e.g. animal migrations). By contrast, the functioning of the global technosphere today needs the movement of many millions of tonnes of solids (e.g. coal, raw materials for manufacture, manufactured objects, food items) over precisely directed pathways which themselves are often purpose-engineered objects (roads, railways), to allow maximum flux of solids with minimum energy loss. The transport of solids here is directed not by gravity gradients or wind directions, but by human agency through purposive action, which Haff (2012, 2019) sees as having emerged within and as part of the Earth System, rather than as a separate phenomenon that has arisen independently and that now simply uses this Earth as a stage for its operation. In this sense, the technosphere can be viewed as a planet-altering evolutionary novelty akin to the wide emergence of oxygen-liberating photosynthetic organisms around the beginning of the Proterozoic Eon, about 2.4 billion years ago, or the emergence of muscular activity and movement by animals at the beginning of the Phanerozoic Eon.

Within the technosphere, human purpose is mostly directed toward maintaining or extending technospheric structure and function. It is not, though, for the most part, a directing agency that can bend the technosphere to its collective will. The technosphere today, hence, is not evolving because it is being guided or directed by some controlling human force (not least because humanity is divided into too many competing or mutually hostile factions for such overt direction to easily emerge). Rather, it is evolving because the invention and emergence of technological novelties (such as computers or mobile phones) spread through the system, near-universally if unevenly: some societal groups have the latest smartphones, while others scratch a living sorting through toxic e-waste. Technological systems and human actions and behaviors are modified in turn to adapt to this development. It is a kind of coevolution of human and technological systems. Within this relationship, complex technological objects such as mobile phones or aeroplanes are not built by humans *de novo*, but because these objects have been enabled by, and are built using, earlier generations of tools and artifacts, so that "technology appears to have bootstrapped itself into its present state" (Haff 2014, p. 302; 2019). Technological evolution, as with biological evolution, takes place from the base afforded by its earlier history.

The physical products of the technosphere are massive in scale (see chapter 3) and highly diverse. Human technology in itself is old: simple stone tools were made by relatives of our species, millions of years ago. But there has been an enormous proliferation of different kinds of machines and tools and manufactured objects since the Industrial Revolution, and especially since the "Great Acceleration" of population growth, industrialization, and globalization of the mid twentieth century. Technology, too, is evolving ever faster. Our pre-industrial ancestors saw little technological change from generation to generation. Now, in the space of little more than one human generation, mobile phones – to take but one example – have been introduced to mass public use and have gone through several generations.

One analogy here may help to show the striking nature of this planetary newcomer. Technological objects, including mobile phones, may be considered geologically as "technofossils" because they are biologically made – or at least biologically directed – constructs that are robust and resistant to decay; they will form future fossils, to characterize the strata of the Anthropocene (Zalasiewicz et al. 2014b). Nobody knows how many different kinds of technofossil "species" there are (a count has been made of one common object, the book, and yielded over 100 million separate titles: Zalasiewicz et al. 2016b). But they already almost certainly exceed the number of fossil species known, while modern "technodiversity," considered this way, also exceeds modern biological diversity. The number of such technofossil "species" is continually increasing too, as techno-logical evolution now far outpaces biological evolution.

Following Haff's concept, the "technosphere" may be thought of as an offshoot of the biosphere and, like it, a complex system with its own emergent properties and dynamics, and an agency which, Haff (2019) argues, is not the same as our own. Important factors in its emergence were the capacity of our species to form sophisticated social structures (Ellis 2015), and to develop and work with tools. However, Haff emphasizes that humans are not so much creators and directors of the technosphere as components within it, and therefore constrained to act to keep it in existence – not least because the technosphere keeps most of the current human population alive, through the supplies of food, shelter, and other resources that it provides. Although a few more or less isolated human societies still exist on Earth, almost all of that human population is now tightly bound within the technosphere. Its development has allowed human population to grow from the few tens of millions that can be kept alive by the hunter-gatherer mode of life in which our species evolved, to the 7.7 billion today.

Currently, the technosphere might be regarded as parasitic on the biosphere, competing with it for energy and resources and altering conditions of planetary habitability. Obvious consequences include greatly increased (and accelerating) rates of extinction of species of plants and animals, and changes to climate and ocean chemistry that are largely deleterious to existing biological communities (though within these, there are both "winners" that exploit the new conditions and numerous "losers" that suffer reductions in their numbers, or extinction). These kinds of changes can in turn damage both the functioning of the biosphere and human populations (in which there will probably be also "winners" and "losers" in relative terms). Ideally, Haff argues, humans should aim to help the technosphere develop into a form that is more sustainable in the long term (with *much* more recycling of resources, for instance, and with less pressure on the biosphere). Nevertheless, humans collectively also have no choice but to try to keep the technosphere operative – because it is now indispensable to our collective existence – even while attempting to adapt and develop it toward greater stability and sustainability.

Near-Future Trajectories for the Biosphere

Human appropriation of energy from the biosphere and the widespread reconfiguration of ecosystems define a wholly reconstructed Anthropocene biosphere. Projections for human population by the end of the twenty-first century have ranged from 6.2 billion to 27 billion, dependent on fertility rates with most forecasting about 1 billion (Barnosky et al. 2012). Currently, the equivalent population of Germany is added to the total human population each year. At the same time, per capita demands on energy consumption are projected to rise during the twenty-first century. The urban population, which is growing rapidly and now exceeds that of the rural population, proportionately uses more energy. Some African cities, such as Lagos and Kinshasa, are projected to become giants, with populations exceeding 80 million inhabitants by the end of the current century. As a result of the increasing population of people, most of the ice-free landscape of the Earth is now modified by humans (Kennedy et al. 2019), and of the order of 10 gigatonnes of vegetation has been turned over to crops (Bar-On et al. 2018). Collectively, these impacts of population growth, agriculture, urbanization, and energy consumption amount to a global forcing mechanism that has begun to produce a state shift in the global biosphere (Williams et al. 2016), a result of ecosystem transformation and fragmentation, and of attendant changes to the global environment from pollution, especially atmospheric carbon dioxide and climate change.

There are two potential future trajectories. The first leads to a wholesale change in global ecosystem structure with attendant collapse of ecosystems and biodiversity from coral reefs to rainforests, and a concomitant mass extinction event, due to uncontrolled energy consumption linked with global environmental degradation. The second trajectory entails human societies rapidly evolving mutualistic relationships with the Earth System, learning to recycle essential materials for the biosphere, and restoring a balance between energy stored and energy consumed via respiration. Trajectory 2, averting a mass extinction event, is undoubtedly preferable from a human perspective to trajectory 1.

How close are we to trajectory 1? Anthony Barnosky and Elizabeth Hadly at Stanford University, and their colleagues, have argued that the scale of human forcing mechanisms at present exceeds the forcing mechanisms of the last major biosphere transition at the end of the most recent ice age, 11,700 years ago (Barnosky et al. 2012). At the local scale, urban and agricultural landscapes have already undergone state shifts. Sometimes this is immediately visible – when, for example, a landscape has been abruptly deforested and converted to grazing cattle. Other times, the state shift results from the accumulation of changes over time, as for example in the Hawaiian landscape of Kauai, where local species were extirpated or became extinct, and where species introduced from elsewhere became dominant (Burney et al. 2001).

Were the state shift to become pervasively global, it would manifest as an irreversible change – for example, to a biosphere with low species diversity, one that might recover its biodiversity to pre-extinction levels but only over millions of years, such as occurred after the mass extinction at the Permian–Triassic boundary 252 million years ago (Chen and Benton 2012). Such a shift might be indicated by a gradual reduction in ecosystem resilience, as displayed, say, in coral reef ecosystems struggling to recover from the combined impacts of global-warming-induced bleaching and heat death, acidification, and pollution. Or a state shift might be signaled by rapid fluctuations of ecosystems between different states, such as occurs during the annual variations in most current marine dead zones, at times allowing bottom-living organisms to recolonize, at other times suffocating them. Past major changes in the biosphere have been characterized by the extinction of dominant species, proliferations of new species, modification of food webs, and pronounced changes in the geographic distribution of organisms. For past state shifts, the causal mechanism was major environmental and evolutionary change. At present, the underlying causal mechanism is human impact.

Can Technosphere and Biosphere Co-exist?

To avoid the potential consequences of trajectory 1, human societies, particularly the most powerful ones, need to recognize the complex interconnectedness of the biosphere with every other component of the Earth System, including human societies themselves, just as Vernadsky did nearly a century ago. There are inherent limits to Earth's life support mechanism – not least that there is a limited quantity of energy available through the biomass of the biosphere. Humboldt and Bonpland began to understand these complex relationships more than 200 years ago, observing how the vegetation in the mountain landscapes of Venezuela was intimately connected with altitude and climate. But, 200 years later, an examination of one of Erle Ellis's maps of anthrome distribution for South America indicates the scale of change in Venezuela. In 1800, most of it was semi-natural or wild, but in the year 2000 vast areas of the country were already converted to "used anthromes" that would be almost unrecognizable to those perceptive nineteenth-century travelers.

At present, humanity's relationship with the biosphere is parasitic. The parasite is removing energy from the biosphere, rather as a leech sucks out the blood of its host. The leech–host relationship survives in ecosystems so long as the leech does not bleed the victim dry. As the human population grows, so does its demands on energy supplies from the biosphere. A more mutualistic relationship with the biosphere, one that is sustainable over long time frames, would be prudent. We might learn from the humble termite, for example, which enhances the quality of soil through the physical transport of material to make mounds, chemical breakdown of clay minerals, and delivery of organic materials within their mounds, increasing fertility. The heterogeneity generated by termite structures can foster habitats for nesting and roosting for birds, or refugia for small invertebrates during times of environmental stress. Human cities and buildings could be configured to attempt the same function (see, for example, Lepczyk et al. 2017; Nilon et al. 2017).

Steps toward developing a more mutualistic relationship with the rest of nature require significant changes in per capita resource use of both land and energy, involving a move away from fossil fuels as the primary source of energy. They require, too, more efficient use of land for food production, avoiding the conversion of yet more semi-natural land to farmland, and so protecting those landscapes that have been less subject to human interference, and acting to preserve and enhance their biodiversity. These steps are in principle straight-forward, but socially and politically they have proved, and remain, extraordinarily difficult. It is this complex human sphere that we turn to next, to explore how people and society can engage with the Anthropocene.

6
The *Anthropos* of the Anthropocene

The first half of "Anthropocene" refers to *anthropos*, the ancient Greek term for "human." Without the presence of humans, the planet would not have entered this new geological epoch. But geology does not have a monopoly on understanding our species. Indeed, for many geologists dealing with Earth time, human time is merely the blink of an eye. The fields of paleoanthropology, archeology, anthropology, and history, working on different scales and with different methods and archives, have much to contribute in coming to terms with the Anthropocene. These disciplines and geology are now in conversation in new ways to explore how, when, and where the *anthropos* came to impact the Earth System. These conversations reveal that human beings are both creatures with a deep past inscribed in rock layers and ice cores, and also a new and overwhelming force on the planet – both a collective unit impacting Earth, and a multitude of disparate individuals and societies with distinctive hopes and ways of living.

This chapter treats the disciplines of paleoanthropology, archeology, and anthropology separately from history, partly because of their differences of scale, methods, and archives. Until very recently, history was almost exclusively devoted to written archives, as opposed to physical and experiential evidence. Historians mostly concerned themselves with conscious actions leaving a paper trail. While some disciplinary differences may be melting in the heat and turmoil of efforts to understand our changing planet, each still gives us a different handle on the two big questions confronted in the Anthropocene: first, how do we understand humanity, in some form or another, as an Earth System force, and, second, does the past suggest alternatives to our headlong trajectory toward "Hothouse

Earth," a planet that will be unlivable for most people and many other species?

Paleoanthropology, Archeology, and Anthropology

Paleoanthropology, archeology, and anthropology are uniquely positioned to understand humanity and the Earth System in three ways. First, the scales at which these disciplines work reveal our embeddedness in geological systems as well as ecosystems. Second, their interest in the physical contexts of societies means that nature has always been part of their analytical frameworks in ways not true in other social sciences, such as history, political science, economics, and sociology. Third, their focus on the particular lifeworlds of small groups has been balanced by an interest in human universals. (Please note that sometimes we use "anthropology" to incorporate all three disciplines, following the North American practice.)

After discussing scale, relations with nature, and the tension between the local and the global in general terms, we will look at the work of paleoanthropologists and archeologists tracing our species in the deep past. Because their research concerns periods long before the Anthropocene emerged, they help us to understand the distinctiveness of our new age of human dominance. Next, we discuss the work of cultural and social anthropologists concerned with contemporary societies, and how the Anthropocene has spurred critical self-reflection in that field. As anthropologists grapple with what it means to be human in our unprecedented situation, some embrace forms of posthumanism, with a special interest in multi-species entanglements, while others investigate forms of knowledge being generated by communities on the frontlines of our overheating planet.

Human Scales

Scales matters. Paleoanthropology, archeology, and anthropology work on dazzling scales of time and space in comparison to other social sciences. Paleoanthropologists concern themselves with the development of all species of *Homo*, whose first representatives walked the planet some 2.8 million years ago; archeologists explore ancient sites of human habitation; and cultural and social anthropologists study contemporary communities. The spatial scale of these disciplines is equally comprehensive today. When anthropology

initially developed, it concentrated on human groups remote from
urban centers and from literate cultures. Its founding fathers include
Bronisław Malinowski (1884–1942), who spent years among the
Trobriand Islanders off the coast of New Guinea, and A. R.
Radcliffe-Brown (1881–1955), who studied Australian Aborigines
and Andaman Islanders. Now, however, anthropologists' interests
are truly global. No place on the planet is off-limits in their quest to
familiarize the exotic and to exoticize the familiar (Eriksen 2017, p.
3). Likewise, anthropology casts a wide net in terms of permissible
evidence. From objects such as stones, bones, ritual implements, and
cell phones, to experiences of all kinds, to relations with other animals
and ecosystems, anthropology is promiscuous in its sources and in
its use of language, concepts, and categories. By contrast, history
still has considerable allegiance to written texts, while mainstream
economics (as discussed in the next chapter) is fairly chaste in its
devotion to numbers. Given anthropology's impressive temporal and
spatial scales and its breadth of evidence, it has much to contribute
to our understanding of the Anthropocene.

The Natural Context of Human Societies

The second great contribution of anthropology to understanding the
Anthropocene (again, unlike other social sciences) is its long-term
awareness of human embeddedness in the natural world. Approaches
ranging from archeological digs to participant observation – where
the researcher breathes and eats with the community under study
– underscore the material aspects of human societies. In general,
anthropologists think of humanity's relationship with nature in two
ways. From the traditional anthropological perspective, societies
emerge from the interplay of nature and culture. Reflecting on his
discipline's distinctiveness, social anthropologist Philippe Descola
(1949–) observes that anthropology is "founded on the belief that
all societies constitute compromises between Nature and Culture
and that its task is to examine the many singular expressions of this
compromise and, if possible, to try to discover the rules of their
formation and destruction" (2013, p. 78). The tug and pull between
nature and culture is of great interest to paleoanthropologists and
archeologists who trace our species over the millennia.

Recently, however, this assumption of an inherent nature–culture
dualism has been critiqued, not least by Descola himself. Yet, even
so, there is no move to jettison nature. If anything, the effort is to
embrace it more fully. Instead of starting with a dualism that societies

must navigate, which Descola and others argue is a recent and solely Western invention, some anthropologists now urge us to understand society as part of complex networks, where each society is a particularity "within a general grammar of cosmologies" (Descola 2013, p. 88). Directly addressing the Anthropocene, cultural anthropologist Anna Tsing (2005, 2015) has developed this approach, erasing the nature–culture dichotomy.

Either way, whether the analysis rests on a nature–culture dualism or on the new networked materialism, paleoanthropology, archeology and anthropology have never been blind to the forces of the nonhuman. Because of this, they have a leg up when it comes to grappling with the Anthropocene. Although the leap from seeing human activities altering environments to seeing them as dominating the Earth System requires effort, it is smoothed by a disciplinary commitment to understanding the physicality of the human experience.

Local Cultures and Universal Culture

Third, these fields explore the scales of the Anthropocene by highlighting the tension between the universal and the particular. We see this tension in the distinction between "culture" and "cultures." In the singular, "culture" highlights a shared human capacity, but the plural form emphasizes unique, variable expressions of culture's "complex whole," famously defined in 1871 by E. B. Tylor (1832–1917), as including "knowledge, belief, art, morals, custom, and any other capabilities and habits acquired by man as a member of society" (cited in Eriksen 2017, p. 26). Stressing culture's universality has been a strategy to combat racism and stage theories of human development and to differentiate our species from other species. This is Culture with a capital "C." Focusing instead on cultures in all their variety highlights human creativity and specificity, detailing the "systemically different social environments" which result in distinctive "life-worlds" (Eriksen 2017, 30). Diverse cultures, in this sense, do not have to be human, but can be found in other species, including dolphins and baboons.

The play between similarity and difference which was once oppositional in anthropology – "us" versus "them," particularly "the West" versus "the other" – has become relational. In a landscape of relationships, anthropologist Tim Ingold argues, "'we' is a community of relations bound, but not bounded, by difference. Here, difference and similarity, becoming other and coming together, go hand in hand" (2018, p. 50). The tension between the solidarity of our shared world and the particularities of different lifeworlds is at the heart of humanistic approaches to the Anthropocene. "The Anthropocene" names, on the one hand, the planetary predicament faced by all beings and, on the other, the uneven responsibilities and experiences that divide us. Anthropology helps us to understand the Anthropocene's many registers.

Paleoanthropology and Archeology

How do paleoanthropology and archeology help us understand the distinctiveness of the Anthropocene? Concerned as they are with the long view of the development of *Homo*, and ultimately of *Homo sapiens*, they show the magnitude and abruptness of the Anthropocene.

For the most part, paleoanthropology paints a picture of *Homo sapiens* and our ancestors as mere playthings in the giant paws of planetary and cosmic forces. The species has been at the mercy of geology, from the movement of tectonic plates to glacial erosion. Indonesia's volcanoes, for instance, have given us a particularly hard time. Just how hard it was 74,000 years ago after the massive Toba explosion on Sumatra is currently being debated (see Daily 2018; Vogel 2018). Anthropologist Stanley H. Ambrose and his colleagues (Williams et al. 2009; Haslam et al. 2010) contend that this disaster made the planet on average 10 °C colder, creating a 6-year-long volcanic winter. The numbers of human beings, by their estimate, was reduced to as few as 3,000 to 10,000 survivors – only enough to constitute the freshman class at most universities today. Others (Yost et al. 2018) argue that the situation was less dire. Studies at sites in South Africa, and earlier in India (Lubick 2010), suggest that the effects of Toba's eruption – one of the largest in the past 2 million years, spewing out about 850 million metric tonnes of sulfur into the atmosphere – may not have been so globally severe. Either way, geological outbursts in Indonesia continue to cause difficulties: Mount Tambora's 1815 eruption created the "year without a summer" in 1816, when crops failed as far away as Vermont; Krakatoa's 1883 eruption disrupted weather patterns and generally cooled the planet; and Mount Pinatubo's 1991 blast temporarily depressed average global temperatures by about 0.5 °C (1 °F).

One of the biggest events in our species' history, when the Pleistocene became the Holocene epoch ~11,700 years ago, also found us on the sidelines, but this time as beneficiaries of forces beyond our control. As discussed in chapter 1, the May 2008 announcement that the Executive Committee of the International Union of Geological Sciences (IUGS) had formally ratified the Holocene with a GSSP located at 1,492.45 m depth by the North Greenland Ice Core Project (NGRIP or NorthGRIP) mentioned neither human forcing nor human forces (Walker et al. 2009, p. 3). Both the beneficence of the Holocene stabilization and the disruptions of Indonesian volcanic explosions are examples of planetary forces working without regard for human actions. Ancient Romans worshipped Demeter for bounteous harvests and blamed Vulcan, the god of fire, for volcanoes, but no scientist credits human beings with launching the Holocene's relative calm or blames humanity for causing Indonesia's seismic restlessness.

In other ways, however, as anthropologists also show, hominin activities have always influenced environmental conditions. It has been suggested (e.g. Chakrabarty 2009) that humanity's impact on the planet was at first biological, and then became geological only very recently, with fossil-fuel-intensive activities. However, anthropologists (Bauer and Ellis 2018) argue otherwise. Paleoanthropology demonstrates that we have always been both geological and biological agents in local and regional ways. We added CO_2 to the atmosphere by burning wood and setting grass fires, as well as eroded soils, stacked rocks, befriended dogs, and dispersed fruit seeds, among a host of other interventions. According to paleoanthropologist Richard Wrangham (2009), this combined geological and biological impact actually began long before *Homo sapiens* emerged on the scene, when our ancestor *Homo erectus* gained control of fire, perhaps 1.8 million years ago, although this claim is contentious (e.g. Roebroeks and Villa 2011; Glikson 2013; Gowlett 2016). In the hands of *Homo sapiens*, fire certainly reshaped ecologies when it was used to drive animals in hunting. Everywhere we went (as with all other species), we altered environments. Indeed, as soon as "the first prehistoric people started to dig for stone to make implements, rather than pick up loose material, humans have modified the landscape through excavation of rock and soil, generation of waste and creation of artificial ground" (Price et al. 2011, p. 1056).

Our presence also made a difference to the other animals, plants, fungi, and microbes around us. Reliable evidence (Miller et al. 2005; Rule et al. 2012; van der Kaars et al. 2017; Smith et al. 2018) suggests that *Homo sapiens* were at least partly responsible for megafauna extinctions and for reducing the size of remaining large-bodied animals in the Pleistocene. Assessing human impact is difficult because the Late Pleistocene, once understood as essentially a static glaciated period, especially in northern latitudes, is now seen as a time of pronounced climate fluctuations (Hofreiter and Stewart 2009). Which extinctions were the result of *Homo sapiens* and which were due to other causes cannot always be ascertained, but it seems likely that we helped usher our own nearest hominin relatives, including the Neanderthals, into oblivion, especially when we developed the "cognitive fluidity" (Mithen 1996, 2007) that allowed for complex thinking and nuanced language around 50,000 years ago. Anthropologist Andrew Bauer is certainly right to argue that "humans modified ecosystems on broad scales well before recent times" (2016, p. 409).

With the Holocene's greater predictability, human impact increased further. Animal domestication, agriculture, the development of cities and writing systems, the creation of complex social and political systems, and population growth added to our power to shape both geospheres and biospheres, locally and even regionally (Wilkinson 2003; Alizadeh et al. 2004; Casana 2008; Morrison 2009; Wilkinson et al. 2010; Fuller et al. 2011; Conolly et al. 2012; Bauer 2013). We developed an increasing, but regional and highly diachronous, influence on the Earth System. These earth-shaping efforts escalated as the centuries passed, until eventually, as geologist Bruce Wilkinson puts it, "humans became the prime agents of erosion sometime during the latter part of the first millennium A.D." (2005, p. 161). With European colonization, humankind became an even more pronounced geological and biological factor, altering landscapes and introducing new species, often with devastating effect on the former biomes. The onset of the Industrial Revolution magnified human impact in western Europe, and later in the rest of the world through Western imperialism. In short, *Homo sapiens* has made itself thoroughly at home on the planet.

If people have always been subject to the forces of nature and have always altered their organic and inorganic surroundings, what then makes the Anthropocene different? "Nothing," say some paleoanthropologists and archeologists. Bauer, along with geographer Erle Ellis, insists that the Anthropocene, in demarcating the contemporary situation from the past, actually prevents us from seeing the long, heterogeneous history of human–environment interactions. They argue that "the Anthropocene divide" should "be dissolved," and offer anthropology's services as teacher and guide in the effort (Bauer and Ellis 2018, p. 23). Archeologist Kathleen Morrison, likewise, argues that "the concept of the Anthropocene is unnecessary – not because humans have not changed the earth, but because we have done so throughout the Holocene" (2015; see also 2013). These critiques voice understandable irritation at the failure of many modernists to recognize that human beings have always modified their environments biologically and geologically.

But, more generally, Bauer, Ellis, and Morrison miss the import of the Anthropocene. Their criticism confuses changing regions of the Earth with transforming the Earth System. All species modify their environments, but only a few organisms, such as ourselves and cyanobacteria (see chapters 1 and 2), have overturned the planetary system. Altering ecosystems so that a few species go extinct is not the same as the Sixth Great Extinction; disturbing landscapes, even large regions, is distinguishable from people becoming "an order of magnitude more important at moving sediment than the sum of all other natural processes operating on the surface of the planet" (Wilkinson 2005, p. 161). The last time there was this much CO_2 in Earth's atmosphere, about 3 million years ago, our species did not exist (Dowsett et al. 2013). Systems science allows us to distinguish particular changes, some of them quite important, from the Anthropocene's systemic transformation.

The significance of the Anthropocene lies not in its discovery of the first traces of our species, but in the magnitude, significance, and future longevity of the planetary system's transformation. It was only in the mid twentieth century that the impact of human systems became both global and near-synchronous, permanently altering the Earth System and leaving an indelible marker on the Earth's crust (Zalasiewicz et al. 2015b). Paleoanthropology and archeology can give us a rich understanding of the vicissitudes and successes of our species in relation to the environments of earlier states of the Earth System, and, in doing so, highlight the unprecedented strangeness of our current predicament.

Cultural and Social Anthropology

The uncanny strangeness of our current predicament has also prompted cultural and social anthropologists to reflect on their discipline's assumptions. How can it be that the human activities they have studied so assiduously have quite suddenly (from a geological perspective) coalesced to transform the workings of our planet? To this question, two approaches, broadly speaking, have emerged. One group flies the banner of posthumanism, which submerges human beings in their physical environments and treats all forces and forcings as co-agents. The other group focuses on the new forms of human power and knowledge that have emerged recently.

Among the first group are many prominent anthropologists (e.g. Anna Tsing; Tim Ingold; Eduardo Kohn; and Elizabeth Povinelli), as well as scholars from other fields, such as political science (e.g. Jane Bennett; Diane Coole and Samantha Frost; William E. Connolly), literature (e.g. Urusla Heise), science and technology studies (e.g. Donna Haraway and Bruno Latour), and ethics and spirituality (e.g. Michael S. Northcott 2014). For them, the nature–culture dualism and the focus on human agency are not aids to understanding the Anthropocene, but lie at the very root of the problem. Using concepts such as "the new materialism" (Bennett 2010; Coole and Frost 2010), "geontologies" (Povinelli 2016), "naturecultures" (Haraway 2003; Fuentes 2010), and the "anthropocosmic" from philosopher Tu Weiming (Tu 1998), they urge anthropologists not to take the separation between nature and culture for granted. Eduardo Kohn (2013), in his work on forests, refers to an "anthropology of life," with its entangled webs of living and nonliving entities all acting as agents or actants. Marisol de la Cadena analyzes the Quechua people of the Andes and their all-encompassing worldview, which guides Mariano Turpo's resistance against the 1969 agrarian reforms, and his son's shamanism (Cadena 2015). The aims of this diverse group of authors might be encapsulated succinctly as twofold: first, to create more inclusive stories; and, second, to suggest a more inclusive politics.

The wager is that expanding the ethnographic field to include different kinds of participants will produce a better way of understanding how modernity's so-called "progress" led to blasted landscapes and bleak prospects. These approaches range from methods such as "multispecies ethnography" (Kirksey and Helmreich 2010) and "multispecies storytelling" (Tsing 2015, p. 162; see also Tsing et al. 2017), to proposals for "geostories" (Latour 2017). These writers distribute agency to all animate and inanimate beings so that their winding tales are powered by assemblages of humans and nonhumans. For example, in *The mushroom at the end of the world*, Tsing takes the elusive matsutake mushroom as her guide through the subtle entanglements of networked biologies, histories, and places. This fungus's idiosyncratic proclivities make it impossible to cultivate, which makes it even more desirable to Japanese connoisseurs, who savor its emblematic "autumn aroma." It flourishes according to its own whims, preferring disturbed landscapes, including Hiroshima after the atomic bomb. Thus, matsutake mushrooms, despite their high value on the global market, escape control by the usual mechanisms of capitalism. Gathering them is the work of people on the margins, often done in secret. Shadowy illicit auctions are held under forest canopies in China, America's Northwest, and elsewhere, before the mushrooms speed along international trade routes. Tsing traces the matsutake's spreading rhizomes of connection in all directions. Hers is no story of progress. Instead, all we have now are tales of "company human and non-human" (2015, p. 282). Tsing's dark testament elevates the resilience of the matsutake and our other companions as we survive in the ruins of modernity's hopes.

Retelling our stories in posthumanist terms is also meant to have political consequences. In *We have never been modern* (1993), Bruno Latour calls for a "parliament of things," meaning the literal participation of all creatures in institutions of democratic deliberation. In *Pandora's hope* (2000), he expresses certainty that one day we will be asking nonhumans, "Are you ready, and at the price of what sacrifice, to live the good life together?" He claims, "That this highest of moral and political questions could have been raised, for so many centuries, by so many bright minds, *for humans only* without the nonhumans that make them up, will soon appear, I have no doubt, as extravagant as when the Founding Fathers denied slaves and women the vote" (2000, p. 297). Likewise, in *Vibrant matter*, Jane Bennett argues:

> If human culture is inextricably enmeshed with vibrant, nonhuman agencies, and if human intentionality can be agentic only if accompanied by a vast entourage of nonhumans, then it seems that the appropriate unit of analysis for democratic theory is neither the individual human nor an exclusive human collective but the (ontologically heterogeneous) "public" coalescing around a problem... . Of course, to acknowledge nonhuman materialities as participants in a political ecology is not to claim that everything is always a participant, or that all participants are alike. Persons, worms, leaves, bacteria, metals, and hurricanes have different types and degrees of power, just as different persons have different types and degrees of power, different worms have different types and degrees of power, and so on. (2010, pp. 108–9)

Including nonhuman creatures in our participatory democracies is also the goal of literary scholar Ursula Heise in *Imagining extinction* (2016). For posthumanists, the Anthropocene reframes anthropology's subject matter and alters its notion of politics as an exclusively human practice. Latour observes that "many anthropologists wish to keep the human in the centre, without always realizing that the centre has shifted, and that the human agent has been put in the centre also by geologists, climatologists, soil scientists and epidemiologists – before being redistributed again" (2017, p. 46).

In contrast to the posthumanists, other social and cultural anthropologists respond to the Anthropocene not by submerging human agency within networks of living and nonliving actants, but by highlighting it. The *anthropos* of the Anthropocene, for these authors, has taken on a qualitatively different power. Their concern is humanity's startlingly recent, systemic domination of the planet and its differential impacts on human communities. Few in this group would deny that human beings have always been, in Bennett's words, "accompanied by a vast entourage of nonhumans," but they are more concerned with the recent emergence of our epoch-making capacities than with dispersing responsibility among companion species and inanimate co-actants. For instance, in *Overheating: An anthropology of accelerated change*, Thomas Hylland Eriksen stresses the qualitative newness of our condition: "Never before has humanity placed its stamp on the planet in ways even remotely comparable to the situation today." No place escapes human influence; as he notes, "even in patches of rainforest or desert where no human has set foot, traces of human activities are present through the local effects of climate change, drought, flooding, the spread of humanly introduced species and so on" (2016, p. 17). The guilt lies, first and foremost, with us, not with other creatures, and the focus is on our particular characteristics.

From this perspective, the extraordinary impact attributable to human societies makes human beings and their uniquely human political systems responsible in heightened ways. The force increasing pressure on the planetary system, argues Eriksen, is accelerated growth: "There are more of us, we engage in more activities, many of them machine-assisted, and depend on each other in more ways than ever before" (2016, p. 10). Energy systems, mobility, communications, urbanization, and global flows of garbage are at the heart of our ever-escalating domination of the Earth. Yet the pace is not the same everywhere: "Different parts of societies, cultures, and life-worlds change at different speeds and reproduce themselves at different rhythms, and it is necessary to understand the disjunctures between speed and slowness, change and continuity in order to grasp the conflicts arising from accelerated globalisation" (2016, p. 9). Ethnography, by this view, is an invaluable tool for showing how the "clashing scales" of the Anthropocene create conflicts.

The skyrocketing number of refugees, from 1 million in 1951 to 60 million in 2014, is compared with increased air flights ferrying the well-to-do. A broad group of anthropologists share Eriksen's understanding of the novelty of our predicament and the usefulness of anthropology's specialized tools for understanding how we got here and what cultural resources we have to meet this challenge. These anthropologists tell gritty stories of predation on Earth's resources, nonhuman species, and vulnerable human communities.

New urgencies reframe their ethnographies to include the impact of climate change, toxins, water insufficiency, rising seas, ecosystem depletion, the energy transition, population growth, and other Anthropocene dangers. For instance, in *Discovering nature: Globalization and environmental culture in China and Taiwan*, cultural anthropologist Robert P. Weller remarks that his notes from his "first period of fieldwork in Taiwan, in the late 1970s, reveal no sign of nature." A decade later, he found that "Taiwan had discovered 'nature' sometime in the mid-1980s," as did the mainland shortly thereafter (2006, pp. 1–2). Something new was afoot: "genuine innovation in how people conceptualize the relationship between humanity and the environment," even before the term "Anthropocene" was available. This innovation was spurred not by pollution alone but by "the combination of global influences and indigenous social and cultural resources [that] ... altered the entire spectrum of daily life in the environment – changing fuel costs, protest movements, the labor requirements of cooking, government regulations, education, leisure activities, and more" (2006, pp. 9–10).

Weller finds that the environmental devastation wrought by Taiwan's capitalism and that due to China's communism are remarkably similar. So too is the environmentalist response at the intellectual centers of these societies. National and international environmentalism tends to be biocentric in its focus and universal in its vision (2006, p. 106). By contrast, at the grassroots level where "the bulk of environmental action" takes place in both Taiwan and the People's Republic of China (PRC), people and their customs tend to take precedence over biota (2006, p. 133). At local temples, resources of resistance can entail spirit possession by Guanyin, the bodhisattva of mercy and nurturance. Divination ceremonies are held to determine the views of Shen Nong, an agricultural god, on how the community should respond to a government plan to build a naphtha cracker (a kind of light oil refinery) in the neighborhood (2006, p. 105). (Shen Nong came down strongly on the side of resistance.) But, as Weller makes clear, there is no simple dichotomy between a local "alternative Chinese environmentalism," on the one hand, and the global juggernaut of environmental destruction and protection, on the other. No unsullied local "Green Orientalism" can be posed against globalization's ruthlessness or modernist environmental consciousness. Instead, Weller reveals the interactions among "multiple locals and globals, remixed and recreated at various crucial nodes and at different scales" (2006, p. 168).

Working at a great distance from steamy, hot Taiwan, anthropologist Julie Cruikshank (2005) tells a similar story. In the ice fields along the Saint Elias Mountain divide between Canada and Alaska, she attends to the friction among human interpretations of glaciers. The indigenous people there tend to anthropomorphize these rivers of ice as thinking, talking beings, while European colonizers arriving first in the eighteenth century saw glaciers as objects of study or as obstacles. Today, scientists seek to incorporate "traditional ecological knowledge" (or TEK as it became known by the 1990s in Canadian government policy circles), but they find that "data" cannot be extracted from local people while disregarding their cultural framework. The place-based understanding of Yukon natives resists being "systematized and incorporated into Western management regimes" (2005, pp. 255–6). Moreover, in our rapidly transforming world, even traditional knowledge evolves to address new challenges. Cruikshank calls for enlarging the "spaces for local knowledge," rather than attempting to meld perspectives into a single data set. No one form of knowledge, she suggests, should predominate as we struggle with complex, interlocking challenges.

Humanity's hybrid motivations, different forms of knowledge production, and makeshift connections form the heart of these ethnographies. Of all the tales of local environmental resistance and scalar friction, one of the most famous is that of the Chipko "tree-hugging movement" told by historian Ramachandra Guha in *The unquiet woods* (2000 [1989]). In the Himalayan uplands, local peasants, intent on defending their customary rights to use the forest, were joined in their resistance to government control of woodlands by outsiders with different ideas. Beginning in the 1970s, Marxists came to help defend the exploited classes, ecofeminists to celebrate the women leading the movement, and environmentalists to protect the woods and their nonhuman inhabitants. Guha reveals a hybrid coalition of incommensurable worldviews and different rationales, yet it effectively protected the forest where a single organization with one clear-cut agenda might have failed.

As these ethnographies make clear, there is no one level of

analysis or subject position that is best suited to understanding the Anthropocene's causes and conditions. "Local knowledge" and "global knowledge" are ever more entangled, not only for indigenous people subject to the forces of modernity, but also for those responsible for its accelerating destruction. Indeed, those subject to the "forces of history" and those responsible for the Anthropocene's "forcings" are often one and the same. Ethnographies of oil-workers in Nigeria (Akpan 2005), studies of Houston residents suffering from Hurricane Harvey (Morton 2018), and participant observations of corporate functionaries (Jordan 2016) reveal that the line between perpetrator and victim can blur in a world of interpenetrating scales.

Igniting Anthropocene History

In contending with the Anthropocene, the discipline of history is no stranger to the problems of scale and causality that confront paleoanthropology, archeology, and anthropology, but it traditionally limited its purview to the written texts, ignoring nature and everything else. Since the oldest known written language is Sumerian, dating only to ~3500 BCE, historical time was quite short – less than half of the Holocene. Few people – generally from small priestly, commercial, or administrative elites – wrote, and, even when they did, their writings succumbed to the ravages of time, war, weather, censorship, insects, and mice. So what does it mean to try to understand "humanity" on the basis of this limited, sparse, and fragile evidence? One thing such evidence does, which is important for understanding the Anthropocene, is to highlight system building – religions, trade networks, and statecraft – and the ideas behind the systems that became a planetary force. Written language allows us to transfer complex knowledge across time and space to coordinate conquest, administer vast territories, and exploit resources and peoples. Arguably, literacy caused the Anthropocene, since, without it, organizing human actions to the extent that they could dominate the Earth System is unimaginable. On a more positive note, it helps us explore our situation and how we might make it better.

Something New under the Sun

At the turn of the millennium, the insights of science and history converged. In 2000, independently of one another, atmospheric chemist Paul Crutzen and world historian John McNeill both declared there was "something new under the sun." As described earlier, Crutzen hit upon the word "Anthropocene" to describe this newness at a scientific meeting in Cuernavaca, Mexico. A few months later, he and biologist Eugene Stoermer presented the term in a two-page article for the *IGBP Newsletter* (2000; see also Carey 2016). McNeill's book *Something new under the Sun* (2000) was just as daring as Crutzen's proposed term, but considerably longer at about 400 pages. While Crutzen pointed to a late-eighteenth-century Anthropocene beginning, McNeill made a convincing case that the twentieth century was "the first time in human history that we have altered ecosystems with such intensity on such scale and with such speed" (2000, p. 3). His dating presaged the 2019 Anthropocene Working Group's overwhelming vote for a mid-twentieth-century boundary.

McNeill also argued that these human-wrought environmental changes dwarfed the importance of "World War II, the communist enterprise, the rise of mass literacy, the spread of democracy, or the growing emancipation of women." Much more consequential than these events – the very events at the center of most modern historians' analyses – was the "screeching acceleration of so many processes" that "the human race, without intending anything of the sort, has undertaken a gigantic uncontrolled experiment on the earth" (2000, p. 4). McNeill's book was extraordinary not in being an environmental history – a field in full swing since the 1970s – but in being an Anthropocene history in all but name. *Avant la lettre*, he laid out many of the central challenges of the human conquest of Earth for a field long dedicated to exploring human endeavors.

In order to understand the "screeching acceleration" of the twentieth century, McNeill delves into the deep past of the genus *Homo* and describes our impact on the lithosphere, pedosphere, atmosphere, hydrosphere, and biosphere, before depicting the 500-year history of stop-and-start developments that historians call the "early modern" and "modern" periods. McNeill argues that, in order to propel ourselves over the mid-twentieth-century threshold, human ingenuity with machines and organizations was critical, but so too was the sheer luck of the Little Ice Age's end (c.1550–1850) and the "gradual adjustment between human hosts and some of our pathogens and parasites" by the eighteenth century (2000, p. 17). Yet even these factors were insufficient. What finally sealed our fate, McNeill contends, "is that in the twentieth century, two trends – conversion to a fossil-fuel-based energy system and very rapid population growth – spread nearly around the world, while a third – ideological and political commitment to economic growth and military power – which was already widespread, consolidated" (2000, p. 268). This combination of physical, social, economic, political, ideological, and demographic factors becoming global in the postwar period is McNeill's "simplest answer." It serves as a precisely calibrated summary of the "multiple, mutually reinforcing causes" revealed in his text (2000, p. 356). While some scholars stress continuity, McNeill stresses change. While some scholars propose single causes of the Anthropocene, such as capitalism or "a clique of white British men [who] literally pointed steam-power as a weapon – on sea and land, boats and rail – against the best part of humankind" (Malm and Hornborg 2014, p. 64; see also Moore 2015 and Malm 2016), McNeill, by contrast, gravitates toward complexity; his Anthropocene history portrays a new and complex systemic dilemma instead of an environmental problem arising from CO_2 alone or a single economic system.

What precisely is the difference between Anthropocene history and environmental history? Most importantly, Anthropocene history offers a different analytical framework, not an additional topic. Some topics of interest may be familiar to environmental historians, but others arise from subfields such as economic or intellectual history. As with other new historical frameworks (labor history, gender history, and structuralism, for instance), Anthropocene history has sent historians back to the drawing board, asking foundational questions about the purpose of history, the appropriate forms of evidence, and how meaningful stories might be crafted out of reality's vast messiness.

The effort to refine "the Anthropocene" for critical historical investigation is still ongoing, but four aspects of this new approach are already evident. The characteristics that distinguish Anthropocene history from environmental history are, first, its unprecedented newness. We have always lived in our environment; never before have we lived in the Anthropocene. While the environment is something we might wish to protect, the Anthropocene is largely unwelcome. Second, the scales that ultimately frame this new form of history are global, with an eye to deep time and to the extraordinary, recent acceleration of human prodigality. Environmental histories need not gesture toward the global or cope with geological time. Third, Anthropocene history responds to a different science: Earth System science rather than ecology. Fourth, Anthropocene history must contend with a radically new concept of human agency as a systemic planetary force, and the fallout from that understanding.

Scale and Anthropocene History

A concern for scale characterizes Anthropocene history. The past is framed with an awareness of the recent rupture of the old Earth System, and concerned ultimately with the speed, intensity, and connectedness of the forces converging in the twentieth century. While environmental histories need not gesture toward the global consequences of particular nature–human interactions, nor speak to the peculiarities of the twentieth century, the defining characteristic of Anthropocene histories is that they keep these vast scales, as well as the pivot of the mid twentieth century, in view, regardless of their immediate focus. It's not that classical Greece or the Pagan dynasty's 250-year rule over the Irrawaddy River valley are irrelevant to Anthropocene history – on the contrary. The point is that, whatever period Anthropocene historians examine, they ask what it might reveal about the "gigantic uncontrolled experiment" in which we all now live (McNeill 2000, p. 4).

That said, the line separating environmental history from Anthropocene history in terms of scale is sometimes murky. Like the difference between weather and climate, the central issue is how the evidence is framed. One scorching summer is not proof of climate change, but it can be used in conjunction with other hot seasons to suggest general patterns. Likewise, environmental histories of cattle drives in medieval Hungary or forestry practices in ancient Japan do not automatically speak to the Anthropocene unless the author deliberately frames the research as part of larger narratives and the changes in the planetary system.

These scalar connections need to be crafted deliberately. McNeill, for instance, constructs scales that link particular events and conditions with global patterns using cumulative aggregates, horizontal webs, charts, and a sense of the *longue durée*. His analysis deploys both of the modes of scaling described in chapter 1: the nested, integrated scale of regularities from little to big; and the sprawling, tangential scale of jarring thresholds. In other words, he argues not only for the importance of the big picture, but also that "differences in quantity can become differences in quality." As he observes, "the cumulation of many increased intensities may throw some grand switches, producing very basic changes on earth" (2000, p. 5). Crossing these thresholds creates unpredictable effects not only in the Earth System but for human communities as well. Societies, like nature, have unknown tipping points – the political, economic, or cultural revolutions that up-end people's worlds. This type of systems-thinking – concerned both with the inner workings of the established Holocene system and the accelerations that tipped Earth into a new system – is essential. Even before Crutzen published the term "Anthropocene," McNeill's *Something new under the Sun* rode these vast temporal and spatial scales. More recent Anthropocene histories do the same.

The Specific Sciences of Anthropocene History

Anthropocene history is not, however, simply environmental history on steroids, attentive to larger scales and greater intensities. A third crucial (and closely related) difference between Anthropocene and environmental history is the type of science in question. While (unsurprisingly) environmental history concerns "the environment," Anthropocene history concerns "Earth System science" as well as geology. The concepts of "the environment" and "the Earth System" both emerged within the sciences as new, disruptive ways of studying the world. Both terms unified several scientific fields, and quickly gained social and political resonance. But they are not identical. In illuminating the rise of environmental history, Paul Warde, Libby Robin, and Sverker Sörlin show that the environment (in our sense of the term) "emerged in the late 1940s as an integrative concept to enable the management of 'natural resources' by scientists" (2017, p. 248). The term then swiftly entered other fields, enabling the "coalescence of practices and thinking by which we now study and manage the natural world" (2017, p. 252). Environmental history then took "the environment" to heart, and pioneered new ways of understanding human development. Like the sciences that informed it, environmental history rarely addressed geology.

The key science behind Anthropocene history is "Earth System science," a term coined in 1983. It views the planet as a single, integrated entity, moving, over the course of 4.54 billion years, from one distinctive system to another. Some past systems were dramatically different from either the Holocene or the Anthropocene. For instance, the Archean, 4 to 2.5 billion years ago, might have been so hot that, early in the eon, "ocean temperatures at times reached above 80 °C [176 °F]" (Robert and Chaussidon 2006). For most of its duration, the atmosphere contained either so little free oxygen – or none at all – that nothing rusted. Then the atmosphere first began to accumulate free oxygen, and this produced another regime with a very different set of feedback loops, including the oxidation of methane. The loss of methane, in the presence of a faint young sun, turned the planet – thankfully, temporarily – into a "Snowball Earth" about 2.3 to 2.2 billion years ago (Kopp et al. 2005). The Anthropocene, at a lower order of magnitude than that of eons, also describes a comprehensive change to planetary functioning. Anthropocene history, in being attuned to Earth System science, grapples with the recognition that human activities have up-ended one Earth System (the regularities of the Holocene, and indeed of the 2.6-million-year span of the Pleistocene before it), and unwittingly produced another Earth System with alternative (and as yet unclear) patterns and relationships among the atmosphere, lithosphere, hydrosphere, biosphere, and much else. Environmental history and Anthropocene history, in other words, are distinct in terms of scale *and* in terms of the scientific concept at the heart of their enterprises.

Understood in this way, even *global* environmental history is not the same as Anthropocene history. Alfred Crosby's groundbreaking *The Columbian exchange: Biological and cultural consequences of 1492* (1972) demonstrates that European domination of the Americas rested on the ecological disruption created by European animals, plants, and microbes; in 1986, he extended this argument, in *Ecological imperialism: The biological expansion of Europe, 900–1900,* to the Norse in Greenland and Iceland, the Crusaders in the Middle East, and, later, Europeans on the mid-Atlantic islands and around Africa all the way to Australia and New Zealand. These field-defining works showed that stories about European political and cultural ascendancy had to account for ecological factors, and that, in fact, these ecological factors were often crucial linchpins. Crosby's work still generates questions and debate. But complex ecological interactions among organisms and their environments, even if aggregated globally, are not the same as the Earth System, which operates beyond the sum of its parts. "The global environment is not the Earth System," as ethicist Clive Hamilton says (2015a, p. 102). How historians might illuminate this difference is still being explored, but a key factor is understanding what it means to be human, in all our variety and complexity, given this startling new power to transform the planet's system.

Reimaging Humanity in Anthropocene History

It follows then that the fourth distinguishing aspect of Anthropocene history, beyond newness, scale, and Earth System science, is its commitment to reimagining humanity. If human systems have for the first time ever transformed the Earth System, then the old humanist ideas about who we are, what we can change and what we can't, and what we might hope to achieve are recast by the astounding and grim discovery of our unwitting power. The Anthropocene is, along with so much else, a strange new prism casting an uncanny light on the human past, present, and future. Historians are still in the midst of the theoretical work necessary to absorb this disruptive concept into their discipline. Indeed, it may be most accurate to describe historians as dabbling in the shallows of this oceanic change – some feeling their way from the shores of environmental history, others approaching from political history, economic history, feminist history, intellectual history, and a host of other subdisciplinary outposts. What does it mean to understand human history in all its richness and variety, if the terminal of history is the Anthropocene? This is the central theoretical conundrum of Anthropocene history.

Intellectual and postcolonial historian Dipesh Chakrabarty has led the way in articulating this unprecedented question and its uncomfortable challenges. His brilliant, densely argued "The climate of history: Four theses" (2009) has shaped subsequent discussion. Chakrabarty stresses the terrifying novelty of our condition, in which the processes of globalization and global warming, capitalism and climate change, have converged. He argues that the "collapse of the age-old humanist distinction between natural history and human history" throws shadows on modern history's story of freedom (2009, p. 201). "In no discussion of freedom in the period since the Enlightenment," he observes, "was there ever any awareness of the geological agency that human beings were acquiring at the same time as and through processes closely linked to their acquisition of freedom." This observation is true beyond Europe. In Japan, as well, freedom (*jiyū*) and nature (*shizen*) were treated as antitheses, and nature became the repressed unconscious of history (Thomas 2001). Yet, from our current perspective, it appears that "the mansion of modern freedoms stands on an ever-expanding base of fossil-fuel use" (Chakrabarty 2009, p. 208). This means that the modern story of hope is simultaneously the modern story of planetary destruction.

Chakrabarty's aim is to explore this devastating paradox both as a political problem and as a formal problem in the writing of history: how do we tell the deep history of "the species" at the same time that we tell the stories of variegated human experiences of longing, fulfillment, and failure? How do we recognize ourselves in our collective impact on the Earth System at the same time that we validate or critique events and personalities shaping societies on comparatively miniature scales? To this dilemma, Chakrabarty resists easy resolutions. Indeed, echoing cultural critic Walter Benjamin (1892–1940), he suggests that "species may indeed be the name of the placeholder for an emergent, new universal history of humans that flashes up in the moment of danger that is climate change. But we can never *understand* this universal figure" as we once understood the striving, hopeful creatures who populated history before our awareness of the Anthropocene (2009, pp. 221–2). The tension between the vastness of geological forcings that have no regard for human hopes and the meaningfulness of human lives, in which history has been invested, has no resolution; it is an antithesis without a synthesis. But it may yet serve to open up a space for action.

In short, Anthropocene history faces the well-nigh impossible task of putting together two stories fundamentally at odds with one another: the deep-time, non-anthropocentric story of the planet where humanity does "not represent any point of culmination," and our own anthropocentric tales of successes and failures, hope and danger (Chakrabarty 2017, p. 42). With Anthropocene history, the problem of finding meaning in human actions is stark. The purposes of human lives, individually and collectively; the political and ethical standards by which we judge the past; and our capacity to create, transform, and choose our circumstances – all are in question. Systems, extending beyond individual control, loom larger than ever.

The problems of causation and meaning in history are not the preserve of Anthropocene narratives alone. All histories face them. In highlighting the environment, environmental historians also confront the challenge of incorporating the natural world into cogent human stories. As environmental historian William Cronon's moving essay on America's Great Plains (1992) demonstrates, ecological change – even human-wrought ecological change – does not have the neat beginnings, middles, and ends that are essential to narratives. Historians' stories "from the point of view of the universe are fictions, pure and simple"; yet stories, Cronon argues, "remain our chief moral compass in the world." The job of environmental history, in his view, is to assert "that stories about the past are better, all other things being equal, if they increase our attention to nature and the place of people within it" (1992, p. 1375). In order to accomplish this task of placing "human agents at the center of events that they themselves may not fully understand but that they constantly affect with their actions," environmental history connects amoral ecologies with the moral human world, although the artifice of narrative can never fully resolve the essential tension between the two (1992, p. 1375; see also Thomas 2010). If "the environment" produces challenges of framing and narrative even for Cronon, working with the relatively limited scales of America's heartland, and twentieth-century stories from Crow Indian Chief Plenty Coups to Roosevelt's New Dealers, how much more so does "the Anthropocene," when larger scales and a different integrated science create greater analytical and rhetorical conundrums?

Both Anthropocene history and environmental history try to craft meaningful narratives while recognizing that these histories "from the point of view of the universe are fictions, pure and simple," as Cronon puts it. In this, they are similar. The crucial distinction between the two is the relation between nature and humans. While Cronon's environmental history speaks of "nature and the place of people within it" (1992, p. 1375), Anthropocene history reconceives humanity so that people are no longer simply *within* nature but are now, collectively, the dominant force on the planet. In other words, we are both inhabitants of the planet – people *within* nature – and a planetary force – people *as* nature. Chakrabarty encapsulates our condition as "simultaneously both human and geological" (2018, p. 22). As he notes, history's "usual disputations about intra-human in/justice, inequalities, oppressive relationships" will continue, but in order to understand our new condition, "our inevitable anthropocentrism will need to be supplemented (not replaced) by 'deep time' perspectives that necessarily escape the human point of view" (Chakrabarty 2017, p. 42). Anthropocene history remains deeply invested in telling political and ethical stories about human beings, while acknowledging that human systems have joined the apolitical and amoral geophysical forces shaping the Earth System. Consciousness of this intractable dualism separates Chakrabarty from the new materialists such as Bennett and Latour, who seek to resolve the dilemma by embracing all things living and nonliving within the political and ethical realm.

In summary, four factors distinguish Anthropocene history from other types of history: first, the unprecedented novelty of the predicament at its heart; second, attentiveness to enormous scales of time and space; third, engagement with Earth System science; and, fourth, a willingness to wrestle with "the human" as a planetary force – a notion alien from all we have hitherto understood ourselves to be – and to consider what that means for our attempts to tell moral and political stories. The Anthropocene is not a topic, but a theoretical lens, bringing with it a new set of questions.

Toward the end of *Something new under the Sun*, John McNeill notes that ours is not the first unsustainable society. Instead, history shows a long succession of locally and regionally unsustainable human societies rising and falling over millennia, long before our own globally unsustainable society pushed against – and in some cases, beyond – planetary boundaries. As McNeill points out, some earlier unsustainable societies vanished, but many "changed their ways and survived. They changed not to sustainability but to some new and different kind of unsustainability... . However, unsustainable society on the global scale may be another matter entirely." Earlier societies benefitted from "ecological buffers – open land, unused water, unpolluted spaces," which today we no longer have. In our near future, "the most difficult passages will probably (or better put, least improbably) involve shortage of clean fresh water, the myriad effects of warmer climate, and of reduced biodiversity." It is even possible, warns McNeill, that "collapse looms" (2000, pp. 358–9). Few of the Anthropocene histories written since 2000 dispute these findings fundamentally.

Conclusion

Through the lens of the disciplines discussed in this chapter, the "human" emerges as far more than just the megaforce overwhelming the Earth System. The *anthropos* here tames the grey wolf, kills mammoths, and develops the cognitive fluidity to manipulate elaborate symbolic systems, from languages and cave paintings to burial rituals. This *anthropos* transforms local environments, learns that seeds can be deliberately planted for harvest, and organizes itself into large, settled societies. Sometimes, these humans talk with deities and sometimes with glaciers. For long periods, some societies managed to live within limited ecosystems. Other societies repeatedly overran their environmental limits. Collectively, the exponentially growing numbers of the *anthropos* have now produced a global society pressing against the planetary boundaries for safe, sustainable human communities. But humanity is not just the sum of its parts. The particularities of cultures and societies and the distinctiveness of complex individuals exceed and defy any singular attempt at representation. No single human subject and no single integrated story emerges from the conflicting roles we humans play in relation to Earth. Combining the sciences of the Anthropocene with the social sciences of the *anthropos* produces an array of ways to understand "the human." These in turn allow us to move beyond a universal "solution" to the "problem," and instead provide a multitude of tools for coping with our predicaments, small and global.

As this chapter shows, the *anthropos* of the human sciences and the *anthropos* of the geological Anthropocene, despite their common Greek root, are not identical. The congeries of local/global interactions, the incommensurable views of society and nature held by different cultures, and the refracted desires of individuals and communities are important to the human sciences' conception of the *anthropos*. Paleoanthropology, archeology, anthropology, and history tend to highlight humanity's multiplicity; Earth System science tends to focus on the convergence of the human activities that changed our planet. One approach focuses on the immense variety of social forms and actions, including those that would not have led to the Anthropocene; the other explains the reality of the Anthropocene in terms of the activities that have come to dominate Earth. The aim of a multidisciplinary approach is to find ways of creating makeshift links between these two understandings of the *anthropos* while acknowledging the irresolvable friction between them.

7

The Economics and Politics of Planetary Limits

In July 1944, US Secretary of the Treasury Henry Morgenthau Jr. opened the Bretton Woods Conference by proclaiming the economic dogma that would propel the postwar world: all people, he said, can enjoy "the fruits of material progress on an Earth infinitely blessed with natural resources" by adhering to "the elementary economic axiom ... that prosperity has no fixed limits" (cited in Rasmussen 2013, p. 242). Half a century later, in 1992, Chief Economist of the World Bank and future US Treasury Secretary Larry Summers reiterated this core tenet of modernity: "There are ... no limits to the carrying capacity of the earth that are likely to bind any time in the foreseeable future." Summers then went further, warning against the very thought of limits: "There isn't a risk of apocalypse due to global warming or anything else. The idea that we should put limits on growth because of some natural limit, is a profound error and one that, were it ever to prove influential, would have staggering social costs" (cited in Bell and Cheng 2009, p. 393). Belief in infinite growth became hegemonic. It structured postwar economic and political institutions in capitalist and communist countries, in non-aligned nations and international organizations. From America's postwar prosperity to Japan's "economic miracle," from Soviet productivity gains to Mao's "Great Leap Forward," all modern nations propounded endless growth and ceaseless bounty. Pursuit of economic growth unified the modern world. Not coincidentally, it also helped propel the Great Acceleration.

Some countries heralded the market as the premier mechanism of growth, a view fervently embraced in Ronald Reagan's America and Margaret Thatcher's United Kingdom in the 1980s. Other nations, such as Japan, pursued growth through state guidance of private enterprise. MITI, Japan's Ministry of International Trade and Industry (1949–2001), sparked admiration (and considerable consternation) when this Asian nation overtook all Western countries except the US to become the world's second-largest economy by the 1980s. Both big industry and big labor loved growth. In capitalist countries, GDP (Gross Domestic Product), measuring all the goods and services on the market, became the dominant metric of economic and political success. Communist countries also wanted growth. The Soviet Union deployed centralized planning, state ownership of the means of production, and collectivization, among other mechanisms of increased productivity. Through a series of "Five Year Plans" beginning in 1928, the USSR transformed itself from an impoverished agrarian backwater to an industrial power, able to triumph against Nazi invaders in World War II and grow even faster in the 1950s and 1960s. It used not GDP but NMP (Net Material Product, leaving out services) to measure its growth. Intellectuals and leaders in many newly liberated African and Asian nations took note of Soviet achievements as they shook themselves free from colonial rule, and sought to emulate centrally planned growth. In short, the creed of growth was embraced by the entire political spectrum, with only a few dissenters, such as Indian independence leader Mahatma Gandhi (1869–1948) and maverick social philosopher André Gorz (1923–2007). The commitment to "growthism" was embedded in modern political, social, and cultural institutions. No idea has been more important in provoking, and then driving, the Anthropocene.

As a way of organizing economies and creating political consensus, economic growth has been phenomenally successful. Global output of goods and services as measured by GDP rocketed from a little over $1 trillion in 1960 to well over $80 trillion by 2018 (Statista 2018; World Bank 2018). Adjusting for inflation, GDP rose in the United States from about $300 billion in 1950 to about $21,429 trillion in 2018 (The Balance). War-torn China had a faltering agrarian economy in 1950, and was only beginning to soar to the $14 trillion economy it is today – the second-largest in the world. In 1950, GDP per capita in Japan was lower than in Mexico or Greece, but its GDP now stands at around $5 trillion, making it the world's third-largest economy. That's nearly half the world's economy in just three countries. All the while, the human population has been rising from about 2.5 billion in 1950 to over 7.8 billion today, mostly due to improved sanitation, more food, and healthcare. More babies thrive, and people live longer lives. Never in the history of the world have production, consumption, and population risen at such high rates and to such levels.

But this good news is also bad news. Rising global GDP came with rising overconsumption by the rich and rising disparities between rich and poor. Demanding more and more of the planet's resources, rich countries, including the US, China, Japan, and the UK, are all in "overshoot," defined by the Global Footprint Network as being "when humanity's demand on nature exceeds the biosphere's supply or regenerative capacity" (cited in Kenner 2015, p. 2). In hyper-demand are physical resources, ranging from rare metals for electronics to sand as an ingredient for concrete, as well as chemical resources, such as phosphorus for fertilizer. The current generation is now literally devouring the sustenance of those who follow. We now consume an estimated 1.7 planet's worth of natural resources each year, sinking ever deeper into ecological debt.

Who are the rich who over-consume in this way? The global 1%, according to the 2018 Credit Suisse *Global Wealth Report*, is anyone with an annual income of US$32,400 or more a year (roughly £25,400, €28,360, ¥3,518,769, 2.4 million Indian rupees, or 24,969 Chinese yuan.) To reach the top 1% in terms of wealth, you'll need a bit more, around $770,000 in assets, including equity in your home; as Thomas Piketty (2014) and others (e.g. Ortiz and Cummins 2011; Byanyima 2015) have shown, wealth is concentrating in the hands of a few even faster than income. Particularly in high-income countries between 1970 and 2010, income disparities rose sharply (Piketty 2014, p. 24). That leaves most of the rest of the world without much income or wealth. In the Introduction to the 2018 Credit Suisse *Global Wealth Report*, Urs Rohner, the Chairman of the Board of Directors, points out that "3.2 billion adults or about 64% of the adult population lives with wealth below USD 10,000, which corresponds to only 1.9% of the global wealth" (Shorrocks et al. 2018, p. 2; see also Kurt 2019). On a per capita basis, this global majority has not overconsumed planetary resources nor benefitted proportionately from growth, yet finds itself more vulnerable to water and food shortages, collapsing ecosystems, climate change, and the violence that accompanies these problems. In this chapter, we examine mainstream economics, which in general denies or ignores the Anthropocene, as well as two alternatives, one called "environmental economics" and the other called "ecological economics," both of which insist that the environment is part of the economy. In different ways, they both reject the neoclassical view eliminating natural resources from market calculations.

Mainstream Economics: Growth as Good

Although economic growth's unwitting environmental and social devastation is now apparent, it is important to acknowledge its original appeal. It wasn't just the greedy few who embraced it. Instead, the reason that the hope of infinite growth beguiled (and still beguiles) so many is that it promised not only the alleviation of crushing poverty but also greater equality within societies and among them. Beginning in the late eighteenth century, and particularly after World War II, the ideology of growth heralded a better, fairer world for all; the Bretton Woods system in the West was designed to generate greater equality among and within nations, and communist ideals in the East served the same purpose. Growth would create more products and services, while the market, government policy, a collective sense of fairness, or some combination of all three would allocate these material benefits in just and socially beneficial ways. In the postwar Western world, at least until the collapse of the Bretton Woods system in the early 1970s, the connection between growth and social wellbeing was axiomatic (e.g. Varoufakis 2016). The gap between rich and poor within the United States and the UK narrowed considerably in the 1950s and 1960s. By the 1980s, however, growth and social welfare were decoupled, and began to be treated in some cases as opposing values. The policies of Ronald Reagan and Margaret Thatcher promoted growth over greater equality, social welfare, and educational commitments. Increasing GDP became the primary political and economic goal in most countries, regardless of its effects on society and the environment. It was inscribed in contemporary economic, political, and social structures all around the world.

Today, belief in the possibility of unlimited growth still reigns supreme in mainstream economics. Now that communist nations such as China, and formerly communist nations such as Russia, have abandoned command economies, some version of "the market" holds sway virtually everywhere. Institutions such as the International Monetary Fund promote "market fundamentalism" around the globe – the belief that "unregulated" markets will solve most economic and social problems through the mechanism of the so-called "invisible hand" of supply and demand. Although impediments to market functions such as oligarchic control, corruption, patriarchy, lack of transparency, and increasing disparities between the haves and the have-nots are noted by most economists, government regulation seems to top their list of worries. Their prescription for most ills is less regulation and more growth. Mainstream economists argue that a growing economy will create better educational and occupational conditions, which will empower a middle class to confront oligarchs, confound corruption, and take control of their destinies, limiting pollution, lowering birth rates, and increasing quality of life for all. This optimistic scenario rests on ignoring planetary limits. Economic journalist David Pilling (2018) refers to this as "the growth delusion." The increasing destabilization of our Earth System is propelled by this dangerous and mistaken view.

Economists, of course, understand that a particular natural resource may run out or get too expensive, but most believe that substitutes can always be found through market pricing and technological innovation. If substitutes can always be found, the argument goes, natural resources will never run out. Therefore, natural resources need not be figured into economic calculations. Economist Robert Solow (1924–) became the poster boy for this view due to a single sentence in a 1974 *American Economic Review* essay. The sentence – "the world could, in effect, get along without natural resources" – is less bizarre in context. In full, Solow writes:

> As you would expect, the degree of substitutability is also a key factor. If it is easy to substitute other factors for natural resources, then there is in principle no "problem." The world can, in effect, get along without natural resources, so exhaustion is just an event, not a catastrophe... . If, on the other hand, real output per unit of resources is effectively bounded – cannot exceed some upper limit of productivity which is in turn not too far from where we are now – then catastrophe is unavoidable. (1974, p. 11)

Having confronted his readers with the appalling disaster of limited resources, Solow quickly pivots around and ends reassuringly: "Fortunately, what little evidence there is suggests that there is quite a lot of substitutability between exhaustible resources and renewable or reproducible resources, though it is an empirical question that could absorb a lot more work than it has so far" (1974, p. 11; see also Bartkowski 2014). The empirical research on planetary boundaries of the last half-century has now largely undermined the broad optimism of Solow's view.

Our increasingly sophisticated (though by no means adequate) understanding of the complex exchanges and feedback loops of the Earth System tells us that in some sectors we are already reaching limits, and may even have crossed certain thresholds. For instance, the ratio of "real output per unit" has diminished in many arenas, meaning that ever greater amounts of energy and materials must be used to produce the same product. In the United States, the EROI (energy return on investment) in oil production has plummeted. In 1919, the return on each unit of energy invested in oil discovery was 1,000:1; by the 2010s, it was 5:1 (Ketcham 2017). As resources become harder and harder to find and extract, more energy goes into obtaining them and the ratio of effort to output rises sharply. Another example of rapidly depleting resources is the rare earth elements, which are vital for technologies that might help reduce carbon emissions, such as hybrid cars, wind turbines, and solar cells (as well as products such as cell phones, iPads, laptops, and televisions). However, these hard-to-substitute minerals are seldom found in sufficient amounts to make extraction easy. Now, at huge cost, deep sea vents and seamounts are being targeted for precious ores (Cho 2012), but such excavation does considerable damage to underwater environments.

On the other hand, for many products the EROI has increased, and new efficiencies in resource use have been achieved. Overall, between 1980 and 2007, "the material intensity of the global economy (i.e. the amount of biomass, minerals, and fossil fuels required to produce a dollar of world GDP) decreased by 33 percent," according to journalist Rob Dietz and economist Dan O'Neill (2013, p. 37). But, as they note, "concurrent with these improvements, world GDP grew by 141 percent, such that total resource use still increased by 61 percent" (2013, p. 37). When greater efficiency and technological improvements use fewer materials, products become cheaper, leading to greater consumption – a phenomenon known as the "Jevons Paradox," named for the English economist William Stanley Jevons (1835–82) who formulated it. Efficiencies also free up capital for further investment and further growth, driving the Great Acceleration ever faster.

If we zoom out from particular economies to take in the planetary picture, the finite nature of Earth's bounty is even more apparent. A 2015 article in *Science* announced that four of the nine planetary boundaries defining a "safe operating space for humanity" have been transgressed: biogeochemical cycles (principally nitrogen and phosphorus), biosphere integrity, land-system use, and climate (Steffen et al. 2015b). The planet, according to these findings, has been pushed beyond sustainable levels. "We are living," warns Harvard economist Stephen A. Marglin, "in a danger zone" (2013, p. 150).

Mainstream Economics and Politics: Separating the Market and Society from Nature

Economics earns its nickname as the "dismal science" (Carlyle 1849) in relation to the Anthropocene because its foundational dogma of infinite growth makes it oblivious to real-world conditions. By and large, it ignores the data on the Earth System and on physical limits that Solow thought missing and that are now available. Mainstream economists' assumptions about nature, time, and evidence blind them to the Anthropocene. The misapprehensions about each of these factors is worth a closer look.

First, nature is treated as an "externality," something that need not figure in calculations about economic activity. Externalities include both the "inputs" of natural resources, such as fresh water, breathable air, and the ozone layer, *and* the "outputs" of waste, including CO_2, nitrogen, phosphorus, toxins, and plastic – the last of these produced at the rate of over 300 million tonnes per year and rising (Plastic Oceans International 2019). Waste also includes rivers of untreated human and farm animal feces; worldwide, roughly 90 percent of sewage is discharged untreated into bodies of water. For mainstream economists, both natural resources and waste are external to the markets and thus irrelevant. The Earth, in this view, is both a never-empty horn of plenty and a fathomless sink able to absorb all we wish to push away. Long ago, one of the founders of political economy, Jean-Baptiste Say (1767–1832), articulated this idea, saying "natural resources are inexhaustible because if that were not the case, we would not obtain them free of charge" (cited in Bonaiuti 2014, p. xviii). This approach to nature has largely held sway ever since.

Second, mainstream economists' approach to time assumes that it flows smoothly into the future without disruption. If market forces are allowed free play, this smooth tide of time will produce ever greater wealth, thereby making everything relatively cheaper in the years to come. Calculating this supposed decline in future costs is called "discounting." Discounting argues against action now to mitigate environmental hazards, protect resources, or cease polluting, because all this will be much cheaper to do in the future. Growth now will take care of problems later. The idea of growth smoothly advancing through time is so rooted in neoclassical economics that British economist Wilfred Beckerman (1925–) claimed that it has been "taking place since the time of Pericles" in the fifth century BCE, waving aside such dips as the collapse of the Roman Empire and the Black Death, perhaps because Europe ultimately recovered. Economies that once flourished along the

Silk Road or in Mali, but lost and never regained their economic vigor, vanish from view. Selecting only current success stories, Beckerman proclaims "there is no reason to suppose that economic growth cannot continue for another 2500 years" (quoted in Higgs 2014, p. 18).

In any case, whether or not there could have been infinite growth in the Holocene Earth System, if properly managed, is now a moot point; we live on an Earth that is increasingly departing from those more predictable conditions. Time's flow has been disrupted by the reality of the Anthropocene. This "rupture" of the Earth System, as Clive Hamilton termed it in 2016, throws a spanner in the works, making it impossible to rely on discounting to automatically lower future costs.

Finally, there is the reliance on metrics as the only kind of evidence admissible when assessing successful economies, people, and societies. Quantifiable data are the gold standard in economics. The elevation of these metrics over humanistic judgments as the basis for policies and programs in all walks of life has obscured our understanding of both natural processes and human values (e.g. O'Neil 2016; Muller 2018). The leading example of such metricized thinking is taking GDP to be the primary measure of progress. GDP takes into account only the goods and services exchanged on markets. It does not consider forms of wellbeing such as health, happiness, and community ties, since these complicated phenomena are difficult to quantify, although efforts are now being made in this direction, as we will see. Activities such as lending a hand in a neighbor's garden, cooking a meal, writing a ditty to sing at a retirement party, taking care of a loved one, or enjoying the beauty of a landscape do not count because they are not bought and sold. Therefore, they do not figure in GDP calculations. Like natural resources in the estimation of Jean-Baptiste Say, actions that strengthen community cohesion and foster individual health should be considered free and without value.

Sometimes, for reasons of insurance or liability assessments, a dollar amount is affixed to things that might seem unquantifiable to non-economists. For instance, calculating the value of the life of an 11-year-old child at 2 dollars, as in one instance (Zelizer 2007), may seem reasonable to a neoclassical economist, who defines "value" in purely monetary terms when assessing the loss of that child. Where no monetary value can be ascribed, the evidence is usually ignored. With examples such as these in mind, Robert Skidelsky (2009), economic historian and biographer of John Maynard Keynes (1883–1946), argues that a reliance on mathematics rather than history is at the root of mainstream economists' inability to situate their thinking in relation to the real world.

In sum, mainstream economics treats "the economy" as separable from the environment, does not acknowledge disruptions in the overall trajectory of growth, and believes in metrics, thereby limiting its grasp of nonquantified, nonmonetary values. Given these assumptions about nature, time, and statistics, it is not surprising that the realities of our new planetary system have not figured in this type of economics, nor in the political systems it supports. The Anthropocene fundamentally undermines orthodox economic paradigms. It brings economic systems and Earth systems together, reveals a break (or extraordinarily rapid transition) in Earth System continuity, and raises the question of values that lie beyond metrics. There are certain cases where the neoclassical model has its uses, as ecological economist Peter Söderbaum (2000, p. xii) argues, but its narrow range of analytical tools makes it a poor guide to the increasingly perturbed and unstable planet we now inhabit.

The premises of neoclassical economics would matter little if the study of economics were an arcane discipline without much bearing on our governing assumptions. But, as Oxford economist Kate Raworth observes, "Economics is the mother tongue of public policy, the language of public life and the mindset that shapes society" (2017, p. 5). This language has been prevalent for so long that sometimes it is hard to see that it is not a neutral description of the natural way things work, but one that emerges only in alliance with powerful institutions and class interests. As economist Stephen Marglin argues, "mainstream economics is the handmaiden of modern culture, its assumptions are the presuppositions of modernity," where a central tenet "is that we live in a world without limits" (2017). Orthodox economics has great bearing on governance, the way we assess potential threats to human societies, and the imagination we bring to bear in our responses. Despite the power of economics as a way of thinking about the world – or, perhaps, because of it – the discipline is little given to pluralism, self-reflection, or to the multidisciplinarity that marks the best efforts to grapple with the Anthropocene; economists generally refer almost exclusively to one another in their publications and disregard other disciplines (Fourcade et al. 2015). With such heavily patrolled intellectual boundaries, mainstream economics rarely examines its assumption of infinitely sustainable growth. However, as environmental perplexities mount and limits to growth assert themselves in various sectors, challenges to this orthodoxy have emerged.

Challenging Belief in Infinite Growth

One of the first powerful challenges to the postwar tenet of infinite growth came from a worried Fiat executive. In 1967, Aurelio Peccei (1908–84) gave a speech outlining his concerns about global environmental and socioeconomic degradation to the Adela Investment Company. This speech landed on the desk of Scottish environmental scientist and civil servant Alexander King (1909–2007), who was so impressed that he joined forces with Peccei to found the Club of Rome in 1968. At first, the Club of Rome was an informal gathering of scientists, economists, and industrialists eager to discuss world problems, but these men soon realized that they lacked basic information on global trends. Their instincts told them that infinite growth on a finite planet was impossible, but they wanted data. With financial backing from Volkswagen, they approached 29-year-old Professor of Systems Dynamics Dennis Meadows, and his team of systems analysts at MIT, asking for a forecast of environmental, social, and economic trajectories. In an earlier age, such a forecast would have consisted of little more than peering into a crystal ball, but the MIT team had designed the World3 computer program on MIT's immense mainframe. For two years, they fed data into their computer. First, they collated retrospective worldwide growth trends from 1900 to 1970. Then, using that data, they modeled 12 potential future scenarios of global development to the year 2100. With each, they focused on the complex feedback loops that connect industry, agriculture, human population, natural resources, and the capacity of sinks to absorb waste. Every realistic scenario showed that planetary limits would force an end to growth sometime during the twenty-first century. If the business-as-usual growth trend continued, they forecasted, "the most probable result will be a rather sudden and uncontrolled decline in both population and industrial capacity" (Meadows et al. 1972, p. 23). This research was published as *The limits to growth* (LTG) in 1972, becoming a bestseller in several countries and translated into around 30 languages.

At that time, members of the LTG team were grave, but optimistic that the world, with 50 years of lead time, would meet the dangers revealed by their research. "Even in the most pessimistic LTG scenario," they pointed out, "the material standard of living kept increasing all the way to 2015" (Meadows et al. 2004, p. xi). The MIT team believed that people, fortified with sufficient information and enough prosperity to reorient their economies and societies, would end relentless growth trends and establish ecological and economic stability. In 1972, it seemed possible that a "state of global equilibrium could be designed so that the basic material needs of each person on earth are satisfied and each person has an equal opportunity to realize his individual human potential" (Meadows et al. 1972, p. 24). However, that happy prospect was derailed. Attacks on *The limits to growth*, the hegemony of neoclassical economics in policy circles, population increase – and, indeed, all the trends of the Great Acceleration – prevented reorientation.

The idea of global ecological equilibrium was anathema to the axiom of infinite growth. Defenders of growth from think tanks, governments, and universities came out swinging against the concept in books, newspapers, and in the pages of *The Economist, Forbes*, and *Foreign Affairs*. Economist Carl Kaysen (1920–2010), who enjoyed a luminous career advising John F. Kennedy and holding posts at MIT, the Institute for Advanced Study, and Harvard, announced that the Earth's available "energy and matter" could support a population of 3.5 trillion people with American standards of living (cited in Higgs 2014, p. 59). Economist Herman Kahn, more modestly, thought that "with current and near current technology, we can support 15 billion people in the world at twenty thousand dollars per capita for a millennium – and that seems to be a very conservative statement" (Meadows et al. 2004). Beckerman, meanwhile, called *The limits to growth* "a brazen, impudent piece of nonsense" (cited in Ketcham 2017).

The doubts cast on the validity of these findings confused public perception, leading many to discount the forecasts in *The limits to growth*. But the study's calculations have proved robust. In 2014, Graham Turner of the Melbourne Sustainable Society Institute of Australia found that the business-as-usual scenario from the 1972 *The limits to growth* tracks closely on current trends; a separate study in 2016 by Professor of Sustainable Development Tim Jackson at the University of Surrey concurred. For neoclassical economists and the policymakers who take their advice, the confirmation that growth has limits is, notes historian Kerryn Higgs, a "massively inconvenient truth" (2014, p. 282).

It has not helped the reputation of *The limits to growth* and related research that, from the 1970s onward, science has been under attack from two additional angles. First, business and political interests have claimed there is widespread scientific disagreement where none exists. This tactic was deployed against anti-smoking campaigns, then against climate-change science, and now against the growing consensus on the Anthropocene. AWG member and historian of science Naomi Oreskes has been instrumental in revealing the networks behind these corporate tactics. In these instances, long after general scientific consensus has been reached, the public remains under the impression that the issues are still hotly debated (Oreskes 2004, p. 1688; see also Oreskes and Conway 2010, Oreskes 2019).

The second angle of attack on science came from within universities for science's purported naivety about its claims to represent reality. In the 1980s, an approach known as science and technology studies (STS) emerged, emphasizing that scientific practices were social practices. These scholars argued that scientific evidence and concepts were not transparent revelations of the real world, but best understood as social constructs. This socially constructed knowledge was beholden to institutional, linguistic, social, and cultural networks. Many took STS to be arguing that scientific findings had no more purchase on reality than any other claims. Some emphasized that scientists are not god-like beings in touch with Truth but parochial operators. Bruno Latour, a leader of this movement with his influential *Science in action* (1987), now looks back on this moment with some chagrin, having become an outspoken defender of science. In 2017, he explained, "I certainly was not antiscience, although I must admit it felt good to put scientists down a little. There was some juvenile enthusiasm in my style" (cited in de Vrieze 2017). These attacks on science were damaging. Unintentionally, the interests of business and politics, social constructivists, and neoclassical economists converged to delay actions recommended by the Club of Rome and others alarmed by the evidence of environmental degradation.

Redesigning Economics and Politics for a Finite Planet

Pessimism overtook the authors of the *The limits to growth* in their 1992 and 2004 updates, but their efforts, along with global realities, helped to put nature back into economics. There are now two primary ways of reuniting "ecosystems" and "economic systems": environmental economics and ecological economics. Their names are similar, and they share some important concepts, such as "ecosystem services," the first iteration of which came out of ecological economics (e.g. Costanza et al. 1997). However, these two approaches have radically different implications for the Anthropocene. In a nutshell, environmental economics treats nature as a subset of the economic system and relies on "the market" to prevent further environmental damage. Ecological economics does the opposite, treating the economy as a subset of the natural world and relying on informed political choice and community input to determine appropriate uses of dwindling resources. Below, this contrast is explored further.

Environmental economics is essentially a branch of neoclassical economics, sharing most of its premises. However, it includes nature within market operations, by pricing and giving a monetary value to species and ecological systems. Once the value of the environment has been established, it then looks to ensure that the market will allocate "ecosystem services" in appropriate ways. For instance, it assumes that industries, if given the correct price signals, will stop harvesting tuna and halibut when these species are endangered, and cease fracking when water supplies are threatened. Environmental economists argue that, if depleting and polluting resources become too expensive due to increased costs or higher taxes, technological innovators will take matters in hand and produce solutions that don't deplete or pollute endangered resources. In this way, the market spurs "green growth" or "sustainable development." Economist Jeffrey Sachs (2015) calls "sustainable development" the "central concept of our age"; it allows us to continue expanding our economy while solving global poverty and ensuring intergenerational justice without environmental harm. As a concept, environmental economics has met with great success. STS scholar Sharon Beder observes that it "is now reflected in government policy around the world including the use of extended cost benefit analyses, contingent valuations, environmental charges and emissions trading" (2011, p. 146).

Ecological economics, on the other hand, has been too far outside the orthodox fold to attract powerful adherents among mainstream economists or policymakers until very recently. It began as a transdisciplinary movement combining economics and ecology and has since forged alliances with behavioral psychology, anthropology, sociology, and a number of other fields. Most importantly, in contrast to environmental economists, leading ecological economists such as Robert Costanza and others assume that "the Earth is materially finite and nongrowing," with the economy "a subset of this finite global system" (cited in Beder 2011, p. 146). In other words, ecological economists see planetary boundaries as true boundaries, beyond which lie unknown and unpredictable conditions unconducive to human societies. From this perspective, the phrases "sustainable development" and "green growth" are oxymoronic in the long term. Instead, ecological economists argue that we need to think in terms such as a "steady-state economy" and even degrowth, valuing things beyond GDP. Although ecological economics and environmental economics are sometimes conflated because the term "ecosystem services" migrated from the former to the latter, the contrast between them can hardly be overstated.

Environmental Economics: Putting Nature on the Market without Changing Politics

In 2000, United Nations Secretary-General Annan announced the UN's "Millennium Ecosystem Assessment" (MA). The goal of this $24 million study was to calculate the harm done to ecosystems around the world and propose ways to protect them. Between 2001 and 2005, 1,360 experts from 95 countries busied themselves with assessing changes in land use, coral reefs, water, nitrogen, CO_2, terrestrial biomes, the rise in human populations, and a host of other factors. Their dire conclusion was that the "world's ecosystems changed more rapidly in the second half of the twentieth century than at any time in human history" (Millennium Ecosystem Assessment 2005, p. 2). One might well ask "dire for whom?" The MA's answer: for human beings. Although the intrinsic value of species and ecosystems is mentioned in the report, human needs are at the center of its calculations of value. "Ecosystem services," as defined by the 155-page synthesis of their five-volume findings, "are the benefits people obtain from ecosystems. These include *provisioning services* such as food, water, timber, and fiber; *regulating services* that affect climate, floods, disease, wastes, and water quality; *cultural services* that provide recreational, aesthetic, and spiritual benefits; and *supporting services* such as soil formation, photosynthesis, and nutrient cycling" (Millennium Ecosystem Assessment 2005a, p. v). Having calculated these ecosystem services, the MA's bottom line "is that human actions are depleting Earth's natural capital, putting such strain on the environment that the ability of the planet's ecosystems to sustain future generations can no longer be taken for granted" (Millennium Ecosystem Assessment 2005b). The year 2000 again appears pivotal: Paul Crutzen improvised the term "Anthropocene"; John McNeill proposed a global history ending with "something new under the sun"; and the UN inaugurated this study of global ecosystem transformation.

The Millennium Ecosystem Assessment, though pioneering in its global reach, was hardly the first – or the last – effort to use an ecosystems services approach. The field's history stretches back to the subdiscipline of resource economics, which emerged in North

American universities after World War II to create models for fisheries, forestry, and agriculture, so that natural resources could be exploited without being depleted. In the 1960s, devastating pollution crises quickened the desire to limit environmental damage caused by industry. At first, governments took the lead. In Japan, for example, the government responded to the so-called big four pollution cases, including the infamous Minamata methylmercury poisonings, with the 1970 Water Pollution Control Act. That same year, by executive order, American President Richard Nixon established the Environmental Protection Agency.

Then, with the rising tide of market fundamentalism in the 1980s and beyond, government efforts in many countries were undermined. In an attempt to remind fellow economists of the importance of natural resources and sinks, Costanza, Herman Daly, and others proposed the concept of "ecosystem services" in the 1990s (Costanza and Daly 1992; Jansson et al. 1994; Costanza et al. 1997; Prugh et al. 1999). This "eye-opening metaphor," as ecological economist Richard B. Norgaard (2010) calls it, originated as a critique of mainstream economics. Building on E. F. Schumacher's earlier concept of "natural capital" (1973), its aim was to draw attention to natural limits ignored by markets. However, the idea of "ecosystem services" morphed into the proposition that markets could protect the environment at least as well as, or even better than, government policies and legal environmental protections. Proponents from environmental economics ignored the basic insight that "natural capital" could be exhausted (Norgaard 2010). This revised definition of "ecosystem services" suggested that the environment could be protected through the mechanism of pricing, without disturbing the belief in infinite growth and its promise of social good. The political status quo could go on with business-as-usual without having to reapportion or protect resources through government action.

Understood in this way, environmental economics readily absorbed "ecosystem services," making it the playbook for a win-win-win situation. How was this triple victory possible? Its most confident advocates, such as economist Jeffrey Sachs, speak of "decoupling," which means that, through ingenious new technologies in concert with market forces, "growth can continue while pressures on key resources (water, air, land, habitat of other species) and pollution are significantly reduced rather than increased" (2015, p. 217). Technological innovation will help "dematerialize" the economy, allowing us to provide for the growing human

population without threatening ecosystem collapse or impover-
ishing future generations.

A favorite example of Sachs and other environmental economists
is substituting wind and solar power for fossil fuels. Through these
initiatives, they argue, the problem of climate change can be solved.
In other words, technological and market-system optimists reduce
our multifaceted predicament to the issue of climate change. Even
more narrowly, they often look only at rising rates of CO_2 from fossil
fuels, without accounting for other greenhouse gases, let alone other
factors affecting the Earth System. Yet climate change is just one
facet of the complex conundrum of the Anthropocene. Assessing
ecological impacts at different temporal and spatial scales is more
complicated than those advocating new technologies readily admit.
The true "price" of technological and market-based solutions is
difficult to gauge, given the planet's systemic complexity and the
unpredictability of Anthropocene conditions.

For instance, most offshore wind turbines require rare earth
metals sourced from China, which supplies about 90 percent of the
world's demand and has a monopoly on some elements. Not only
are the mines of China's primary production site, the southeastern
province of Jiangxi, being rapidly depleted, but such mining entails
great environmental and social costs. According to investigative
journalist Liu Hongqiao (2016), "Research has found that producing
one tonne of rare earth ore (in terms of rare earth oxides) produces
200 cubic metres of acidic waste water. The production of the rare
earths needed to meet China's demand for wind turbines up to 2050
(in a scenario of radical wind power expansion) will result in the
release of 80 million cubic metres of waste water – enough to fill
Hangzhou's West Lake eight times over" – and at a time when fresh
water is a major problem for the Chinese people. But that is not
all. Manufacturing and installing the turbines produces emissions,
due to smelting, separation, processing, and transportation, often
to places as distant as the UK. Once in place, the turbines require
monitoring and upkeep. In the North Sea, for instance, maintenance
requires teams of technicians to spend alternate months at sea in
fossil-fuel-powered boats and planes. All along the line, there are
biological costs, as habitats are disturbed or destroyed, as well as
human costs, due to poorly paid labor, work hazards, local pollution,
corruption, illegal mines, and broken social ties.

So, while wind power may seem like salvation, producing carbon-
free, "dematerialized" energy, this is true only when the emissions
from functioning turbines alone are calculated, while the other aspects

of their production, maintenance, and eventual decay are ignored. Only by this one metric is wind power one of the "non-emission sources" that economist Paul Krugman (2013) says it is. Without a systemic evaluation of all the costs – economic, environmental, and social – it is not clear that a "decoupling" of natural resources and the economy has occurred, or even that CO_2 emissions have been diminished. Reducing our predicament to the problem of climate change, then reducing climate change to CO_2 emissions, and finally measuring emissions at the point of energy production is an inadequate simplification of our dilemma. Such reduction rests on three factors: it assumes that our knowledge of how the planet works is sufficient, that natural and human capital are interchangeable, and that industrial products can be substituted for natural resources. So far, there is little evidence of any significant "decoupling" when all these factors are accounted for. There is a good case for promoting wind and solar power, but these technologies have downsides too. Decisions on how to weigh the costs and benefits of these technologies to various communities are political, not technocratic.

The Difficulties of Assigning Market Value to Ecosystem Services

Do we know enough about ecosystem services to assign monetary value to them? It seems that the answer is "no." We're nowhere near having the basic facts we need for such calculations. Take the seemingly simple question of the number of species on Earth. About 1.4 million species have been identified and named, but "estimates as to the true total vary hugely from 2 million to 100 million" (Goulson 2013, p. 44). A 2011 study "predicts –8.7 million (±1.3 million SE) eukaryotic species globally" and suggests "some 86% of existing species on Earth and 91% of species in the ocean still await description" (Mora et al. 2011). Without even this basic knowledge, pricing the services of particular species would have been challenging, to put it mildly, under Holocene conditions. Now that biodiversity is under threat and ecosystems are changing quickly under pressure from the Anthropocene's new biogeochemical cycles, the value of any particular species or the biome's total services becomes a moving target that is impossible to pin down.

Moreover, maintaining biodiversity, while vitally important, is not the only issue. Biologists talk not only of species diversity, but also of species disparity. Disparity is a measure of the range of body plans available in nature. For instance, all insects share the same general body plan, but have huge species diversity (basically variation on the same theme), whereas insects and onychophorans have different body plans. There are only about 200 onychophoran species, compared with over 1 million insects. While losing 200 insect species is a great setback, losing all 200 onychophoran species would be disastrous from the point of view of evolution, in that a whole phylum would be gone forever (see chapter 5). Such a loss is literally incalculable by "the market," economists, or scientists. As the altered Earth System of the Anthropocene produces unpredictable tipping points and unforeseen interactions, we cannot price most ecosystem services with any sensible degree of precision.

The Millennium Ecosystem Assessment, while embracing the language of environmental economics and building on some of its concepts and research, introduced cautionary observations, repeatedly mentioning "gaps in knowledge" and "non-linear processes" such as sudden disease emergence (as in the 2020 COVID-19 crisis), abrupt alterations in water quality, the creation of "dead zones" in coastal waters, the collapse of fisheries, and shifts in regional climates. It also suggested that growth in GDP may not be the only necessary metric for ensuring thriving societies on an unpredictable planet. As the MEA dryly notes, "Human well-being depends on ecosystem services but also on the supply and quality of social capital, technology, and institutions. These factors mediate the relationship between ecosystem services and human well-being in ways that remain contested and incompletely understood" (Millennium Ecosystem Assessment 2005a, p. 49). The implication of such statements is that hubris is dangerous. What we do not know – and cannot yet know – about the emerging planetary system precludes confidence in solutions through market pricing.

A second trait of environmental economics is that it treats the "products" of nature as being interchangeable with products of human manufacture. The "services" provided by nature and by human industry are both considered forms of capital and thus exchangeable on the market. As long as capital overall is growing, all is well. By this logic, it made sense when one mathematician argued in 1973: "kill every blue whale left in the oceans as fast as possible and reinvest the profits in growth industries rather than wait for the species to recover to the point where it could sustain an annual catch" (as described in Beder 2011, p. 142). Back in the early 1970s, the calculation of greater overall wealth by killing whales may have worked mathematically with the information available at the time. But, more recently, Earth System science has shown that whales have a much wider value than their blubber, playing a triple role in carbon sequestration: their feces provide nutrients to phytoplankton that absorb carbon and produce oxygen; their movements churn nutrients in the sea, helping feed organisms below the surface; and their enormous bodies themselves store carbon. When whales die, about 2 metric tonnes in the average 40-tonne carcass fall to the ocean floor (Subramanian 2017). In other words, the natural capital of whales is now recognized as considerably more valuable than was realized in the 1970s. Had the dictates of environmental economics been followed earlier, we would have squandered a valuable asset and now been poorer even in market terms. In short, even were we to accept growth in GDP as our paramount value, we do not yet know enough to treat natural and human products and services as equivalent forms of capital.

Finally, the real bottom line is that the market cannot evaluate goods and services for which there is no substitute and therefore no exchange value. We can't decide to swap breathable oxygen for something else and expect to live. We cannot do without fresh water, no matter how much cash we have in the bank. The list also includes "the climate-regulating functions of ocean phyto-plankton, the watershed protection functions of tropical forests, the pollution-cleaning and nutrient-trap functions of wetlands," and much else (Beder 2011, p. 143). Since such environmental assets have no substitutes and therefore no exchange value, there can be no market for them. If there can be no market for these natural benefits, then the foundational premise of environmental economics crumbles. Tweaking neoclassical economics and including nature in market calculations is inadequate to meeting the challenge of the Anthropocene. The Millennium Ecosystem Assessment report acknowledges that our current systems are not up to the task: "Reversing the degradation of ecosystems while meeting increasing demands for services can be partially met under some scenarios" but "will involve significant changes in policies, institutions and practices that are not currently under way" (2005b). Even partial success, in other words, requires radical changes to business-as-usual.

There can be little doubt that environmental economics is an improvement over the neoclassical view espoused by Jean-Baptiste Say and Robert Solow, which claims that natural resources, being infinite, have no value and therefore lie outside the purview of economists. Giving market value to natural resources and sinks, however speculatively, at least makes them visible to economists, and economists working in this vein have produced useful proposals on aspects of the Anthropocene, particularly climate change. These proposals include a revenue-neutral carbon tax, cap-and-trade, or some mix of the two that might ultimately reduce CO_2 emissions if full and complete assessments were made. For his work along these lines, environmental economist William Nordhaus (1941–) won the Nobel Prize in Economics in 2018. As of July 2018, when China expanded its carbon pricing system to include the whole country, fully a quarter of the world's carbon emissions were priced at some level. Overall, 40 countries participate in such schemes. But, as we know, climate change is only one facet of Earth System transformation. Environmental economists tend to be less interested in other aspects, such as land-use change, biome collapse, population growth, water scarcity, and nitrogen overload, presumably because these problems cannot be framed as "solvable" by the market or by new technologies. Most crucially, environmental economists fail to acknowledge planetary limits to growth. Using market forces to redirect our impact on the environment, their proposals tweak the system without changing it. As such, these proposals may be modest ways forward in the interim before we really tackle systemic change – but "the interim" is getting shorter with each passing year. Since 2000, the Millennium Ecosystem Assessment's call for "significant changes in policies, institutions and practices" has gone largely unheeded.

Ecological Economics: Subordinating the Market to Nature and Politics

The third group in our taxonomy of economic approaches comprises the ecological economists, who subordinate the market to ecological limits and who posit that decisions regarding the use and distribution of resources are ultimately political rather than technical. For decades, they have called for systemic transformation to align politics and economics with environmental constraints, and they are now addressing the Anthropocene directly. Recent work includes *Ecological economics for the Anthropocene* (2015), edited by Canadians Peter G. Brown and Peter Timmerman, and *Economics in the Anthropocene age* (2017) by Peruvian economist Adolfo Figueroa. Ecological economists argue that environmental economists don't go nearly far enough in addressing the complexity of the Anthropocene. Norgaard encapsulates this view: "We are in a global ecological-economic crisis that threatens human well-being through climate change, ecosystem degradation, and species loss driven by our economic choices.

Marginal adjustments in the economy will not suffice" (2010, p. 1223). New political and economic systems are essential.

Imagining these necessary new systems is difficult. Our growth-intensive economic and political systems have transformed not only the environment, but the way we think. "Markets," observes Stephen Marglin, "shape our values, beliefs, and ways of understanding in line with what makes for success in the market" (2013, p. 153). Costanza et al. (2007) point out that "our values, knowledge, and social organization have coevolved around fossil hydrocarbons." This energy system, they continue, "has selected for individualist, materialist values; favored the development of reductionist understanding at the expense of systemic understanding; and preferred a bureaucratic, centralized form of control that works better for steady-state industrial management than for the varied, surprising dynamics of ecosystem management." These words resonate with ideas discussed in earlier chapters.

Thinking "outside the box" in these conditions requires verve. The Anthropocene's dark light recasts many modern values, ways of thought, and social organizations as the culprits – forces that are destroying community resilience and the environment, instead of being the tools of progress we once took them for. The first step toward renewed hope for Marglin, Costanza, and other ecological economists is turning business-as-usual on its head. They begin with the proposition that the economy is subordinate to the biogeophysical systems of the planet, not independent of these systems or their controller. As such, economic activities must be alert to the physical constraints of the planet and to potential tipping points, especially as the Earth System evolves into the no-analogue state of the Anthropocene. Difficult political choices will need to be made at all levels, from the global to the local.

Ecological Economics as a Multidisciplinary Endeavor

The field of ecological economics arose from serendipitous contacts between Sweden and the American state of Florida. In 1970, ecologist AnnMari Jansson (1934–2007), a specialist in the energy flows of the Baltic Sea's green algae ecosystem, and her marine biologist husband Bengt-Owe Jansson (1931–2007) invited American systems ecologist Howard T. Odum (1924–2002) to Stockholm University. In turn, Odum invited the Janssons to the University of Florida the following year. This collaboration eventually included growing ranks of graduate students, including Costanza. This collective endeavor pioneered the incorporation of human systems, especially the economy, within ecosystems. In 1982, the Janssons and their collaborators hosted the Wallenberg Symposium held at Saltsjöbaden, and invited economist Herman Daly. Their theme, "Integrating ecology and economics," might have resulted in mutual bafflement given the different training and approaches of these disciplines, but friendship helped create common ground. In 1987, a similar symposium was hosted in Barcelona, Spain, by economist Joan Martinez-Alier (1939–). The field of ecological economics was then formalized through the International Society for Ecological Economics (ISEE) and its journal *Ecological Economics*, launched in February 1989. By the 1990s, there were organizations dedicated to ecological economics in Europe, the Americas, and the Antipodes.

The Proposals of Ecological Economics

So what do ecological economists propose? As a pluralistic multidisciplinary field drawing on both physical sciences and social sciences, ecological economists don't all speak the same language. While neoclassical and environmental economists tend to have clear ideas about who belongs in their ranks, which university departments are best, what forms of analysis are credible, and how the levers of government serve their purposes, ecological economics is a comparatively loose grouping of individuals in a variety of departments and public positions. Notably, its practitioners include substantially more women than do the fields of neoclassical or environmental economics.

This intellectual and institutional flexibility and gender diversity has produced a host of ideas. Proposals from the first generation of ecological economists include Daly's (1973, 1977) "steady-state economics," Schumacher's (1973) "small is beautiful" approach, and Gorz's (1980) "ecology as politics." Other important ideas include Vandana Shiva's (2008) "soil not oil" and Masanobu Fukuoka's (1978) "one-straw revolution" to create non-fossil-fuel-based agriculture; Juliet Schor's (2010) "true wealth," arguing for a "time-rich, ecologically light, small-scale, high-satisfaction" economy; Tim Jackson's (2009) "prosperity without growth"; the degrowth paradigms of Martinez-Alier (2002) and Serge Latouche (2012); O'Neill's (Dietz and O'Neill 2013) "enough is enough"; Kozo Yamamura's (2018) "too much stuff"; and Kate Raworth's (2017) "Green Doughnut" model, in which the lower boundaries of social welfare are inserted within the model of planetary boundaries for safe, sustainable societies.

Market mechanisms and metricized measurement are often the target of ecological economists. Marglin (2010) argues that thriving communities protect both human and ecosystem health but are currently being undermined by market relations. He further suggests that richer nations may need to lower standards of living to allow poorer countries to have enough. Schor likewise emphasizes the centrality of thriving, egalitarian human communities to maintaining functional ecologies. She pits "plenitude" against GDP's narrow focus on market exchanges (2010; see also Schor 1998). To replace GDP as the standard metric, new ways of measuring prosperity have been proposed, such as the Index of Sustainable Economic Welfare (ISEW), the Genuine Progress Index (GPI), the Human Development Index (HDI), and the Happy Planet Index (HPI). Names for the desired new economy include "just sustainabilities" (Agyeman 2013), as well as "green economy, ecological economy, sustainable economy, stationary state, dynamic equilibrium, eco-economy, biophysical economy" (Dietz and O'Neill 2013, p. 45), among others.

Despite this variety, ecological economics shares three common denominators. First, it posits that natural systems have limits. Distort a local ecosystem or the entire Earth System with too much of anything – nitrogen, carbon dioxide, pig excrement, or plastic Lego building blocks – and that system will be pushed into a different state. This tenet makes ecological economics compatible with the understanding put forward by Earth System science. Second, it replaces modernity's old goal of growth with the goal of wellbeing. Since the planet cannot support infinitely growing human demands for resources and sinks, and since studies have shown that, beyond a certain minimum, ever-rising rates of growth don't actually make people happier, the rational choice is to aim for healthy sustainable communities rather than "productivity" measured by GDP's market exchange. Third, the discoveries that wellbeing increases in societies that are more equal, and that more equal societies are less destructive of their natural environments, mean that equitable sharing, both within nations and among them, becomes the prime economic and political goal of most ecological economists (e.g. Wilkinson and Pickett 2009). Instead of relying on economic growth and the market to succor the poor, ecological economists argue for actively restructuring economic and political systems so that each person has a fair Earth share.

This concept of a "fair Earth share" means that proposals for the Global North and the Global South are different. On the one hand, the well-fed Global North needs to direct its attention to building thriving communities, eliminating pockets of internal poverty, and limiting consumption for those already replete. On the other hand, the vastly greater populations of the Global South need new kinds of development that will provide adequate food, shelter, and livelihoods without replicating the environmentally damaging development patterns of the Global North. Roughly speaking, then, these three tenets – ecological limits, the goal of wellbeing, and greater equity – define the approach of ecological economics as it seeks to establish new economic and political systems.

Equality and Environmental Protection

The evidence linking social stability, relative equality, and ecological sustainability has been growing over the last 40 years. In 1980, the "Brandt Report," nicknamed for former German Chancellor Willy Brandt (1913–92), who led the international committee responsible for this report, responded to three problems arising in the turbulent 1970s: economic instability after the collapse of the Bretton Woods system, when America withdrew from the gold standard in 1971; increasing global inequality despite international aid programs; and heightened environmental concern in the wake of the 1960s and 1970s pollution cases, *The limits to growth*, and Earth Day. The official name of the Brandt Report is *North–South: A programme for survival.* "North" was shorthand for wealthy nations, including the US, Canada, Europe, Japan and other developed Asian countries, as well as Australia and New Zealand. All members of what was then the G7 hailed from the Global North, as did four out of the five permanent members of the UN Security Council. (China was the lone non-North nation by the reckoning of the time.) "South" referred to all the other countries, home to three-quarters of the world's population and its greatest poverty. What made the Brandt Report notable was that it made political and economic stability, social equity, and ecological sustainability inseparable from one another.

One couldn't be had without the others, so the world suffered in all three ways. The cause of this misery, the report said, was the North's domination of "the international economic system, its rules and regulations, and its international institutions of trade, money and finance." In creating inequality, the North harmed not only the South but also itself, and this unequal system degraded natural resources everywhere. Environmental damage was mainly caused by "the growth of the industrial economies," but the expanding populations principally in the South were also to blame. Only through "international management of the atmosphere and other global commons" could irreversible ecological damage be avoided (cited in Share the World's Resources 2006). In short, the Brandt Report recommended bold political action to restructure the global economy for the sake of stability, equity, and the environment. To our cost, little came of this 1980 initiative. In subsequent governmental and non-governmental reports, its conjoined themes would emerge again and again.

Over the next four decades, more evidence emerged linking instability, inequality, and environmental degradation. In *The spirit level: Why greater equality makes societies stronger* (2009), medical researchers Richard Wilkinson and Kate Pickett show that greater inequality produces poorer health for rich and poor alike, more violence, higher infant mortality rates, increased illegal drug use, and lower educational outcomes, as well as higher demands for natural resources and sinks. In unequal societies, Wilkinson and Pickett argue, people are goaded to consume more because of status concerns. Being social creatures, we tend to want to have what our neighbors have. Consumer debt levels rise in sync with social disparities. Due to pressures to consume, more inequality also results in longer working hours (2009, p. 223). More consumption, more debt, more work, and more pollution all contribute to the Great Acceleration. Another reason that inequality produces greater environmental damage is that asymmetries in political power concentrate toxic waste and polluting industries in poorer neighborhoods, instead of regulating them for the benefit of all. This "out of sight, out of mind" approach shields the wealthy, at least temporarily, from the smelly, ugly by-products of industry. But pollutants eventually work their way into air and water cycles, which may be one reason why the rich in unequal affluent societies are less healthy than their counterparts in more equal affluent societies (Cushing et al. 2015).

Statistics produced by geographer Danny Dorling also indicate that greater equality benefits both society and the environment. More equitable affluent countries – such as South Korea, Japan, France, Italy, Norway, and Germany – tend to emit less CO_2, produce less garbage, consume less meat, drive less, and use less water (Dorling 2017a; see also 2017b). His claim is that while the correlations aren't perfect, they are striking. Even the rich in more equal affluent countries pollute less than the rich in unequal countries such as the US, Canada, and Britain. Inequality appears to reduce leisure time, health, happiness, landfill space, clean air and water, and other species. Dorling's work is a morality tale told with numbers.

As a result, even organizations dedicated to protecting nonhuman animals, such as the World Wild Fund for Nature (WWF, formerly the World Wildlife Fund), focus on human disparities. The WWF's 2000 *Living planet report* measured the "ecological footprint" of people in different societies, with a focus on the stark consequences for nonhuman beings. The summary of the report announced, "If every human alive today consumed natural resources and emitted carbon dioxide at the same rate as the average American, German or Frenchman we would need at least another two earths" (WWF 2000). Since 2000, inequality around the world has increased further. To try to capture the systemic pressures of human societies on the living world around them, the WWF's 2016 *Living planet report* embraced the concept of the Anthropocene and the findings of Earth System science as framing concepts, arguing for fair distribution of Earth's resources to reduce consumption and therefore reduce demands on natural resources (WWF 2016).

There are at least six different pathways, involving cross-scale interactions and feedback loops, that link inequality and the degradation of the biosphere (Hamann et al. 2018). Wilkinson and Pickett argue: "Given what inequality does to a society, and particularly how it heightens competitive consumption, it looks not only as if the two are complementary, but also that governments may be unable to make big enough cuts in carbon emissions without also reducing inequality" (2009, p. 215). In short, when it comes to resources use, dancing to the tempo of an egalitarian community is much less destructive than marching to the drumbeat of the unfettered market.

Adjusting for the Anthropocene: Proposals for the Global North

There are many proposals for weaning the "Global North," and more recently developed economies such as China and Brazil, off their addiction to growing demands for resources and sinks. One of them is simply to reduce working hours. The purpose is not to create more time to consume but to free up time for activities that strengthen communities and support ecological wellbeing, such as gardening, canning, composting, making, mending, participating in the arts, caring for others, playing outdoors, and sharing goods and services, while slowing down economic growth. Mandatory limits on work could help diffuse the drive toward longer hours for more pay to consume more stuff, a drive particularly strong in unequal affluent societies. Another proposal is a universal basic wage with a minimum subvention uplifting the poor and a cap on maximum income for top earners (usually a multiple of the bottom earners' wages in the company or society). The aim is greater equality and less pressure on natural resources as growth is ramped down.

Ending the current financial mechanism by which private banks create money through lending has been proposed as a means to stem the cycle of debt, inflation, and an ever-expanding money supply. If 100 percent reserves were required for loans, commercial banks could only lend as much money as had been saved by their depositors. A related proposal urges centralized control of the money supply by the national government. There are calls as well for downgrading the power of the World Trade Organization (WTO) and World Bank. The argument is that the blunt financial instruments of these organizations encourage environmentally destructive growth rather than sustainable local initiatives. Many have argued that we need "cap-auction-trade systems for basic resources." This phrase is shorthand for putting caps on the use of natural resources and auctioning off the right to use them to individuals and firms who can then trade these rights so that they go to the highest users. The idea is to protect renewable natural resources and severely limit the use of nonrenewable resources, while providing flexibility. All these proposals – and others – are aimed at redirecting our energies and resource use to activities that build more egalitarian communities that demand less of the Earth's bounty.

Carbon taxes can address the relationship among social stability, fairness, and environmental quality, though their primary purpose is to reduce GHG emissions. As a policy measure, it almost always means a tax on fossil fuels used in transportation and power plants, as opposed to a tax on other sources of GHG emissions, such as burning forests and peat land, producing concrete, melting tundra that releases methane, or disturbing soil for agriculture or building. Since the Kyoto Protocols, signed in 1997, many nations have implemented higher taxes on fossil fuels to limit their use. In most places, this tax has been effective, but its social impact is regressive, with the heaviest burden borne by those least able to pay. If you own a private jet, a few thousand dollars more in fuel costs will make negligible impact on your standard of living, but if you have to commute to a minimum-wage job in an inefficient old car, a few hundred dollars in taxes may be the last straw. The inequality embodied in these taxes can breed political resistance. In France in the winter of 2018, President Emmanuel Macron imposed a universal carbon tax while cutting taxes for businesses and the wealthy. This action led to national demonstrations, some of which were violent.

Not all carbon taxes, however, are structured to place a heavier burden on the less well-to-do. Revenue-neutral carbon taxes provide a means of dampening demand for fossil fuels, while sharing the burden more fairly. In 2008, British Columbia instituted a particularly effective revenue-neutral carbon tax that returned every dollar generated to British Columbians in the form of personal and business tax relief. A 2015 study estimated that the tax reduced emissions in the province by up to 15 percent, without adverse effects on the province's economy. In fact, "between 2007 and 2014, British Columbia's real GDP grew 12.4% more than the Canadian average," with equally strong job growth in clean-energy jobs (United Nations, Climate Change 2019). Simultaneously, in the United States, the Citizens' Climate Lobby (CCL) asked Congress to pass a bipartisan measure similar to British Columbia's plan. Their aim is to create a Carbon Fees Trust fund that will collect the tax and return it directly to households as a monthly dividend. They estimate that "about two-thirds of Americans will receive more in dividends than they will pay in higher prices" (Citizens' Climate Lobby 2019). The UN and the World Bank have supported revenue-neutral plans as models for others to follow. Helpful though some new carbon taxes may be, they address only one aspect of the Anthropocene, sometimes ignoring other aspects such as biodiversity collapse and land-use change as corn and palm oil trees replace forests.

More recently, as the problems of relentless growth mount, the idea of degrowth – or *la décroissance* – has emerged, particularly in France, to underscore the necessity that the Global North scale back its economic production and consumption. The goal is to increase human wellbeing and equality while ratcheting down the demands on materials and energy in developed countries (D'Alisa et al. 2014). Dan O'Neill distinguishes between steady-state economists, who are more comfortable using market mechanisms to stabilize resource use, and degrowth advocates, who tend to be skeptical of capitalist institutions and stress social outcomes. Nevertheless, he concludes that their concepts are compatible. In the Global North, where "resource use and waste emissions exceed ecosystem limits, ... a process of degrowth may be needed before a steady-state economy can be established" (2015, p. 1214).

Adjusting for the Anthropocene: Proposals for the Global South

The challenges of the "Global South" are another matter entirely. Individually, most people in these vast regions live modestly at best. As summarized by journalist Corinne Abrams, a 2015 Oxfam report titled *Extreme carbon inequality* found that "India's wealthiest 10% emit one-quarter the amount of carbon produced annually by the poorest 50% living in the U.S." (Abrams 2015). They also consume fewer carbon-producing goods and services, live in smaller houses, eat less meat, and may not own a car. India's poorest 50 percent – around 600 million people – have a carbon footprint almost the same size as Japan's richest 10 percent, about 12 million people. The reason India is the third-largest carbon emitter behind the US and China is not due to overconsumption by most individuals, but to inefficient use of resources, lagging technologies, the economic divide between rich and poor, and its enormous population. According to these statistics, systems matter more than individual choices.

As the 1980 Brandt Report indicated and more recent work demonstrates (Hickel 2018), the current global economic and political system does actively favor the Global North at the expense of the Global South. Some have traced this imbalance to imperialism, since most areas of the Global South were either directly controlled as colonies or heavily pressured by the Global North from at least the early nineteenth century. Through imperial domination, the Global North extracted resources and destroyed local structures of social and ecological welfare in the colonies (Austin 2017). For instance, it was only after British domination that famines in India became truly deadly (Davis 2001). In Ghana and some other parts of Africa, land-extensive methods used by indigenous peoples were more suited to the local environment than the land-intensive methods imported by European cocoa planters (Austin 1996). The same is true in the case of rubber in Southeast Asia. Local planters understood their particular biophysical conditions, and knew that rubber trees could withstand leaf blight if they were grown in complex ecosystems rather than planted in straight lines in the monocropped fields of the early twentieth century (Ross 2017). Although these places were far from being ecological utopias before the coming of the West, societies had developed values, economic practices, and social systems responsive to their particular local ecosystems. Historically, the connections between relatively egalitarian communities and ecological preservation are fairly clear, and, in many places, what broke these connections was the coming of the West.

The Global North continued to reshape life in the Global South even when formal colonialism ended. After World War II, medical advances lengthened lifespans and diminished infant mortality; technological advances improved sanitation, transportation, and communication. With the support of the American government, the Ford Foundation, and the Rockefeller Foundation, the so-called Green Revolution of the 1950s and 1960s was launched in Mexico, and then elsewhere. As Shiva describes, in South Asia, this program entailed vast quantities of taxpayer-subsidized NPK fertilizers (nitrogen–phosphorus–potassium), high-yielding cereal varietals, modern water-intensive irrigation systems, and mechanized cultivation techniques. The initial leap in crop yields looked promising, saving many lives and persuading farmers to change their methods and go into debt to buy fossil-fuel-based, artificially produced fertilizers, irrigation pumps, and other expensive equipment. Then the boomerang effect set in as these fertilizers degraded the soil's micronutrient and fungal structures, polluted water supplies, and harmed human health. The situation was further exacerbated in 1991 when the World Bank imposed a structural adjustment program in India that, combined with the WTO rules of 1995, dismantled "the public framework for food sovereignty and food security" and forced "the integration of India's food and agricultural systems with those of rich countries" (Shiva 2008, p. 95). The result was an agrarian crisis, skyrocketing prices, and desperate farmers.

The conundrum of the Green Revolution is the conundrum of growth meeting physical constraints. In Asia, for example, although cereal production doubled between 1970 and 1995, the ratio of crops produced to energy input decreased over time, while the population continued to rise. This result came as no surprise to the brilliant plant scientist behind the Green Revolution, Norman Borlaug (1914–2009). In his speech accepting the 1970 Nobel Peace Prize, he pointed out that his scientific breakthroughs in agriculture provided merely a temporary cushion against the growing human population. As he put it, "there can be no permanent progress in the battle against hunger until the agencies that fight for increased food production and those that fight for population control unite in a common effort" (Borlaug 1970).

The Anthropocene challenge for the Global South is to create pathways to wellbeing that do not replicate the Global North's damaging patterns of growth. These alternatives need to be sufficiently flexible to cope with rapidly changing environments and with rising demographic pressures – a difficult feat. In theory, the Global South can bypass older, dirtier technologies for newer, more energy-efficient ones: such leapfrogging would allow these communities to avoid becoming trapped in high-carbon paradigms. In practice, transfer and adoption of green technologies from developed to developing nations is hindered by intellectual property laws, technical know-how of the recipients, compatibility of the systems and institutions, trade barriers, and the high cost of imported technologies (Hasper 2009). In response to these obstacles, products have been developed specifically for the Global South, such as cheap, solar-powered laptops for areas with unreliable electricity, and low-cost, low-maintenance ceramic and "slow sand water filtration" systems. Some of these alternatives still add to the Anthropocene waste stream when they are discarded, but other alternative technologies rely on renewable materials and local manufacture to avoid transportation emissions. Moreover, these alternatives are designed to be repaired and recycled. While high-tech options get the most attention, low-tech options are often more effective when their total impact is taken into account, which means they often get overlooked because they fall outside the usual categories of economic analysis. Small repairs to leaking clay pipes to save water never feature in GDP statistics, while building desalinization plants to produce potable water makes a statistical splash.

Scientific knowledge combined with local, ecologically sensitive production and recycling can be particularly effective in farming. In India, which has the greatest number of organic farmers according to the International Federation of Organic Agriculture Movements (IFOAM), sophisticated agriculture that doesn't use fossil-fuel-based fertilizers and equipment has been shown to be as productive in terms of crop yields per acre as conventional agriculture, while sustaining insects (a key and growing concern) and protecting soil structure, clean water, and air (Shiva 2008). Africa, where the Green Revolution did not take hold to the same extent as in South Asia, is also improving agricultural efficiency while limiting environmental damage. Uganda now has the second-highest number of organic farmers, and their crops command premium prices.

Gender equity enters into the picture here, as elsewhere. Policy expert Moustapha Kamal Gueye of the International Labour Organization argues that, with greater access to land rights and capital, African "women could increase yields on their farms 20–30 percent. This could raise total agricultural input in developing countries by 2.5–4 percent which could, in turn, reduce the number of hungry people in the world by 12–17 percent" (Gueye 2016). Organic farming in these new forms is not the same as traditional farming since they rely not just on customary knowledge, but on scientific research and outreach from laboratories. These operations are knowledge- and labor-intensive, as opposed to capital- and fossil-fuel-intensive. While the Global North may now be mostly caught within a technosphere, some people in the Global South might be seen to move in and out of it – at times trapped in megaprojects of oil extraction in, for instance, Nigeria, and the garbage heaps of megacities – and at other times living on its margins or beyond.

Although the Global South leads the way in terms of numbers of organic farmers, the Global North also has practitioners. Japanese microbiologist and plant scientist Masanobu Fukuoka became a proponent of cultivating rice without tilling and without herbicides. His book *The one straw revolution*, published in Japanese in 1975 then translated into 25 other languages (including English in 1978), shows how he improved not only yields but also the soil and biodiversity of his fields. Other supporters and practitioners of organic farming agree that healthier soil containing complex microbial life produces more nutritious grains, fruits, nuts, and vegetables. In *Animal, vegetable, miracle* (2007), American novelist and farmer Barbara Kingsolver chronicles the year her family of four ate locally, sustained almost entirely by their own garden and those of neighboring organic farmers in southwest Virginia. She found that, even counting the off-farm purchases of organic animal feed and 300 pounds of bread flour unavailable near her mountain home, her "family's food footprint for the year was probably around one acre." By contrast, the average American family of four requires 4.8 acres, partly to grow corn for the corn syrup used in processed foods that helps to fuel the obesity crisis and related health risks. As Kingsolver points out, her family's low acreage is significant given the estimate that, by 2050, "the amount of U.S. farmland available per citizen will be only 0.6 acres" (2007, p. 343).

Currently, government policies support unsustainable agribusiness techniques that temporarily produce cheap, less nutritious food and harm small farmers and their communities. Could they evolve to support sustainable agriculture and strong communities? Surveying the globe's many challenges and proposals for remedy, Raworth suggests that, rather than obsessing about green growth, a steady-state economy, or degrowth, we should frame our goal as creating "economies that make us thrive" and are genuinely sustainable

(2017, p. 209). Unfortunately, the work of ecological economists has not gained much traction in the halls of power, and indeed some assessments suggest that ecological economics is moving toward the market-driven growth models and ecosystem services pricing adopted by environmental economists (Beder 2011).

Conclusion

Modernity, and the economic and political ideas at its core, are premised on a separation of humanity from nature. Political and economic thinkers presented our destinies as remote from the networked flows of materials and energy on our planetary home. Humanity could defy the laws of entropy and grow forever, even though the Earth System remained beholden to those laws. Belief in this separation between human destiny and planetary destiny is no longer tenable. The Anthropocene is the unintended consequence of the delusion that the human trajectory and the planetary trajectory had nothing to do with one another. What we know now is that we are part of the Earth System, and always will be.

Successful economic and political strategies in the Anthropocene will necessarily be diverse, different in different places, and at different scales ranging from international efforts to neighborhood actions. There is no single "fix" that will result in thriving human communities sufficiently resilient to the impacts of rapidly changing climates and biomes, accelerating and decelerating human population growth rates, new disease threats and toxic overloads, the movement of refugees, and the pressures on social cohesion. The economic predicament of the Global South necessitates more food, energy, and jobs for rapidly growing populations, while the Global North must wrestle with creating steady-state or degrowth economies for declining populations. Politically, the challenge is the approximate coordination of new measures at all levels of governance: international agreements to restrain more planetary overshoot and aid in the transformation of international norms, practices, and institutions; national reorientation of economies and social institutions to build resilience; and local community empowerment to cope with frontline challenges.

Our best hope lies in taking a diversity of approaches. But all these approaches must recognize that, on a finite planet, infinite growth is not possible; that social and natural systems are enmeshed; that human life can never be dematerialized, although we can develop ways to use resources and energy less intensively; and greater equity creates not only stronger, healthier, and more just societies, but ones with lighter demands for natural stocks and sinks. As we discuss these many options for reshaping human societies, the question of our values comes to the fore. Ultimately, the question raised by the Anthropocene is not about which technologies, policies, or institutions to adopt, but what sort of societies we wish to live in. The Earth System strongly delimits our choices, but it does not decide them.

8

The Existential Challenges of the Anthropocene

After a brush with death at the age of 36, Montaigne, the sixteenth-century French nobleman, left his public duties to contemplate the grand question of "how to live" (Bakewell 2011). This question presents itself now with even greater urgency because the Anthropocene introduces novel existential challenges on every level: physical and philosophical; political, economic, and cultural; individual and collective. Montaigne sought his answers by cultivating an intense awareness of "self" in relation to the world and to others. His effort earned him the epithet of "the first completely modern man" from Leonard Woolf. Today, the Anthropocene calls into question that modern strategy of self-creation, by presenting us with a new understanding of "the human" as a planetary force rupturing the Earth System. This approach frames "the human" as "the species" or "human activities" writ large, rather than the individual that became so central to modern thought. This understanding of the human lies outside Montaigne's capacious imaginings; few, even now, can grasp our species as a collective, Earth System-altering force (Chakrabarty 2009). While the death that Montaigne attuned himself to was personal, we confront the accelerating extinction of species, the collapse of ecosystems, and deep suffering of billions of human beings. Some of the earlier existential challenges and joys of being human at smaller scales remain, but now they exist in an uneasy relationship with our global predicament. Here, in this final chapter, we explore the Anthropocene's many existential challenges, beginning with the dangers to our physical wellbeing in the very near future.

A 2018 paper (Steffen et al. 2018) nicknamed "Hothouse Earth" paints a particularly clear – and deeply worrying – picture of the prospects before us. Anthropocene Working Group member Will Steffen and his colleagues point to evidence suggesting only two possible Anthropocene trajectories. In the next few years, the one we're on, "business-as-usual," may push the Earth System over "a planetary threshold that could lock in a continuing rapid pathway toward much hotter conditions – Hothouse Earth. This pathway would be propelled by strong, intrinsic, biogeophysical feedbacks difficult to influence by human actions, a pathway that could not be reversed, steered, or substantially slowed" (Steffen et al. 2018, p. 8252). These runaway, uncontrollable changes would delay a stable state; that distant state, once achieved, would have a significantly higher global average temperature than any interglacial in the past 1.2 million years, with enormous human consequences (Xu et al. 2020), compounded by sea level rises of tens of meters. Once the planetary threshold is crossed, even reducing human emissions would make little difference. This trajectory might even take Earth out of the late glacial–interglacial cycle of the Quaternary Period for millions of years. Another 2018 study shows that tipping points – or "regime shifts" as Juan Rocha of the Stockholm Resilience Centre calls them – are amplified by mutually reinforcing feedbacks and domino effects in 45 percent of all potential environmental collapses (Rocha et al. 2018). Biosphere degradation due to land-use change and human predation, and the buildup of toxins and waste products of all kinds, would intensify (Williams et al. 2016). This "unmitigated Anthropocene" would be characterized by conditions that *Homo sapiens*, and even the immediate ancestors of our species, have never confronted. Only the darkest literary, artistic, and religious imaginings can summon up the potential human suffering in such radically different and highly degraded conditions.

On the other hand, human societies might choose to cooperate in managing the planet, artificially stabilizing the Earth System with a rise of less than 2 °C and keeping it there. In order to deliberately redirect the planet's trajectory away from thresholds and redirect feedback loops, the authors argue "that a deep transformation based on a fundamental reorientation of human values, equity, behavior, institutions, economies, and technologies is required" (Steffen et al. 2018, p. 8252). Yet even this revolution in human affairs would deliver no nirvana. At best, a so-called "Stabilized Earth" pathway will still "involve considerable changes to the structure and functioning of the Earth System" (Steffen et al. 2018, p. 8258). The result will still be warming more intense than that of any of the interglacial intervals of the later Quaternary, with higher sea levels, a greatly diminished biosphere, and the need for constant political and administrative skill in resilience-building measures, both technological and social. Stabilized Earth conditions hold little allure, but they are a far sight better than the completely unknown and hostile world of Hothouse Earth.

Climate scientist Michael Mann sums up our challenge this way: "It's late in the game, but not too late." The damage we've created is permanent, but, so far, it's still limited. We still have the opportunity to avoid the worst, truly terrifying levels of disruption (Mann and Toles 2016, p. xii). This harsh but more livable Anthropocene is our best hope. According to Steffen and his colleagues, the choice then is between an unmitigated Anthropocene and a mitigated one, between Hothouse Earth and Stabilized Earth. As both chronostratigraphy and Earth System science indicate, "the Earth has entered the Anthropocene, and the mid-20th century is the most convincing start date" (Steffen et al. 2016, p. 337). We cannot go back; the least bad option is to cultivate a new understanding of ourselves in relation to the world.

Other reports underline the scale of the challenge, and the risks. In October 2018, the United Nations Intergovernmental Panel on Climate Change (IPCC) warned that carbon emissions needed to be cut 45 percent by 2030, and to zero by 2050, to avoid global average temperatures rising above the danger threshold of 1.5 °C (2.7 °F) (Davenport 2018; IPCC 2018). At the time, this gave the world only 12 years to alter its course and prevent catastrophes ranging from the effective disappearance of coral reefs to the displacement of tens of millions of people escaping rising seas, drought, and fire. As one news story observed, "Coral reefs cover a mere 0.1% of the world's ocean floor but they support about 25% of all marine species. They also provide nature with some of its most beautiful vistas. For good measure, coral reefs protect shorelines from storms, support the livelihoods of 500 million people and help generate almost £25bn of income" (McKie 2018). The report concludes with the accurate yet dismaying observation that there is "no documented historical precedent" for the required magnitude of institutional change in such a brief period (IPCC 2018, p. 17).

Also in October 2018, another UN organization, the UN Convention on Biological Diversity headed by Cristiana Paşca Palmer, pointed to the swift decline of other species and the danger to humans of biome collapse. The phrase "Sixth Great Extinction Event" indicates the potential loss of 75 percent of species diversity if humanity does not change its approach to the biosphere. We are not there yet, but extinction rates have significantly increased as a result of human activities. Extinction, though, is only part of the problem. The number of individuals within each surviving species is also dwindling due to continued destruction of their habitats. A 2017 World Wildlife Fund report, co-authored by 59 scientists from across the globe, revealed that "humanity has wiped out 60% of mammals, birds, fish and reptiles since 1970" (Carrington 2018b). Another 2017 study showed that nearly half of the 177 mammal species surveyed lost more than 80 percent of their distribution between 1900 and 2015 (Ceballos et al. 2017).

Losing biological diversity threatens our food supplies, as pollinators for current staples and potential future food sources vanish. Science reporter Damian Carrington points out, "Three-quarters of the world's food today comes from just 12 crops and five animal species and this leaves supplies very vulnerable to disease and pests that can sweep through large areas of monocultures, as happened in the Irish potato famine when a million people starved to death" (Carrington 2017). Alternative edible species may have already gone extinct, despite the efforts of seed banks to archive the world's botanical diversity. Moreover, swift climate changes are likely to cut crop yields just as human population growth peaks (Fowler 2017).

Sufficient calories are only part of the problem. Another worry is loss of nutrients from the soil and hence from the plants and animals we eat. According to the UN Food and Agriculture Organization (FAO), a third of the world's food supply is currently vitamin-deficient, due to agricultural systems that are based on producing cheap food on depleted soil through artificial fertilizers, rather than nutritious food through careful husbandry (Carrington 2018a). As agricultural production based on artificial fertilizers and other such methods is ramped up to provide calories, complex nutrients necessary for health are lost.

The last decade has already seen a rise in food scarcity. Even though the percentage of people living in dire poverty (defined as less than $1.90 per day) has decreased, the number of people going without adequate food has increased, according to a study conducted by five UN agencies. By 2018, it had increased to 821 million (1 in 9 people), the highest in a decade, due to climate change and the dramatic rise in the number of conflicts. The report emphasized that climate variability and extremes are undermining food production in some regions and forcing people to migrate (UN News 2018). Between 1981 and 2013, the headcount of those living on less than $7.40 per day rose from 3.2 billion to 4.2 billion, or 58 percent of the global population (Hickel 2018). To feed rising populations, we need to produce more – as much as 50 percent more – food, while making fewer demands on the ecosystem if there is to be any hope of avoiding widespread starvation (Pope 2019).

Due to less nourishing and insufficient food supplies, people will likely become less resistant to disease, at the same time as antibiotics are losing their potency. Rampant use of antibiotics in feedlots, and their uncontrolled human use elsewhere, have accelerated the emergence of resistant bacteria – sometimes called "superbugs" – against which modern medicine is largely defenseless. While the overuse of antibiotics undermines our capacity to resist disease, the misuse of hormones to speed growth in domestic livestock creates cancers and developmental disorders in the reproductive organs of humans and wild animals alike. From polar bears to snails, a variety of species are unable to breed easily due to the synthetic oestrogen that now courses through the global environment (Langston 2010). Another source of disease is the diminished wildlife populations. Even as we became a predominantly urban species in 2007, people have increased pressures on forest ecosystems, in part in search of bush meat. In these conditions, zoonotic diseases emerge, such as Ebola, HIV, and the coronaviruses SARS and COVID-19, moving from nonhumans to humans, and in some cases spreading around the world with lethal effect.

Along with rising food scarcity and vulnerability to disease, other UN studies demonstrate that water scarcity is already a major threat to human wellbeing and will only get worse as the population grows. A 2017 report from the World Health Organization (WHO) and the United Nations Children's Fund (UNICEF) showed that 2.1 billion people lack access to safe drinking water, and 4.5 billion people lack safely managed sanitation services. The same year, the United Nations Educational, Scientific and Cultural Organization (UNESCO) reported that 80 percent of wastewater flows back into the ecosystem without being treated or reused. It is little wonder, then, that 340,000 children under 5 die every year from diarrheal diseases. According to the FAO, agriculture accounts for 70 percent of global water withdrawal. Of the water used for industrial purposes, roughly 75 percent is for energy production, including fracking, as reported in 2014 by UNESCO. In other words, about 4 out of every 10 people currently suffer from water scarcity. Desperation for water easily becomes a source of political and even military conflict when only about a third of the world's transboundary rivers are currently governed by cooperative management frameworks. These statistics and forecasts are unlikely to improve as populations grow.

We face a crisis with no easy answers. In the next few decades, we need to support a growing human population *and* dramatically lessen demands on the planet's already overtaxed resources. Doing both at the same time is a daunting challenge. The world's human population continues to rapidly expand; by 2050, it's expected to grow from its current level of about 7.8 billion to 9.8 billion; even if global reproduction rates continue to drop as expected, the total population will reach 11.2 billion in 2100 (UN, Department of Economic and Social Affairs 2017). Our ecological demands already overrun the planet's capacity to renew its ecological assets. According to the Global Footprint Network, created in 1990 by ecological engineer Mathis Wackernagel and ecologist William Rees, "more than 80 percent of the world's population lives in countries that are running ecological deficits, using more resources than what their ecosystems can renew" (Global Footprint Network n.d.). For the year 2018, the scientists of the Global Footprint Network calculated that the global human population consumed 1.7 times the planet's natural resources, including plant-based food and fiber products, livestock and fish products, timber and other forest products, and space for urban infrastructure, along with the resources necessary to absorb and recycle waste, especially carbon emissions. Levels of consumption are very unequal, with some countries consuming considerably more than others (e.g. Alexander et al. 2016). Looking ahead, "under a business-as-usual path, human demand on the Earth's ecosystems is projected to exceed what nature can regenerate [each year] by about 75 percent by 2020" (Global Footprint Network n.d.). Energy needs, too, will rise in some areas of the globe. Today, an estimated 14 percent of the global population live without electricity; addressing that problem will require expanding energy output in places with growing populations, particularly in sub-Saharan Africa and southern Asia, even as other places need to be encouraged to curtail their demands (International Energy Agency 2017).

Increasing some forms of production while decreasing impact on the Earth System is challenging for two additional reasons. First, the environment is already less predictable than in the past. As the evolving Anthropocene produces unexpected challenges, planning ahead will become even more difficult. Flexibility and resilience will have to be built into all our systems, from infrastructure and agriculture to the social interactions of politics and economics, including the framework of law (Vidas 2015; Vidas et al. 2015). Second, inequality is rising rapidly, both within societies and globally. This situation means that the democratic energies necessary to deliberate acceptable choices may be hijacked by the wealthy, who have the tightest grip on power and influence and who can best protect themselves from the dangers of the emergent Anthropocene. Conversely, the impoverished often resist environmental policies they see as unfair, such as those demanding austerity before they have sufficiency.

More equal distribution of planetary bounty and greater equalization of risk is not just an ethical abstraction – it may be a necessity. As Wilkinson and Pickett show, "governments may be unable to make big enough cuts in carbon emissions without also reducing inequality" (see discussion in chapter 7; Wilkinson and Pickett 2009, p. 215 – a longer version of this passage appears above). Furthermore, research suggests that more egalitarian societies, in creating greater trust and transparency, are more likely to use resources wisely and effectively. Yet the ideological commitment to inequality remains strong. The planetary goals for a mitigated Anthropocene are fairly clear: building a green economy, which will also mean a smaller economy (especially in the Global North); encouraging a green politics, which will distribute resources and power more equitably; and lowering the human birth rate, which will allow for healthier lives within changing planetary boundaries. The question is whether we can get through the tight bottleneck of the next few years and stabilize the Earth System before dangerous thresholds are crossed, while meeting these economic, political, and population goals.

Different World, Different Hopes

"The biggest problem we face," writer Roy Scranton observes, "is a philosophical one: understanding that this civilization is *already dead*" (Scranton 2013; see also Scranton 2015, p. 23). By "this civilization," Scranton means the one he learned to die for in Iraq during his military service in the US Army from 2003 to 2004. "This civilization," in his sense, is the relentless, power-seeking, fossil-fuel-based, neoliberal behemoth apparently bent on a "forever war" (Filkins 2008). But "this civilization" also refers to the bright hopes of modernity, to the increased knowledge that has allowed many more of us to survive childhood and childbirth, to enjoy improved sanitation and diet, to wear better clothing, and to withstand famines and disease. And not only that. "Modernity" is shorthand for the spread of literacy and education, increased social mobility and opportunities for women, the wonders of science, greater access to the arts, the elevation of democratic ideals and self-determination, and the hope that everyone might enjoy these things. If "this civilization" referred only to horrors, we would want it dead. What makes it hard to accept that modernity was a "deluded fantasy," as Scranton calls it, is that it was – and still is – so alluring. To recognize the Anthropocene is to kill a dream; to understand our new world is to accept that the old one is dead. The challenge is to figure out what elements of the old dream might still be viable in the new world. Can we salvage hopes for wellbeing and self-determination in the new Earth System?

Anthropocene Morality and Individual Actions

Fortunately, realistic trajectories leading away from the siren narrative of ever-increasing power and infinite economic and population growth can, albeit with difficulty, be discerned. Most of us, the authors of this book included, want "to do something" that makes a real difference. We want to live lives of decency and compassion without appropriating an unfair share of Earth's resources. But, in the developed world, the advice given by school science textbooks and government resources is often misleading. According to a recent study (Wynes and Nicholas 2017), recommended actions include recycling bottles and paper, hang-drying laundry, upgrading light bulbs, driving fuel-efficient cars, and buying green energy. Yet these measures have low or medium impact on reducing carbon emissions. If the goal is to empower individuals in developed countries to make the most effective changes in their behavior, these recommendations fail. Indeed, assurances that "making a difference doesn't have to be difficult," as one textbook advocating reusable shopping bags asserts, can create the impression that the issue is trivial, asking of us only a modest effort (Wynes and Nicholas 2017, p. 074024).

The four most impactful choices that reduce individual carbon emissions, according to comprehensive research, are "having one fewer child, living car free, avoiding air travel, and eating a plant-based diet." The authors of this study, Seth Wynes and Kimberly Nicholas, calculate that "each of these actions was high-impact (reduces an individual's greenhouse gas emissions by at least 0.8 t carbon dioxide per year, about 5% of current annual emissions in the US or Australia) regardless of study parameters" (2017, p. 074024). Although the most effective action by far is choosing to have fewer children, this possibility was not mentioned in any Canadian high school science textbook they examined (Wynes and Nicholas 2017; see also Murtaugh and Schlax 2009).

From an Earth System perspective, the four individual actions recommended by Wynes and Nicholas would go beyond reducing individual GHG emissions to mitigate effects on other flows and materials. For instance, choosing smaller families could leave more space for other creatures, helping to check biodiversity loss and curb land-use change. Along the same lines, given that 40 percent of the planet's ice-free land is used for farms and animal grazing, moving to a largely plant-based diet, especially for those living in the 15 richest countries – where meat consumption per capita is 750 percent higher than in the poorest 24 nations – could leave more land for other species and stem the overuse of antibiotics in feedlots (Tilman and Clark 2014). If enough people were to decide to live car free, their actions would not only reduce emissions but potentially reduce urban sprawl. In turn, this would free up land for the filtration of water; the maintenance of soil structure; the capturing of carbon in peat, soil, and forest; and other life-enabling processes. Living car free could also produce tighter, healthier, more egalitarian human communities that tend, as studies show, to be more careful about their environmental impact.

Similarly, fewer air passengers would lessen demand not only for aviation fuel but also for other resources and sinks. According to the International Air Transport Association, in 2017 cabin waste (much of it plastic) weighed in at 5.2 million tonnes; by 2030, this amount is expected to rise to 10 million tonnes. In other words, taken together, these four high-impact individual actions might be the foundation not just of a climate morality, but also of an Anthropocene morality. They are responsive to today's global-scale forcing mechanisms, which Anthony Barnosky and his colleagues sum up as: "human population growth with attendant resource consumption, habitat transformation and fragmentation, energy production and consumption, and climate change" (Barnosky et al. 2012, p. 53). But can individual choices, however important, create sufficient force to mitigate global forcings?

With this question of forcings and forces, we return to the issues raised in chapter 1 – how to grapple with the relationship between the physical sciences and human sciences, and how to move between the scales of geological and human time that overlap in the Anthropocene. Constructing a multidisciplinary approach to the Anthropocene, the effort at the heart of this volume, requires understanding the relationship between the enormous geophysical forcing of combined human activities and the many, various forces of particular human actions. As the study by Wynes and Nicholas suggests, the predominant way of looking at that relationship is to focus on the individual. Modernity has accustomed us to think of ourselves primarily as individual actors, and so we tend to seek morally defensible individual choices, hoping that in aggregate they will alter the planetary trajectory.

This approach linking the person directly to the planetary is what novelist and critic Amitav Ghosh points to as "the individual moral adventure" at the heart of modern literary, historical, and political thinking (2016, p. 77). Yet there is a huge gulf between, on the one hand, our daily decisions about families, food, and transportation and, on the other, the long evolution of human activities that suddenly converged in little more than a human lifetime to transform the planetary metabolism and produce the Anthropocene. Even if every person chose a cloth shopping bag, it would not make our political and economic systems accord with planetary constraints. It's not that individual choices don't matter. They do. But our over-reliance on them is an artifact of the very civilization that Scranton shows to be dead. Making the individual central has helped undermine the ecological foundation of our lives. It is unlikely, then, that individual choices alone can create viable, decent societies within the Anthropocene.

The very fact that individuals feel they bear responsibility to "save the planet" is not an accident. In the early 1970s, as environmental consciousness in the Global North rose and governments and communities began to respond, corporate and political interests deliberately reframed "the environment" as an arena of individual moral concern rather than a matter of political and social responsibility. In the United States, for instance, powerful corporations including Coca-Cola, PepsiCo, and the US Brewers Association found themselves tasked with reusing their bottles. Laws were passed encouraging customers to bring back empties for a nickel, or, in some places, a dime. The drink producers would then collect and refill these empties with more drink. Corporations rebelled. Not wishing to shoulder this burden, they began to promote antilitter campaigns aimed at making individuals and local governments responsible for recycling. No longer were Coke bottles washed and refilled by Coca-Cola Inc. Instead, the glass, much less efficiently, was trucked away at public expense to municipal recycling centers to be sorted by color, crushed, and melted for new uses. Effectively, municipal curbside recycling came to work as a corporate subsidy. This "green liberalism," as historian Ted Steinberg (2010) argues, protects corporate interests and capitalist markets while consumers and taxpayers pick up the tab for less effective environmental protections. Green liberalism promotes individual choice as the key to a sustainable system, but many consumers feel the futility of these gestures and become cynical or despairing. Something more is needed.

Wynes and Nicholas, even while promoting effective individual choices, recognize that "knowledgeable and willing individuals may not reduce meat intake or adopt other high impact actions if cultural norms or structural barriers act as obstacles" (2017, p. 6). Accordingly, they call for shifts in public attitudes and public policy. Social norms, sculpted by misleading textbooks as well as corporate and political imperatives, create a world where being seriously "green" requires antisocial postures. It is no wonder, then, that the Anthropocene provokes an existential crisis for many. In the developed world, true Anthropocene morality is nearly impossible. The few individualists who buck social norms and skirt laws in order to live lightly on the Earth provide a picaresque counterpoint to mainstream "green consumers." Living off the power grid in intentional communities, sustaining themselves through gathered foods and roadkill, building homes from scrap, and wearing only homespun clothing or animal skins accord closely with necessary environmental constraints. However, these choices are the target of law enforcement and mockery. Living in cob houses with DIY solar panels, creating art from debris in abandoned buildings, and planting a garden on property zoned for other uses may be planetarily appropriate, but such actions come up against "endless red tape, detrimental laws and ridicule" (Hren 2011, p. 181).

Carpenter and teacher Stephen Hren, after surveying alternative lifestyles in the United States, from Detroit's D-Town Farm founded in a food desert by an African-American community to neoprimitivist encampments in western North Carolina, argues in favor of these efforts: "We need to be as flexible and exploratory as possible, yet the momentum of the juggernaut of unquestioning conformity embedded in our laws and mores has created a rigidity that impedes us" (2011, p. 181). Even the less extreme measures recommended by Wynes and Nicholas, such as choosing vegetarianism, can raise hackles. Those who choose them risk seeming like awkward, inflexible ideologues. The conundrum of what to do and how to live in the Anthropocene makes decisions that once seemed easy, perplexing. In the essay "Raising a daughter in a doomed world," Scranton struggles with both joy and sorrow at the birth of his child into a "broken world" where "in all the most important ways, it's already too late" (2018, p. 327).

Technological "Fixes" in the Anthropocene

If well-informed individual choices are unlikely to counteract the planetary forcings of the Anthropocene, perhaps new technologies can. These proposals work at different scales, from geoengineering the entire planet to altering national power grids, and on down to more modest "green" technologies for homes and communities. While appealing, by and large, current efforts address climate change rather than the Anthropocene *per se*, sidestepping engagement with the Earth System in all its dimensions. They also often fail to account for the timescales involved: for instance, even were decarbonization technologies to be successful, it would still take millennia for the marine environment to recover (Mathesius et al. 2015). Another problem is the tendency to overlook the political import of techno-logical proposals. The critiques of green technology, particularly geoengineering, have been swift and often persuasive. But many, including environmental policy specialist Simon Nicholson, argue that, although there is no "techno-fix," new technologies can be "one small part of an effort to steer the world to a state of rightness and fitness in ecological and social terms" (2013, p. 331; see also Nicholson and Jinnah 2016). It is important to weigh each specific technology, both for ecological efficacy in the larger Earth System sense and for its political, economic, and social ramifications. A "fix" can produce new problems.

Geoengineering the planet is the most flamboyant idea. The term has sometimes been defined as "deliberate large-scale intervention in the Earth's climate system, in order to moderate global warming" (Royal Society 2009, p. ix). By 2006, Paul Crutzen had despaired of the political efforts attempting to stem greenhouse gas emissions, calling them "grossly unsuccessful" (cited in Lane et al. 2007). Other scientists and engineers, supported by institutions such as the IPCC, the Pentagon, NASA, universities, and the private sector, agree with Crutzen's judgment that the dangers of climate change are so severe and pressing that they may require geoengineering solutions, even though, like Crutzen, they are well aware of the risks. In *This changes everything*, Naomi Klein describes the UK Royal Society's March 2011 meeting at Chicheley Hall as a celebration of these geoengi-neering possibilities (2015, p. 277), but their report acknowledges that geoengineering is "bedevilled by much doubt and confusion. Some schemes are manifestly far-fetched; others are more credible, and are being investigated by reputable scientists; some are being promoted over-optimistically" (Royal Society 2009). The two basic classes of geoengineering methods are carbon dioxide removal (CDR) and solar radiation management (SRM). Carbon dioxide removal techniques would suck carbon dioxide from the atmosphere, either through novel mechanical arrays or by deliberately augmenting existing biological or chemical processes. Some of the mechanical techniques being developed involve capturing carbon as it is being released from smokestacks. Other techniques would "scrub" the air of its excessive carbon. In both cases, the carbon would have to be stored, though where and how are questions still to be answered. Atmospheric carbon dioxide might also be removed by techniques modeling themselves on naturally existing carbon recycling. These include large-scale tree planting, tilling methods that enable the soil to capture more carbon, fostering peat, and seeding oceans with iron dust to encourage the growth of carbon-dioxide-absorbing phytoplankton (Hamilton 2013).

The second class of geoengineering techniques, called solar radiation management, seeks to reflect a "small percentage of the sun's light and heat back into space" (Royal Society 2009, p. ix). SRM techniques include physicist Roger Angel's (2006) "cloud of many spacecraft," which trails a solar-reflecting transparent material to shade the planet; David Keith's proposal that we spray sulfate aerosols into the stratosphere (2019, see also Klein 2015); and Crutzen's (2006) proposal for stratospheric sulfur injections to reduce the amount of sunlight striking Earth's surface. For the lower atmosphere, engineers are working on methods to whiten the clouds to make them more reflective, perhaps with a fleet of wind-powered, ocean-going vessels spraying salt water into the air. At the ground level, suggestions include painting roofs white; genetically engineering plants for shinier, more reflective leaves; creating more ocean foam and reflective bubbles; and shielding polar ice and deserts with reflective materials.

As Nicholson notes, the problem is that, while solar radiation management options might turn down the heat, they would do nothing about the build-up of greenhouse gases and would have to be continued indefinitely, at the risk of sending temperatures soaring very quickly if stopped (2013, p. 332). Many of these efforts are still in early experimental phases, but already concerns have been raised about such things as unknown side effects on living species, altered rain patterns, reversibility should problems arise, and questions of international law. Skeptics also draw parallels between the overweening hubris that re-engineered the Earth System unintentionally in the first place and these deliberate attempts to continue to dominate it. Pro-geoengineering "earthmasters" (as Hamilton [2013] calls them) counter that there is a global emergency that threatens human welfare, and we need to respond accordingly. Most understand that talk of geoengineering is "unpleasant," as Cambridge Professor of Engineering Hugh Hunt puts it. He continues, "Nobody wants it, ...but it could very well turn out to be the least bad option we have going" (cited in Nicholson 2013, p. 324).

Other advocates of technological solutions see a deliberately hyper-engineered environment not as a last-ditch effort, but as a way to "solve" the problem of global warming so that they can get on with business-as-usual. Some are even gleeful at the prospect. One group, the ecomodernists of the Breakthrough Institute, celebrate the possibility of a "good, or even great, Anthropocene." Their "Ecomodernist manifesto" proposes that "urbanization, aquaculture, agricultural intensification, nuclear power, and desalination are all processes with a demonstrated potential to reduce human demands on the environment, allowing more room for non-human species" (Asafu-Adjaye et al. 2015). The primary obstacle to a good Anthropocene, in their view, is the environmental movement and its premise that resources are finite. Cofounders of the Institute, policy analysts Michael Shellenberger and Ted Nordhaus (the nephew of economist William Nordhaus), first attacked environmentalists in an essay that was released at a meeting of the Environmental Grantmakers Association in 2004, then reprinted in 2005 by *Grist* (and later updated with supplementary postings). In the essay, they state, "We believe that the environmental movement's foundational concepts, its method for framing legislative proposals, and *its very institutions* are outmoded. Today environmentalism is just another special interest" (Shellenberger and Nordhaus 2005). Technology, in their view, will allow us to live in a new world that is "postenvironmental, not environmental, and postmaterial, not material" (Nordhaus and Shellenberger 2007, p. 160). Breakthrough Institute members include entrepreneur Stewart Brand, author of *Whole Earth discipline* (2009); journalist Matt Ridley, author of several books including *The rational optimist: How prosperity evolves* (2010); and journalist Mark Lynas, author of *The god species: Saving the planet in the age of humans* (2011) – all of whom advocate for nuclear energy. Dutch journalist Marco Visscher also promotes their message that we can have it all (Visscher 2015a,b).

Others outside the Breakthrough Institute community share their beliefs (e.g. Kahn 2010). Such ideas are, not surprisingly, popular among some business leaders as well. For instance, businessman Richard Branson, chair of Virgin Atlantic and other companies, believes that technological innovation will circumvent planetary constraints. To support these efforts, Branson gave $25 million to kick off research on pulling carbon directly out of the air. "If we could come up with a geoengineering answer to this problem," Branson said, "we could carry on flying our planes and driving our cars" (cited in Nicholson 2013, p. 324). As with the environmental economists discussed in chapter 7, some businesspeople and policy-makers propose technological megaprojects such as large-scale carbon dioxide removal as a way to avoid tough political decisions about how to end our increasing resource use and energy output. In Scranton's terms, these advocates of business-as-usual fail the philosophical challenge of understanding that the old civilization is dead.

A third group embraces technological megaprojects as a way to lessen the social burdens as we transition from the globalized growth economy to a dynamic steady-state economy within ecological constraints. If that's the aim, the difficulty is financing. Private firms will not invest in new technologies if the expectation is little or minimal return on their investment as the economy slows and steadies; indeed, in some cases they *cannot* do this, under law, due to their responsibility to shareholders. For this reason and others, Dutch economist Servaas Storm argues that private firms can't be the force behind downsizing the global economy. "What must be understood," Storm says:

> is that the radical innovation needed to stop global warming is beyond the capacities of small and even large firms, because it is very costly, takes at least 20–25 years to fully develop, is an uncertain – nonproba-bilistic – process with "odds" of success or failure that cannot be objectively calculated in advance, and always features potential gains to society that cannot be appropriated by the innovator. (2017, p. 1314)

Along similar lines, Hamilton argues that there is a fundamental "mismatch between the short timescales of markets and the political systems tied to them, and the much longer timescales that the Earth System needs to accommodate human activity... . Put another way, the tempo of the market's metabolism is much faster than that of the Earth System, yet in the Anthropocene they no longer operate independently" (2015b, p. 35). According to both Storm and Hamilton, the market cannot do the job; we need alternative ways of promoting the emergence of a steady-state or degrowth economy, while minimizing human suffering.

One such alternative is large public works or public–private initiatives in green technology, where immediate returns from investment are less crucial. In the power sector, solar, wind, thermal, nuclear, biofuels, and hydrogen have all been proposed as attractive, government-supported alternative energy sources. With each alternative, the calculations as to costs and benefits are complex, both socially and environmentally. The "no free lunch" principle applies. One issue is how to measure the carbon emissions of any large-scale alternative energy source. This is easier said than done since emissions from the entire manufacturing, transport, maintenance, and decay cycle need to be calculated. Furthermore, large-scale green energy plants impact on the biosphere, and land use must also be accounted for, as discussed in chapter 7. Other issues involve social and economic costs. How does each form of energy build on established grids, or will it require new modes of delivery that could shift power relations within the society? Which communities will bear the brunt of new installations?

Immediate benefits must be weighed against long-term disadvantages, this being a particular problem with the radioactive waste from nuclear energy and emissions from nuclear meltdowns (Brown 2019). Some radioactive isotopes decay quickly but others linger for years, even thousands of years. (Plutonium-239, for instance, has a half-life of 24,000 years.) Fierce and still unresolved debates erupted in Japan concerning nuclear energy after the triple disaster of the earthquake, tsunami, and Fukushima nuclear plant meltdown in March, 2011 – a meltdown still ongoing as we write (Aldrich 2019). Finally, new sources of green energy should not be added to already existing fossil-fuel sources for a net increase in global energy use. Instead, the overall goal must be to increase energy availability in under-resourced communities while decreasing demand elsewhere (Chatterjee 2020). As we push through the bottleneck of rising human population and rapidly diminishing resources, choosing the right technologies presents a series of difficult trade-offs, especially when the projects are massive and expensive.

Smaller-scale technologies, such as passive solar home design, modern composting toilets, and innovative water-and-soil conservation techniques can be minimalist in their resource use and in the sinks they require. Often, they emerge locally, in response to the cultures and to the particular environmental challenges of a community. They are modern, as they rely upon advanced scientific knowledge, but their careful material usage, production methods, and waste recycling set them apart; by building these specifications into their designs, they minimize some of the attendant problems of large-scale techno-fixes. Earth-sheltered home construction, for instance, draws on principles evolved by our distant ancestors millennia ago. These small-scale innovations have the advantage of being amenable to democratic political control and easily reversible if the technology produces unforeseen problems or if tipping points in the environment produce abrupt changes in conditions that the community faces. Small-scale technologies also avoid the problem of the enormous "sunk costs" incurred with megaprojects, yet implementing and coordinating a patchwork of local initiatives is challenging, given the need for a cumulative transformation of the whole system. Again, there is no free lunch.

Better technologies, like better individual choices, are essential. But they are insufficient to change the system. Resource-minimizing techniques and mindful consumer efforts are not enough, say Steffen and his colleagues, without "new governance arrangements and transformed social values" (Steffen et al. 2016, p. 324). Political scientist David Orr also argues that "in the long emergency ahead, the challenges to be overcome are first and foremost political" (2013, p. 291; see also Orr 2016). Sociologist Juliet Schor observes that:

> solving our problems in the time we have available is not possible if all we do is change our technology. We will not arrest ecological decline or regain financial health without also introducing a different rhythm of work, consumption, and daily life, as well as alterations in a number of system-wide structures. We need an alternative economy not just an alternative energy system. (Schor 2010, p. 2)

These calls for systemic social, cultural, economic, and political transformation are becoming increasingly urgent. They ask us to direct our attention not to individual choices or technological salvation, but to the task of reorganizing the power structures and values of our societies.

Are New Human Systems Possible?

The aim is to create human societies dedicated to wellbeing within ecological limits on a rapidly changing planet. Is this a reasonable goal? Can we alter our current social, political, and economic systems in time to avoid an unmitigated Anthropocene, or will forcings and tipping points dictate the future? Can communities flourish in a state of dynamic equilibrium responsive to changing environmental constraints without collapsing into famine and violence?

Given contemporary polarization, mistrust of government, and antagonism at all levels, many have thrown in the towel and resigned themselves to doom or to watching, with bemused detachment, the collapse of humanity's final, unsustainable global civilization. Former activists such as Paul Kingsnorth (2017) have turned their backs on frontline environmental efforts. Some of our best writers explore apocalyptic scenarios, as in *The road* by novelist Cormac McCarthy. In an exhibition accompanied by a catalogue and film, photographer Edward Burtynsky and filmmakers Jennifer Baichwal and Nicholas de Pencier capture nightmarish landscapes where human destruction stretches to the horizon (Burtynsky et al. 2018a,b; Baichwal et al. 2019). Others argue that the only way to avoid self-destruction is to relinquish modern liberties and consign ourselves to eco-authoritarianism. In the famous 1968 essay "The tragedy of the commons," biologist Garrett Hardin famously called for "mutual coercion, mutually agreed upon" to avoid complete destruction of the environment. He forthrightly argued that "injustice is preferable to total ruin" (1968, p. 1247). Economist Robert Heilbroner followed up in 1974, arguing that populations accustomed to affluence would never willingly embrace the self-discipline and austerities of a steady-state economy. He wrote, "I not only predict but I prescribe a centralization of power as the only means by which our threatened and dangerous civilization will make way for its successor" (1974, p. 175). Many have followed this reasoning, urging much more powerful nation-states combined with international governance (e.g. Giddens 2009; Rothkopf 2012). Perhaps almost everyone who has thought about our prospects feels hopeless resignation from time to time or reaches for eco-authoritarian dictates as the last-ditch solution. Despair may be reasonable; it is certainly easy.

But another approach is possible. Willed optimists argue that creating good societies that enjoy eco-economic equilibrium with limited autonomy is neither impossible nor all that radical. A deeper grounding in history and anthropology undermines the idea that the conjuncture of human forces that created the Anthropocene was predestined, or that their unrestrained continuance is inevitable. Knowledge of human societies in all their wondrous inventiveness and quirky choices of rules and goals shows that there is not just one way to live, nor one notion of a good life. Certainly, things look bleak now, but optimists have evidence on their side too. Here, we consider three factors: the historically recent advent of "growth" as the defining social, economic, and political value; the many groups and sectors around the world currently living in something very like a steady state, which in some cases is not only sustainable locally, but could be scaled up; and the scientific and social knowledge already at our command about our predicament. These offer, in turn, three historical and sociological foundations for hopeful action: the scale of our collective rapaciousness is recent; not all of us live lives that put increasing pressure on natural resources; and much is already known about our physical circumstances and social resources. In short, there are three grounds on which to argue that modest wellbeing within environmental constraints need not be a pipe dream. A moderated Anthropocene rather than an unmitigated Anthropocene is a reasonable aim.

The Recent Advent of the Current Global System

The first hopeful factor is this: modern civilization is an anomaly in the long history of human beings. It follows that there is reason to believe that we can live without its particular splendors, squalor, and delusions. As Anthropocene historians, political scientists, sociologists, and ecological economists point out, the notion of endless growth is a recent one, becoming a goal of modernizing nations only in the nineteenth century, and even then often questioned. It has taken some time to spread this idea around the globe, and it continues to meet with resistance. Before fossil fuels enabled rapid global exchange, few doubted the constraints on human enterprise. Likewise, the view that the political system's primary purpose is to ensure economic growth is quite recent. The very concept of "the economy" as "the totality of the relations of production, distribution and consumption of goods and services within a given country or region" is an invention of the 1930s, as political scientist Timothy Mitchell has shown (1998, p. 82). Only after "the economy" was invented could it become the standard by which governments were judged.

Furthermore, it wasn't until the 1970s and 1980s, with the rise of finance capitalism, that the idea emerged that the economy could transcend the planet's biogeochemical limits and defy the laws of entropy forever. For the wealthy, this restless globalization obscures planetary limits. New resources, new markets, and new, distant garbage heaps seem always at hand, while any violence perpetrated in the service of this new financial system is rendered invisible, often through metrics that hide poverty and deprivation. For the less fortunate, the costs and constraints of growth remain apparent. In other words, the ideology and experience of cornucopianism and its centrality to economic and political life are historically and geographically bounded; it emerged strongly only as the Holocene gave way to the Anthropocene, and it has only ever been true for a small percentage of people. It is an anomaly, revealing nothing definitive about human nature or what drives most people. As with the extremely long-toed shoes called crakows in fifteenth-century Europe, very popular despite tripping up their wearers, belief in infinite growth has tripped us up. And like crakows, the aberration of our current economic system is inherently temporary.

Much more common in human history has been the understanding that production, trade, and consumption are necessarily responsive to energy and material flows and limitations. Anthropologists, historians, and sociologists have produced a wealth of examples of people who understand their communities as embedded physically, culturally, and spiritually within the limitations of a particular locale. For instance, the early modern commercial rope-making works in Germany's Black Forest were always at the mercy of the environment; their craft depended on sufficient grasses of the right pliability, enough water in mountain streams to power modest water wheels, the right metals out of which to fashion combing mechanisms, and a host of other factors. A spell of dry weather that withered grasses and diminished water flows, a sudden outbreak of illness weakening or felling laborers, the depletion of a seam of iron, and much else provided immediate feedbacks that limits had been reached. Without access to rope, other activities were stymied; people could not haul goods, handle horses, pull water buckets, or ring church bells. At local scales, production and social wellbeing were necessarily responsive to the environment's contraints.

Even as fossil-fueled growth began to take off in the nineteenth century, and the imperative to accumulate and reinvest began to spread, many argued that societies would – and should – tire of incessant work for unnecessary goods. Once people had acquired enough, it was reasoned, who would want grim labor rather than enjoyment, productivity gains rather than pleasure? Sociologist Max Weber (1864–1920) decried the "iron cage" of so-called "reason" arising from the legacy of the "Protestant work ethic" and propelling capitalism, with all its loneliness (Weber 1958 [1905]). He argued that it was hard to escape, but others have been more optimistic about a prison break from the treadmill of endless economic growth. An eventual steady state of wellbeing dedicated to the accumulation of friends, skills, and outdoor enjoyments, rather than the accumulation of wealth, was, they argued, only rational. In 1848, political economist John Stuart Mill (1806–73) famously articulated this future, arguing that:

> a stationary condition of capital and population implies no stationary state of human improvement. There would be as much scope as ever for all kinds of mental culture, and moral and social progress; as much room for improving the Art of Living, and much more likelihood of it being improved, when minds ceased to be engrossed by the art of getting on. (1965 [1848], p. 756)

Nor did the idea of substituting enriched leisure for ceaseless monetary gain die away in the twentieth century. In 1930, the founder of macroeconomics, John Maynard Keynes, wrote an essay called "Economic possibilities for our grandchildren," in which he envisions the world of 2030. By that time, he predicted, leisure, rather than work, would characterize national lifestyles (Keynes 1932). Keynes reasoned that most people would want more time rather than more stuff. A steady-state economy was championed outside the Western world. Most famously, Mahatma Gandhi urged India not to succumb to modernity's trajectory. Recognition that growth was a historical and sociological aberration, with a defined shelf life, emerged long before Crutzen uttered the word "Anthropocene." Today, some economists with no discernible interest in environmental questions argue that a stagnant economy is a sign of success (e.g. Vollrath 2020).

Current Steady States

The second reason for thinking that wellbeing without increasing demands on natural resources might be possible is that many places and people either have never experienced modern growth rates or have returned to something close to a steady state in terms of population, personal income, and the materials and energy flows consumed. Much of the Global South has never enjoyed fast-paced, expansive economic growth, partly because improved healthcare has permitted fast-paced population growth. Many people live pretty much at the same level as their ancestors, though the gap between the rich and the poor in their societies escalates, as it does globally.

These environments have also become degraded, and urban lifestyles continue to replace rural ways. Rebecca Solnit (2004, 2007, 2010), among other writers (e.g. Lapierre 1985), has investigated these communities. With deliberate, willed optimism, Solnit celebrates human resilience, and underscores what we might learn about lives not defined by material abundance.

In the Global North, the "Golden Age" of postwar high economic growth with increasing equality ended in the recession of 1973. The 36 member countries of the Organisation for Economic Co-operation and Development (OECD) "enjoyed real GDP growth averaging over 4% per year in the 1950s, and nearly 5% per year in the 1960s, compared with 3% in the 1970s and 2% in the 1980s" (Marglin and Schor 1990, p. 1). While there has since been some uptick in growth rates, the 2008 crash wiped out much of those gains. Currently, there are many pockets of little or no growth, and some places and classes are even experiencing degrowth. At the national level, "economic stagnation," a relative term defined as a long period of slow growth in relation to economists' expectations, characterizes many countries. By this definition, Japan, the third-largest economy in the world, has persisted in a state of economic stagnation since the economic bubble burst decades ago in 1989. Using 16 biophysical and social indicators to examine 180 countries over a 10-year period, economist Daniel W. O'Neill located several countries with stable stocks and flows (e.g. Japan, Poland, Romania, and the US) and four experiencing biophysical degrowth (Germany, Guyana, Moldova, and Zimbabwe). This research suggests that "biophysical stability and strong democracy" tend to go hand in hand, and that "continuous growth is not needed in order to maintain a high level of social performance" (2015, pp. 1227–8).

Not only countries, but also certain classes, are already experiencing a steady state – US wage earners among them. Although, according to the International Monetary Fund, "widening income inequality is the defining challenge of our time" and, "in advanced economies, the gap between the rich and poor is at its highest level in decades," those who are not rich are not experiencing increasingly high standards of living (Dabla-Norris et al. 2015). In the United States, the "real average wage (that is, the wage after accounting for inflation) has about the same purchasing power it did 40 years ago," reports the Pew Research Center (DeSilver 2018). Degrowth is also apparent in several sectors of the Global North. Younger generations are less wealthy than their parents in most developed countries. In the United Kingdom, research in 2018 by the Trades Union Congress showed that average wages in London and some other places were worth a third less than before the 2008 economic crash.

Instead of visualizing economic growth in the form of the hockey stick or J-curve, where growth is stagnant for most of human history and then speeds up very rapidly, historians Iris Borowy and Matthias Schmelzer suggest that current "economies seem to be transitioning into a development more adequately described as an S-curve, in which rapid acceleration slows down and eventually comes to a halt" (2017, pp. 9–10). Borowy and Schmelzer argue that "on a global scale future growth rates will be nowhere near what they have been in the recent past," because those earlier growth rates were due to "exceptional and non-reproducible circumstances" (2017, p. 14). Only developing countries such as China have high growth rates, and even there they are falling. By the end of the century, America must brace for the loss of hundreds of billions of dollars and at least a 10 percent decline in GDP, according to US government reports, if there is no significant environmental mitigation nationally and globally. The 2018 National Climate Assessment predicts that thousands will die prematurely due to increasing wildfires, rising seas, toxins, and a host of other environmental factors (US Global Change Research Program 2018).

The global system, as we finish writing this book, is undergoing the profound shock of COVID-19, a pandemic whose origin was made more likely – and its speed of spread far more rapid – by the conditions of the Anthropocene. Amid the fear, loss of life, and dislocated economies, new and painfully won insights have emerged. Bruno Latour quickly noted that it showed that the "train of progress," formerly thought unstoppable, could be not only slowed, but actually brought to a screeching halt; in the aftermath, he said, a new kind of economy might be built, based on what we decide we really need – or the old one reinstated with its power structures reinforced. This was framed as not so much a choice as an invitation to engagement (Latour 2020).

In considering such possibilities, it is important to distinguish economies with flat or nearly flat growth rates from true steady-state economies attuned to ecological flows. Most economies nearing a steady state, such as those mentioned above, have unsustainable ecological footprints per capita. They demand more than their "Fair Earth Share," currently estimated at around 1.4 hectares productive land and 0.5 hectares fresh water per person per year (dividing the total area of productive land and fresh water by the number of people). According to O'Neill (2015), while no countries have stabilized their resource use within ecological limits, some places (e.g. Colombia and Cuba) come near to achieving a balance of wellbeing, stability, equitable democracy, *and* sustainability. He argues that achieving a steady-state economy, even if at unsustainable levels, is a step in the right direction toward degrowth. According to the 2003 UN Human Development Index, which combines life expectancy, education, and GDP per capita, Cuba actually succeeded in creating a society where people lived well without consuming more than their Fair Earth Share (Wilkinson and Pickett 2009, p. 217). According to another measure, which takes life expectancy, self-reported life satisfaction, and ecological footprint into account, Costa Rica tops the charts (Agyeman 2013, p. 14). What these studies suggest is that ecological and social sustainability are achievable, once the goal of capitalist growth for its own sake is discarded and replaced by the goals of social wellbeing and greater equity. Making this choice, like making the choice for growth, is a deliberate action. The transformed social values, behavioral changes, new governance arrangements, technological innovations, decarbonized economies, and enhancements of the biosphere called for by Earth System scientists will not emerge of their own accord (Steffen et al. 2018, p. 8252). They take political will. Economist Stephen Marglin argues: "It is not, as Keynes suggested, that we can rethink the premises of society once we have 'enough.' Rather, we shall have enough when we rethink the premises of modernity" (Marglin 2010, p. 222).

There is hope, too, that population growth rates, with concerted effort, can fall in beneficial ways, rather than through disease, famine, or war. For example, Botswana, unlike neighboring countries, has a healthcare program offering family planning services, education, and contraception. Government-supported outposts exist in even the smallest communities, giving women control over their fertility. A mere 50 years ago, Botswanan women had, on average, seven children, but "now they have fewer than three. It's one of the fastest falling fertility rates anywhere in the world" (Davis 2018). These efforts have improved maternal health, allowed women more liberty, and lowered rates of infant mortality. As the global population is poised to hit 8 billion in 2023, the Botswanan example demonstrates what thoughtful, fully funded, and noncoercive policies can achieve. These policies better the lives of women and children. By contrast, according to statistics from 2016, in Niger, the average number of births per woman is over seven; in Nigeria, it's over five (World Bank 2019). As this evidence shows, it is possible to live decent lives within ecological constraints. Whether speaking in terms of resource use or human numbers, degrowth is not just about *less*, but about *different* whether it be slower, less material-rich lives or giving women control over their fertility (D'Alisa et al. 2014).

Multidisciplinary Knowledge and Multiscalar Institutions

The final reason for thinking that human societies could make it through the bottleneck of the next few decades – coping with demands for more food, water, shelter, and energy while lowering impacts on planetary resources – is knowledge and our capacity for reinvention. There is, given our predicament, no "solution" to be found through altered individual choices or new technologies. Nor is it likely that an authoritarian government, however well disposed, would have either the flexibility or the necessary grasp of local conditions to respond to our unpredictable and multiscalar challenges. Besides, as political scientist David Orr (2016) argues, the track record of powerful authoritarian states in coping with long-term complex emergencies is not particularly encouraging. Large bureaucracies lack the nimbleness required to respond to changing conditions and tend to seek large-scale solutions in lieu of more appropriate responses. In short, there is no single "fix" at hand.

Instead, there is an epistemological shift. Both the planetary sciences and the human sciences are becoming more flexible and multidisciplinary. Both forms of knowledge are starting to recognize that the probabilistic world of the Holocene, in which Earth Systems and social systems seemed to function relatively predictably and separately from one another, is in the rearview mirror. We are moving rapidly away from a planet where we can assume that "nature varies in knowable ways around an invariable mean," while social development progresses linearly upward toward longer lifespans and greater material abundance for all (Norgaard 2013, p. 2). Indeed, in both the US and Britain, life expectancy is beginning to drop. Modernity's delusions and dreams no longer hold.

Just as we are now relinquishing the idea that nature and society are probabilistic, we are also relinquishing the idea that the best way to study phenomena is to treat each one separately from the others, moving from empirical details to abstract, encompassing concepts. As ecological economist Richard Norgaard observes, a modern bureaucracy is "a hierarchy of wastebaskets. At each level, managers simplify the information they have about the complexity of the system" before communicating to the next level. This pyramid of simplification, he argues, was based on "preconceived notions of nature's divisibility" (2013, p. 3). Our current understanding of the Earth System's networked complexities argues for a new form of social knowledge, equally complex and networked. This understanding is already emerging, as Anna Tsing's (2015) study of the networked, non-hierarchical world of matsutake mushrooms makes clear (see chapter 6). As neatly nested hierarchies of knowledge are replaced by networked, not-always-commensurate multiscalar perspectives, power is no longer concentrated at a central point at the top of the pyramid. The knowledge legible at the global level – the kind of statistics and understanding produced by the Anthropocene Working Group and the United Nations – is essential. Just as essential, and far less legible to states and international bodies, is local knowledge, which at times may be at odds with worldwide aggregates.

The relationship between these global and local forms of knowledge – and many intermediate forms – is complex; both need to be respected. Local communities are the frontline interface with our changing planet. As their particular ecosystems change, communities will be the first to know and the first to respond. Women walking 3 miles each way for water as Himalayan glaciers recede; British gardeners fostering tropical plants as the UK's climate changes; South Korean children raised indoors as air pollution endangers health; Louisiana petrochemical workers enduring unprecedented rates of cancer; Mexican indigenous leaders defending forest – all have particular and important knowledge of their environments. Their experience will not necessarily be applicable everywhere, and yet it is vital to the overall goal of understanding the Anthropocene and working to mitigate it.

And the knowledge at local levels is often starkly different from the knowledge at the global level. While those at the top of the pyramid of wealth and in command of international averages are not yet (or only rarely) touched by Anthropocene death, those possessed of local knowledge and in touch with local transformations are already suffering – not only from environmental change but from the forces driving it. We must remember the losses: the murders of activists defending their lands and forests from mining, pipelines, illegal logging, and dam building, as well as the murders of journalists reporting on these deaths; the dumping of chemicals and debris; and the devastation of wild animal populations. In the twenty-first century, more than 100 defenders, mostly indigenous activists, have been killed each year (Holmes 2016; Watts 2018). Their knowledge and experience are also the essence of the Anthropocene.

To support and act upon knowledge that is multidisciplinary and multiscalar, institutions will also need to be multiscalar, less hierarchical, and more flexible. Economist Elinor Ostrom, the first of only two women to have been awarded the economists' Nobel Memorial Prize, argues that "institutional diversity may be as important as biological diversity for our long-term survival" (1999, p. 278). Looking at small communities, such as farmers in Nepal, who are able to solve problems within ecological limits, she underscores the trust enabling their success. She observes that scaling up these equitable, trusting communities can be difficult, but it is not impossible. Even at the international level, non-coerced agreements can be achieved if trust among representatives has been created. A prime example is the 2016 Paris Agreement, which was reached at COP 21. Behind the scenes, Tony de Brum (1945–2017), among others, worked tirelessly to persuade around 100 countries to join the High Ambition Coalition, dedicating themselves to trying to limit Earth's warming to 1.5 °C (2.7 °F) above pre-industrial levels. As a Marshallese politician, de Brum could have adopted an accusatory stance against the nations responsible both for the nuclear tests he witnessed as a boy and for the greenhouse gases causing the oceans to rise and endanger his homeland. Instead, through force of personality and persuasion, he won over allies. The Paris Climate Accord that entered into force in 2016 was the result of this practice of building trust. As Brum's work and Ostrom's research show, Anthropocene ethics requires the building of new alliances across old wounds. Yet the frailty of such trust-building must be acknowledged. In the years since the Accord, few nations beyond Morocco and the Gambia have met their commitments, and the United States has begun withdrawal procedures (Erickson 2018).

Conclusion

The Anthropocene is real. The science confirming it has gained clarity. The social sciences and humanities have begun their work of understanding how human beings, in all our great variety, have arrived at this collective predicament. We also know what is required for a mitigated Anthropocene as opposed to an unmitigated one: a smaller, green economy; a green politics that distributes power and wealth more equitably; and a livable planet that hosts fewer human beings and greater biodiversity. Finally, we are also beginning to understand the philosophical challenge of the Anthropocene. The

Anthropocene has produced an existential crisis in proposing a new, and hitherto unknown, figure of "the human" as a planetary force. No consideration of what being human means can ignore this vision of the *anthropos* as the sum total of human impacts on the planet. Yet this singular figure does not erase the many other *anthropos* operating at multiple scales of time and place, contributing differently to the Anthropocene trajectory, and suffering its effects unequally. The new existential challenge is global, but many of our attempts to understand and cope with it will be local. The challenge is also political, but the type of politics needed is networked and non-hierarchical; it must be conscious that resilience will require buffers, redundancy, and a diversity of institutions. The only way to achieve such uncoerced coordination appears to be by building trust through dispersing power and embracing many forms of knowledge. As scholar of religion Lisa Sideris notes, no single discipline can define what it means to be human in the Age of the Human. Nor can anyone know just what will work, given the thresholds, tipping points, and positive feedback loops driving Earth's dangerous trans-formation (2016, p. 89). Yet the future no longer offers the unlimited array of possibilities promised by modernity. Instead, we face a very limited range of options: either we create radically different societies in keeping with our new planetary circumstances, or we continue with the status quo – to our peril.

Bibliography

Abrams, C. (2015). India's rich have a smaller carbon footprint than rich countries' poor. [Blog] *India Real Time, The Wall Street Journal*: https://blogs.wsj.com/indiarealtime/2015/12/03/indias-rich-have-a-smaller-carbon-footprint-than-rich-countries-poor.

Agyeman, J. (2013). *Introducing just sustainabilities: Policy, planning, and practice*. London: Zed Books.

Akpan, W. (2005). Putting oil first? Some ethnographic aspects of petroleum-related land use controversies in Nigeria. *African Sociological Review / Revue Africaine de Sociologie*, 9, pp. 134–52.

Aldrich, D. P. (2019). *Black wave: How networks and governance shaped Japan's 3/11 disasters*. University of Chicago Press.

Alexander, P., Brown, C., Arneth, A., Finnigan, J., and Rounsevell, M. D. (2016). Human appropriation of land for food: The role of diet. *Global Environmental Change*, 41, 88–98.

Alizadeh, A., Kouchoukos, N., Wilkinson, T., Bauer, A., and Mashkour, M. (2004). Human–environment interactions on the Upper Khuzestan Plains, Southwest Iran: Recent investigations. *Paléorient*, 30, pp. 69–88.

Angel, R. (2006). Feasibility of cooling the Earth with a cloud of small spacecraft near the inner Lagrange point (L1). *Proceedings of the National Academy of Sciences of the United States of America*, 103, pp. 17184–9.

Asafu-Adjaye, J., Blomquist, L., Brand, S., et al. (2015). An ecomodernist manifesto: www.ecomodernism.org.

Austin, G. (1996). Mode of production or mode of cultivation: Explaining the failure of European cocoa planters in competition with African farmers in colonial Ghana. In W. Clarence-Smith, ed., *Cocoa pioneer fronts: The role of smallholders, planters and merchants*. New York: St. Martin's Press, pp. 154–75.

Austin, G., ed. (2017) *Economic development and environmental history in the Anthropocene: Perspectives on Asia and Africa*. London: Bloomsbury Academic.

Autin, W. J. and Holbrook, J. M. (2012). Is the Anthropocene an issue of stratigraphy or pop culture? *GSA Today*, 22, pp. 60–1.

Babcock, L. E., Peng, S., Zhu, M., Xiao, S., and Ahlberg, P. (2014). Proposed reassessment of the Cambrian GSSP. *Journal of African Earth Sciences*, 98, pp. 3–10.

Bacon, K. L. and Swindles, G. T. (2016). Could a potential Anthropocene mass extinction define a new geological period? *The Anthropocene Review*, 3, pp. 208–17.

Baichwal, J., de Pencier, N., and Burtynsky, E. (2019). *Anthropocene: The human epoch, the documentary*: https://theanthropocene.org/film.

Bakewell, S. (2011). *How to live, or, A life of Montaigne in one question and twenty attempts at an answer*. New York: Other Press.

The Balance. US GDP by year compared to recessions and events: www.thebalance.com/us-gdp-by-year-3305543.

Bar-On, Y. M., Phillips, R., and Milo, R. (2018). The biomass distribution on Earth. *Proceedings of the National Academy of Sciences of the United States of America*, 115, pp. 6506–11.

Bardeen, C. G., Garcia, R. R., Toon, O. B., and Conley, A. J. (2017). On transient climate change at the Cretaceous–Paleogene boundary due to atmospheric soot injections. *Proceedings of the National Academy of Sciences of the United States of America*, 114, pp. E7415–24.

Barnosky, A. D. (2008). Megafauna biomass tradeoff as a driver of Quaternary and future extinctions. *Proceedings of the National Academy of Sciences of the United States of America*, 105, pp. 11543–8.

Barnosky, A. D. (2014). Palaeontological evidence for defining the Anthropocene. In C. N. Waters, J. Zalasiewicz, M. Williams, et al., eds., *A stratigraphical basis for the Anthropocene*. Special Publications, 395. London: Geological Society, pp. 149–65.

Barnosky, A. D. and Hadly, E. (2016). *Tipping point for planet Earth: How close are we to the edge?* London: Thomas Dunne Books.

Barnosky, A. D., Matzke, N., Tomiya, S., et al. (2011). Has the Earth's sixth mass extinction already arrived? *Nature*, 471, pp. 51–7.

Barnosky, A. D., Hadly, E. A., Bascompte, J., et al. (2012). Approaching a state shift in Earth's biosphere. *Nature*, 486, pp. 52–8.

Bartkowski, B. (2014). The world can, in effect, get along without natural resources. [Blog] *The Skeptical Economist*: https://zielonygrzyb.wordpress.com/2014/02/15/the-world-can-in-effect-get-along-without-natural-resources.

Baucom, I. (2020). *History 4° Celsius: Search for a method in the age of the Anthropocene*. Durham: Duke University Press.

Bauer, A. (2013). Impacts of mid- to late-Holocene land use on residual hill geomorphology: A remote sensing and archaeological evaluation of human-related soil erosion in central Karnataka, South India. *The Holocene*, 24, pp. 3–14.

Bauer, A. (2016). Questioning the Anthropocene and its silences:

Socioenvironmental history and the climate crisis. *Resilience: A Journal of the Environmental Humanities*, 3, pp. 403–26.

Bauer, A. and Ellis, E. (2018). The Anthropocene divide: Obscuring understanding of social-environmental change. *Current Anthropology*, 59, pp. 209–27.

Bax, N., Williamson, A., Aguero, M., Gonzalez, E., and Geeves, W. (2003). Marine invasive alien species: A threat to global biodiversity. *Marine Policy*, 27, 313–23.

Beder, S. (2011). Environmental economics and ecological economics: The contribution of interdisciplinarity to understanding, influence and effectiveness. *Environmental Conservation*, 38, pp. 140–50.

Bell, D. and Cheung, Y. eds. (2009). *Introduction to sustainable development*, vol. I. Oxford: EOLSS Publishers.

Bennett, C. E., Thomas, R., Williams, M., et al. (2018). The broiler chicken as a signal of a human reconfigured biosphere. *Royal Society Open Science*, 5, p. 180325: http://dx.doi.org/10.1098/rsos.180325.

Bennett, J. (2010). *Vibrant matter: A political ecology of things*. Durham: Duke University Press.

Berry, E. W. (1925). The term Psychozoic. *Science*, 44, p. 16.

Blanchon, P. and Shaw, J. 1995. Reef drowning during the last deglaciation: Evidence for catastrophic sea level rise and ice-sheet collapse. *Geology*, 23, pp. 4–8.

Blaxter, M. and Sunnucks, P. (2011). Velvet worms. *Current Biology*, 27, pp. R238–40.

Bonaiuti, M. (2014). *The great transition*. London: Routledge.

Borlaug, N. (1970). Norman Borlaug acceptance speech, on the occasion of the award of the Nobel Peace Prize in Oslo, December 10, 1970. The Nobel Prize: www.nobelprize.org/prizes/peace/1970/borlaug/acceptance-speech.

Borowy, I. and Schmelzer, M. (2017). Introduction: The end of economic growth in the long-term perspective. In I. Borowy and M. Schmelzer, eds., *History of the future of economic growth*. Abingdon, Oxon: Routledge, pp. 1–26.

Bostrom, N. (2002). Existential risks: Analyzing human extinction scenarios and related hazards. *Journal of Evolution and Technology*, 9: http://jetpress.org/volume9/risks.html.

Brand, S. (2009). *Whole Earth discipline: An ecopragmatist manifesto*. New York: Viking Penguin Books.

Breitburg, D., Levin, L. A., Oschlies, A., et al. (2018). Declining oxygen in the global ocean and coastal waters. *Science*, 359, p. 46.

Brocks, J. J., Jarrett, A. J. M., Sirantoine, E., et al. (2017). The rise of algae in Cryogenian oceans and the emergence of animals. *Nature*, 548, pp. 578–81.

Brown, K. (2019). *Manual for survival: A Chernobyl guide to the future*. New York: W. W. Norton & Company.

Brown, P. and Timmerman, P., eds. (2015). *Ecological economics for the anthropocene*. New York: Columbia University Press.

Buffon, G.-L. L. de (2018). *The epochs of nature*. Ed. and trans. J. Zalasiewicz, A.-S. Milon, and M. Zalasiewicz. University of Chicago Press.

Burney, D. A., James, H. F., Grady, F. V., et al. (2001). Fossil evidence for a diverse biota from Kaua'i and its transformation since human arrival. *Ecological Monographs*, 7, pp. 615–41.

Burtynsky, E., Baichwal, J., and de Pencier, N. (2018a) *Anthropocene*. Toronto: Art Gallery of Ontario and Goose Lane Editions.

Burtynsky, E., De Pencier, N. and Baichwal, J. (2018b). The Anthropocene project: https://theanthropocene.org.

Byanyima, W. (2015). Another world is possible, without the 1%. [Blog] *Oxfam International, Inequality and Essential Services Blog Channel*: https://blogs.oxfam.org/en/blogs/15-03-23-another-world-possible-without-1/index.html.

Cadena, M. (2015). *Earth beings: Ecologies of practice across Andean worlds*. Durham: Duke University Press.

Canfield, D. E., Glazer, A. N., and Falkowski, P. G. (2010). The evolution and future of Earth's nitrogen cycle. *Science*, 330, pp. 192–6.

Carey, J. (2016). Core concept: Are we in the "Anthropocene?" *Proceedings of the National Academy of Sciences of the United States of America*, 113, pp. 3908–9.

Carlyle, T. (1849). Occasional discourse on the Negro question. *Fraser's Magazine for Town and Country*, 40, pp. 670–9.

Carrington, D. (2017). Sixth mass extinction of wildlife also threatens global food supplies. *The Guardian*: www.theguardian.com/environment/2017/sep/26/sixth-mass-extinction-of-wildlife-also-threatens-global-food-supplies.

Carrington, D. (2018a). Global food system is broken, say world's science academies. *The Guardian*: www.theguardian.com/environment/2018/nov/28/global-food-system-is-broken-say-worlds-science-academies?CMP=Share_iOSApp_Other.

Carrington, D. (2018b). Humanity has wiped out 60% of animal populations since 1970, report finds. *The Guardian*: www.theguardian.com/environment/2018/oct/30/humanity-wiped-out-animals-since-1970-major-report-finds.

Casana, J. (2008). Mediterranean valleys revisited: Linking soil erosion, land use and climate variability in the Northern Levant. *Geomorphology*, 101, pp. 429–42.

Ceballos, G., Ehrlich, P. R., Barnosky, A. D., et al. (2015). Accelerated modern human-induced species losses: Entering the sixth mass extinction. *Scientific Advances*, 1, p. e1400253.

Ceballos, G., Ehrlich, P., and Dirzo, R. (2017). Biological annihilation via the ongoing sixth mass extinction signaled by vertebrate population losses and declines. *Proceedings of the National Academy of Sciences of the United States of America*, 114, pp. E6089–96.

Certini, G. and Scalenghe, R. (2011). Anthropogenic soils are the golden spikes for the Anthropocene. *The Holocene*, 21, pp. 1269–74.

Chakrabarty, D. (2009). The climate of history: Four theses. *Critical Inquiry*, 35, pp. 197–222.

Chakrabarty, D. (2017). The future of the human sciences in the age of humans: A note. *European Journal of Social Theory*, 20, pp. 39–43.

Chakrabarty, D. (2018). Planetary crises and the difficulty of being modern. *Millennium: Journal of International Studies*, 46, pp. 259–82.

Chatterjee, E. (2020). The Asian Anthropocene: Electricity and fossil fuel developmentalism. *Journal of Asian Studies*, 79(1), pp. 3–24.

Chen, Z.-Q. and Benton, M. J. (2012). The timing and pattern of biotic recovery following the end-Permian mass extinction. *Nature Geoscience*, 5, pp. 375–83.

Cho, R. (2012). Rare earth metals: Will we have enough? [Blog] *State of the Planet, Earth Institute, Columbia University*: https://blogs.ei.columbia.edu/2012/09/19/rare-earth-metals-will-we-have-enough.

Citizens' Climate Lobby (2019). The basics of carbon fee and dividend: https://citizensclimatelobby.org/basics-carbon-fee-dividend.

Clark, P. U., Shakun, J. D., Marcott, S. A., et al. (2016). Consequences of twenty-first-century policy for multi-millennial climate and sea-level change. *Nature Climate Change*, 6, pp. 360–9.

Coen, D. (2018). *Climate in motion: Science, empire, and the problem of scale*. University of Chicago Press.

Cohen, A. S., Coe, A. L., and Kemp, D. B. (2007). The late Paleocene – early Eocene and Toarcian (early Jurassic) carbon isotope excursions: A comparison of their time scales, associated environmental changes, causes and consequences. *Journal of the Geological Society*, 164, pp. 1093–1108.

Conolly, J., Manning, K., Colledge, S., Dobney, K., and Shennan, S. (2012). Species distribution modelling of ancient cattle from early Neolithic sites in SW Asia and Europe. *The Holocene*, 22, pp. 997–1010.

Coole, D. and Frost, S. (2010). *New materialisms: Ontology, agency, and politics*. Durham: Duke University Press.

Corlett, R. T. (2015). The Anthropocene concept in ecology and conservation. *Trends in Ecology and Evolution*, 30, pp. 36–41.

Costanza, R. and Daly, H. (1992). Natural capital and sustainable development. *Conservation Biology*, 6, pp. 37–46.

Costanza, R., d'Arge, R., de Groot, R., et al. (1997). The value of the world's ecosystem services and natural capital. *Nature*, 387, pp. 253–60.

Costanza, R., Norgaard, R., Daly, H., Goodland, R., and Cumberland, J., eds. (2007). *The encyclopedia of Earth*, ch. 2: An introduction to ecological economics: http://editors.eol.org/eoearth/wiki/An_Introduction_to_Ecological_Economics:_Chapter_2.

Creutzig, F., Baiocchi, G., Bierkandt, R., Pichler, P.-P., and Seto, K. C. (2014). Global typology of urban energy use and potentials for an urbanization mitigation wedge. *Proceedings of the National Academy of Sciences of the United States of America*, 112, pp. 6283–8.

Cronon, W. (1992). A place for stories: Nature, history, and narrative. *The Journal of American History*, 78, pp. 1347–76.

Crosby, A. (1972). *The Columbian exchange: Biological and cultural consequences of 1492.* Westport, Conn.: Greenwood Press.

Crosby, A. (1986). *Ecological imperialism: The biological expansion of Europe, 900–1900.* Cambridge University Press.

Crowe, A. A., Dossing, L., Beukes, N. J., et al. (2013). Atmospheric oxygenation three billion years ago. *Nature*, 501, pp. 535–8.

Cruikshank, J. (2005). *Do glaciers listen? Local knowledge, colonial encounters & social imagination.* Vancouver: UBC Press.

Crutzen, P. J. (2002). Geology of mankind. *Nature*, 415, p. 23.

Crutzen, P. J. (2006). Albedo enhancement by stratospheric sulfur injections: A contribution to resolve a policy dilemma? *Climatic Change*, 77, pp. 211–20.

Crutzen, P. J. and Stoermer, E. (2000). Anthropocene. *IGBP* [*International Geosphere–Biosphere Programme*] *Newsletter*, 41, pp. 17–18.

Cushing, L., Morello-Frosch, R., Wander, M., and Pastor, M. (2015). The haves, the have-nots, and the health of everyone: The relationship between social inequality and environmental quality. *Annual Review of Public Health*, 36, pp. 193–209.

Dabla-Norris, E., Kochhar, K., Suphaphiphat, N., Ricka, F., and Trounta, E. (2015). Causes and consequences of income inequality: A global perspective. *IMF Staff Discussion Notes* [online], SDN/15/13. Washington, DC: International Monetary Fund.

Daily, J. (2018). Ancient humans weathered the Toba Supervolcano just fine. *Smithsonian.com*: www.smithsonianmag.com/smart-news/ancient-humans-weathered-toba-supervolcano-just-fine-180968479.

D'Alisa, G., Demaria, F., and Kallis, G., eds. (2014). *Degrowth: A vocabulary for a new era.* New York: Routledge.

Daly, H., ed. (1973). *Toward a steady-state economy.* San Francisco: W. H. Freeman.

Daly, H. (1977). *Steady-state economics: The economics of biophysical equilibrium and moral growth.* San Francisco: W. H. Freeman.

Davenport, C. (2018). Major climate report describes a strong risk of crisis as early as 2040. *The New York Times*: http://nytimes.com/2018/10/07/climate/ipcc-climate-report-2040.html.

Davies, N. S. and Gibling, M. R. (2010). Cambrian to Devonian evolution of alluvial systems: The sedimentological impact of the earliest land plants. *Earth Science Reviews*, 98, pp. 171–200.

Davies, N. S. and Gibling, M. R. (2013). The sedimentary record of Carboniferous rivers: Continuing influence of land plant evolution on alluvial processes and Palaeozoic ecosystems. *Earth Science Reviews*, 120, pp. 40–79.

Davis, L. W. and Gertler, P. J. (2015). Contribution of air conditioning adoption to future energy use under global warming. *Proceedings of the*

National Academy of Sciences of the United States of America, 112, pp. 5962–7.

Davis, M. (2001). *Late Victorian holocausts*. London: Verso.

Davis, N. (2018). How to grapple with soaring world population? An answer from Botswana. *The Guardian*: www.theguardian.com/world/2018/ oct/10/how-to-grapple-with-soaring-world-population-an-answer-from-down-south.

de Vrieze, J. (2017). Bruno Latour, a veteran of the "science wars," has a new mission. *Science*: www.sciencemag.org/news/2017/10/ bruno-latour-veteran-science-wars-has-new-mission.

Descola, P. (2013). *Beyond nature and culture*. University of Chicago Press.

DeSilver, D. (2018). For most U.S. workers, real wages have barely budged in decades. [Blog] Fact Tank, Pew Research Center: www. pewresearch.org/fact-tank/2018/08/07/for-most-us-workers-real-wages-have-barely-budged-for-decades.

Dietz, R. and O'Neill, D. (2013). *Enough is enough: Building a sustainable economy in a world of finite resources*. London: Routledge.

Dorling, D. (2017a). Is inequality bad for the environment? *The Guardian*: www.theguardian.com/inequality/2017/jul/04/is-inequality-bad-for-the-environment.

Dorling, D. (2017b). *The equality effect*. Oxford: New Internationalist.

Dowsett, H., Robinson, M., Stoll, D., et al. (2013). The PRISM (Pliocene palaeoclimate) reconstruction: Time for a paradigm shift. *Philosophical Transactions of the Royal Society A: Mathematical, Physical and Engineering Sciences*, 371, p. 20120524.

Dutton, A. and Lambeck, K. 2012. Ice volume and sea level during the last interglacial. *Science*, 337, pp. 216–19.

Edgeworth, M. (2014). The relationship between archaeological stratigraphy and artificial ground and its significance to the Anthropocene. In C. N. Waters, J. Zalasiewicz, M. Williams, et al., eds., *A stratigraphical basis for the Anthropocene*. Special Publications, 395. London: Geological Society, pp. 91–108.

Edwards, M. (2016). Sea life (pelagic) systems. In T. P. Letcher, ed., *Climate change: Observed impacts on planet Earth* (2nd edn.). Amsterdam and Oxford: Elsevier, pp. 167–82.

Edwards, P. (2010). *A vast machine: Computer models, climate data, and the politics of global warming*. Cambridge, Mass.: MIT Press.

Ellis, E. C. (2015). Ecology in an anthropogenic biosphere. *Ecological Monographs*, 85, pp. 287–331.

Ellis, E. C. and Ramankutty, N. (2008). Putting people in the map: Anthropogenic biomes of the world. *Frontiers in Ecology and the Environment*, 6, pp. 439–47, DOI: 10.1890/070062.

Elsig, J., Schmitt, J., Leuenberger, D., et al. (2009). Stable isotope constraints on Holocene carbon cycle changes from an Antarctic ice core. *Nature*, 461, pp. 507–10.

EPICA Community Members (2006). One-to-one coupling of glacial climate variability in Greenland and Antarctica. *Nature*, 444, pp. 195–8.

Erickson, A. (2018) Few countries are meeting the Paris climate goals. Here are the ones that are. *The Washington Post*: www.washingtonpost.com/world/2018/10/11/few-countries-are-meeting-paris-climate-goals-here-are-ones-that-are.

Eriksen, T. (2016). *Overheating: An anthropology of accelerated change*. London: Pluto Press.

Eriksen, T. (2017). *What is anthropology?* (2nd edn.). London: Pluto Press.

Fagan, B. (2001). *The Little Ice Age: How climate made history 1300–1850*. New York: Basic Books, 272 pp.

Feldman, D. R., Collins, W. D., Gero, P. J., et al. (2015). Observational determination of surface radiative forcing by CO_2 from 2000 to 2010. *Nature*, 519, pp. 339–43.

Figueroa, A. (2017). *Economics of the Anthropocene age*. New York: Palgrave Macmillan.

Filippelli, G. M. (2002). The global phosphorus cycle: past, present, and future. *Elements*, 4, pp. 89–95.

Filkins, D. (2008). *The forever war*. New York: Knopf.

Finney, S. C. and Edwards, L. E. (2016). The "Anthropocene" epoch: Scientific decision or political statement? *GSA Today*, 26, pp. 4–10.

Fourcade, M., Ollion, E., and Algan, Y. (2015). The superiority of economists. *Journal of Economic Perspectives*, 29, pp. 89–114.

Fowler, C. (2017). *Seeds on ice: Svalbard and the Global Seed Vault*. Westport, Conn.: Prospecta.

Frank, A. (2018). www.liebertpub.com/doi/10.1089/ast.2017.1671.

Frank, A., Albert, M., and Kleidon, A. (2017). Earth as a hybrid planet: The Anthropocene in an evolutionary astrobiological context: https://arxiv.org/ftp/arxiv/papers/1708/1708.08121.pdf.

Frank, A., Carroll-Nellenback, J., Alberti, M., and Kleidon, A. (2018). The Anthropocene generalized: Evolution of exo-civilizations and their planetary feedback. *Astrobiology*, 18, pp. 503–18.

Fuentes, A. (2010). Naturalcultural encounters in Bali: Monkeys, temples, tourists, and ethnoprimatology. *Cultural Anthropology*, 25, pp. 600–24.

Fukuoka, M. (1978). *The one-straw revolution: An introduction to natural farming*. Emmaus, Pa.: Rodale Press.

Fuller, D., van Etten, J., Manning, K., et al. (2011). The contribution of rice agriculture and livestock pastoralism to prehistoric methane levels. *The Holocene*, 21, pp. 743–59.

Galloway, J. N., Leach, A. M., Bleeker, and Erisman, J. W. (2013). A chronology of human understanding of the nitrogen cycle. *Philosophical Transactions of the Royal Society of London. Series B, Biological Sciences*, 368(1621), 20130120. DOI: 10.1098/rstb.2013.0120.

Galuszka, A. and Wagreich, M. (2019). Metals. In J. Zalasiewicz, C. Waters,

M. Williams, and C. Summerhayes, eds., *The Anthropocene as a geological time unit*. Cambridge University Press, pp. 178–86.

Ganopolski, A., Winkelmann, R., and Schellnhuber, H. J. (2016). Critical insolation – CO_2 relation for diagnosing past and future glacial inception. *Nature*, 529, pp. 200–3.

Gervais, P. (1867–9). *Zoologie et paleontology générales: nouvelles recherches sur les animaux vertébrés et fossiles*. Paris.

Geyer, R., Jambeck, J. R., and Lavender Law, K. (2017). Production, use, and fate of all plastics ever made. *Science Advances*, 3, p. e1700782.

Ghosh, A. (2016). *The great derangement: Climate change and the unthinkable*. University of Chicago Press.

Gibbard, P. and Head, M. (2010). The newly-ratified definition of the Quaternary System/Period and redefinition of the Pleistocene Series/Epoch, and comparison of proposals advanced prior to formal ratification. *Episodes*, 33, pp. 152–8.

Gibbard, P. L. and Walker, M. J. C. (2014). The term "Anthropocene" in the context of formal geological classification. In C. N. Waters, J. A. Zalasiewicz, M. Williams, et al., eds., *A stratigraphical basis for the Anthropocene*. Special Publications, 395. London: Geological Society, pp. 29–37.

Giddens, A. (2009). *The politics of climate change*. Cambridge: Polity.

Glikson, A. (2013). Fire and human evolution: The deep-time blueprints of the Anthropocene. *Anthropocene*, 3, pp. 89–92.

Global Footprint Network (n.d.). *Ecological Footprint*: Global Footprint Network. www.footprintnetwork.org/our-work/ecological-footprint.

Gorz, A. (1980). *Ecology as politics*. Boston: South End Press.

Goulson, D. (2013). *A sting in the tale: My adventures with bumblebees*. New York: Picador.

Gowlett, J. (2016). The discovery of fire by humans: A long and convoluted process. *Philosophical Transactions of the Royal Society B: Biological Sciences*, 371, p. 20150164.

Grinevald, J. (2007). *La Biosphère de l'Anthropocène: climat et pétrole, la double menace. Repères transdisciplinaires (1824–2007)*. Geneva, Switzerland: Georg / Éditions Médecine & Hygiène.

Grinevald, J., McNeill, J., Oreskes, N., Steffen, W., Summerhayes, C., and Zalasiewicz, J. (2019). History of the Anthropocene concept. In J. Zalasiewicz, C. Waters, M. Williams, and C. Summerhayes, eds., *The Anthropocene as a geological time unit*. Cambridge University Press, pp. 4–11.

Griscom, B. W., Adams, J., Ellis, P. W., et al. (2017). Natural climate solutions. *Proceedings of the National Academy of Sciences*, 114(44), pp. 11645–50.

Gueye, M. (2016). Five facts you should know about green jobs in Africa. [Blog] Green Growth Knowledge Platform: www.greengrowthknowledge.org/blog/five-facts-you-should-know-about-green-jobs-africa.

Guha, R. (2000 [1989]). *The unquiet woods: Ecological change and peasant resistance in the Himalaya.* Berkeley: University of California Press.

Gutjahr, M., Ridgwell, A., Sexton, P. F., et al. (2017). Very large release of mostly volcanic carbon during the Paleocene–Eocene Thermal Maximum. *Nature,* 548, pp. 573–7.

Haff, P. K. (2012). Technology and human purpose: The problem of solids transport on the Earth's surface. *Earth System Dynamics,* 3, pp. 149–56.

Haff, P. K. (2014). Technology as a geological phenomenon: Implications for human wellbeing. In C. N. Waters, J. A. Zalasiewicz, M. Williams, et al., eds., *A stratigraphical basis for the Anthropocene.* Special Publications, 395. London: Geological Society, pp. 301–9.

Haff, P. K. (2019). The technosphere and its relation to the Anthropocene. In J. Zalasiewicz, C. Waters, M. Williams, and C. Summerhayes, eds., *The Anthropocene as a geological time unit.* Cambridge University Press, pp. 138–43.

Hamann, M., Berry, K., Chaigneau, T., et al. (2018). Inequality and the biosphere. *Annual Review of Environment and Resources,* 43, pp. 61–83.

Hamilton, C. (2013). *Earthmasters: The dawn of the age of climate engineering.* New Haven: Yale University Press.

Hamilton, C. (2015a). Getting the Anthropocene so wrong. *Anthropocene Review,* 2, pp. 102–7.

Hamilton, C. (2015b). Human destiny in the Anthropocene. In C. Hamilton, C. Bonneuil, and F. Gemenne, eds., *The Anthropocene and the global environmental crisis: Rethinking modernity in a new epoch.* New York: Routledge.

Hamilton, C. (2016). Anthropocene as rupture. *Anthropocene Review,* 3, pp. 93–106.

Hamilton, C. and Grinevald, J. (2015). Was the Anthropocene anticipated? *Anthropocene Review,* 2, pp. 59–72.

Hansen, P. H. (2013). *The summits of modern man: Mountaineering after the Enlightenment.* Cambridge, Mass.: Harvard University Press.

Haraway, D. (2003). *The companion species manifesto: Dogs, people, and significant otherness.* Chicago: Prickly Paradigm Press.

Hardin, G. (1968). The tragedy of the commons. *Science,* 162, pp. 1243–8.

Haslam, M., Clarkson, C., Petraglia, M., et al. (2010). The 74 ka Toba super-eruption and southern Indian hominins: archaeology, lithic technology and environments at Jwalapuram Locality 3. *Journal of Archaeological Science,* 37, pp. 3370–84.

Hasper, M. (2009). Green technology in developing countries: Creating accessibility through a global exchange forum. *Duke Law and Technology Review,* 7, pp. 1–14.

Haug, G. H., Ganopolski, A., Sigman, D. M., et al. (2005). North Pacific seasonality and the glaciation of North America 2.7 million years ago. *Nature,* 433, pp. 821–5.

Haughton, S. (1865) *Manual of Geology.* Dublin and London: Longman & Co.

Hawking, S. and Mlodinow, L. (2013). The (elusive) theory of everything. *Scientific American*, 22, pp. 90–3.

Hazen, R. M., Papineau, D., Bleeker, W., et al. (2008). Mineral evolution. *American Mineralogist*, 93, pp. 1639–1720.

Hazen, R. M., Grew, E. S., Origlieri, M. J., and Downs, R. T. (2017). On the mineralogy of the "Anthropocene Epoch." *American Mineralogist*, 102, pp. 595–611.

Hecht, G. (2018). Interscalar vehicles for an African Anthropocene: On waste, temporality, and violence. *Cultural Anthropology*, 33, pp. 109–41.

Heilbroner, R. (1974). *An inquiry into the human prospect*. New York: W. W. Norton.

Heise, U. (2016). *Imagining extinction: The cultural meanings of endangered species*. University of Chicago Press.

Heron, S. F., Maynard, J. A., van Hooidonk, R., and Eakin, C. M. (2016). Warming stress and bleaching trends of the world's coral reefs 1985–2012. *Scientific Reports*, 6, p. 38402.

Hickel, J. (2018). *The divide: Global inequality from conquest to free markets*. New York: W. W. Norton.

Higgs, K. (2014). *Collision course: Endless growth on a finite planet*. Cambridge, Mass.: MIT Press.

Himson, S., Kinsey, N. P., Aldridge, D. C., Williams, M., and Zalasiewicz, J. (2020). Invasive mollusk faunas of the River Thames exemplify potential biostratigraphic characterization of the Anthropocene. *Lethaia*, 53, pp. 267–79..

Hodgkiss, M. S. W., Crockford, P. W., Peng, Y., Wing, B. A., and Horner, T. J. (2019). A productivity collapse to end Earth's Great Oxidation. *Proceedings of the National Academy of Sciences of the United States of America*, 116, pp. 17207–12.

Hofreiter, M. and Stewart, J. (2009). Ecological change, range fluctuations and population dynamics during the Pleistocene. *Current Biology*, 19(14), pp. R584–94.

Holmes, O. (2016). Environmental activist murders set record as 2015 became deadliest year. *The Guardian*: www.theguardian.com/environment/2016/jun/20/environmental-activist-murders-global-witness-report.

Holtgrieve, G. W., Schindler, D. E., Hobbs, W. O., et al. (2011). A coherent signature of anthropogenic nitrogen deposition to remote watersheds of the northern hemisphere. *Science*, 334, pp. 1545–8.

Homann, M., Sansjofre, P., Van Zuilen, M., et al. 2018. Microbial life and biogeochemical cycling on land 3,220 million years ago. *Nature Geoscience*, 11, pp. 665–71.

Hren, S. (2011). *Tales from the sustainable Underground: A wild journey with people who care more about the planet than the law*. Gabriola Island, Canada: New Society Publishers, Limited.

Hughes, T. P., Anderson, K. D., and Connolly, S. R. (2018). Spatial and temporal patterns of mass bleaching of corals in the Anthropocene. *Science*, 359, pp. 80–3.

Hutton, J. (1899 [1795]). *Theory of the Earth with Proofs and Illustrations (in Four Parts)*, vols. I–II, Edinburgh, 1795; London: Geological Society, 1899.

Ingold, T. (2018). *Anthropology: Why it matters*. Cambridge: Polity.

International Energy Agency (2017). Energy Access Database: www.iea.org/ energyaccess/database.

IPCC (2013). Summary for policymakers. In [T. F. Stocker, D. Qin, G.-K. Plattner, et al., eds.,] *Climate change 2013: The physical science basis*. Contribution of Working Group I to the Fifth Assessment Report of the Intergovernmental Panel on Climate Change. Cambridge and New York: Cambridge University Press.

IPCC (2018). Summary for policymakers. In V. Masson-Delmotte, P. Zhai, H. Pörtner, et al., eds., *Global warming of 1.5 °C: An IPCC Special Report on the impacts of global warming of 1.5 °C above pre-industrial levels and related global greenhouse gas emission pathways, in the context of strengthening the global response to the threat of climate change, sustainable development, and efforts to eradicate poverty*. Geneva: World Meteorological Organization: www.ipcc.ch/site/assets/uploads/ sites/2/2018/07/SR15_SPM_version_stand_alone_LR.pdf.

Jackson, S. (2019). Humboldt for the Anthropocene. *Science*, 365, pp. 1074–6.

Jackson, T. (2009). *Prosperity without growth? The transition to a sustainable economy*. London: Sustainable Development Commission: https:// research-repository.st-andrews.ac.uk/bitstream/handle/10023/2163/ sdc-2009-pwg.pdf?seq.

Jagoutz, O., Macdonald, F. A., and Royden, L. (2016). Low-latitude arc-continent collision as a driver for global cooling. *Proceedings of the National Academy of Sciences of the United States of America*, 113, pp. 4935–40.

Jansson, A., Hammer, M., Folke, C., and Costanza, R., eds. (1994). *Investing in natural capital: The ecological economics approach to sustainability*. Washington, DC: Island Press.

Jenkyn, T. W. (1854a). Lessons in Geology XLVI. Chapter IV. On the effects of organic agents on the Earth's crust. *Popular Educator*, 4, pp. 139–41.

Jenkyn, T. W. (1854b). Lessons in Geology XLIX. Chapter V. On the classi- fication of rocks section IV. On the tertiaries. *Popular Educator*, 4, pp. 312–16.

Jensenius, A. (2012). Disciplinarities: intra, cross, multi, inter, trans. [Blog] Alexander Refsum Jensenius: www.arj.no/2012/03/12/disciplinarities-2.

Jordan, B. (2016). *Advancing ethnography in corporate environments: Challenges and emerging opportunities*. London: Routledge.

Kahn, M. E. (2010) *Climatopolis: How our cities will thrive in the hotter future*. New York: Basic Books.

Keith, D. (2019) Let's talk about geoengineering. Project Syndicate: www.project-syndicate.org/commentary/solar-geoengineering-global-climate-debate-by-david-keith-2019-03.

Kemp, D. B., Coe, A. L., Cohen, A. S., and Schwark, L. (2005). Astronomical pacing of methane release in the Early Jurassic Period. *Nature*, 437, pp. 396–9.

Kennedy, C. M., Oakleaf, J. R., Theobald, D. M., Baruch-Mordo, S., and Kiesecker, J. (2019). Managing the middle: A shift in conservation priorities based on the global human modification gradient. *Global Change Biology*, 25, pp. 811–26.

Kenner, D. (2015). *Inequality of overconsumption: The ecological footprint of the richest*. GSI Working Paper 2015/2. Cambridge: Global Sustainability Institute, Anglia Ruskin University.

Ketcham, C. (2017). The fallacy of endless economic growth. *Pacific Standard*: https://psmag.com/magazine/fallacy-of-endless-growth.

Keynes, J. M. (1932). Economic possibilities for our grandchildren. In *Essays in persuasion*. New York: Harcourt Brace, pp. 358–73.

Kingsnorth, P. (2017). *Confessions of a recovering environmentalist*. London: Faber & Faber.

Kingsolver, B. (2007). *Animal, vegetable, miracle: A year of food life*. New York: Harper Perennial.

Kirksey, S., and Helmreich, S. (2010). The emergence of multispecies ethnography. *Cultural Anthropology*, 25, pp. 545–76.

Klein, N. (2015). *This changes everything: Capitalism vs. the climate*. New York: Penguin.

Knoll, A. H., Walter, M. R., Narbonne, G. M., and Christie-Blick, M. (2006). The Ediacaran Period: A new addition to the geological time scale. *Lethaia*, 39, pp. 13–30.

Kohn, E. (2013). *How forests think: Toward an anthropology beyond the human*. Berkeley: University of California Press.

Konrad, H., Shepherd, A., Gilbert, L., et al. (2018). Net retreat of Antarctic glacier grounding lines. *Nature Geoscience*, 11, pp. 258–62.

Kopp, R., Kirschvink, J., Hilburn, I., and Nash, C. (2005). The Paleoproterozoic snowball Earth: A climate disaster triggered by the evolution of oxygenic photosynthesis. *Proceedings of the National Academy of Sciences of the United States of America*, 102, pp. 11131–6.

Kramnick, J. (2017). The interdisciplinary fallacy. *Representations*, 140, pp. 67–83.

Krugman, P. (2013). Gambling with civilization [review of *The climate casino: Risk, uncertainty, and economics in a warming world* by W. D. Nordhaus]. *The New York Review of Books*: www.nybooks.com/articles/2013/11/07/climate-change-gambling-civilization.

Kurt, D. (2019). Are you in the world's top 1 percent? [Blog] Investopedia: www.investopedia.com/articles/personal-finance/050615/are-you-top-one-percent-world.asp.

Lambeck, K., Rouby, H., Purcell, A., Sun, Y., and Sambridge, M. (2014). Sea level and global ice volumes from the Last Glacial Maximum to the Holocene. *Proceedings of the National Academy of Sciences of the United States of America*, 111, pp. 15296–303.

Lane, L., Caldeira, K., Chatfield, R., and Langhoff, S. (2007). Workshop report on managing solar radiation. [online] NASA/CP-2007-214558: https://ntrs.nasa.gov/archive/nasa/casi.ntrs.nasa.gov/20070031204.pdf.

Langston, N. (2010). *Toxic bodies: Hormone disruptors and the legacy of DES*. New Haven: Yale University Press.

Lapierre, D. (1985). *City of joy*. Garden City: Doubleday.

Latouche, S. (2012). *Farewell to growth*. Cambridge: Polity.

Latour, B. (1987). *Science in action: How to follow scientists and engineers through society*. Cambridge, Mass.: Harvard University Press.

Latour, B. (1993). *We have never been modern*. New York: Harvester Wheatsheaf.

Latour, B. (2000). *Pandora's hope: Essays on the reality of science studies*. Cambridge, Mass.: Harvard University Press.

Latour, B. (2017). Anthropology at the time of the Anthropocene: A personal view of what is to be studied. In M. Brightman and J. Lewis, eds., *The anthropology of sustainability: Beyond development and progress*. London: Palgrave Macmillan.

Latour, B. (2020). Imaginer les gestes-barrières contre le retour à la production d'avant-crise, https://aoc.media/opinion/2020/03/29/imaginer-les-gestes-barrieres-contre-le-retour-a-la-production-davant-crise.

Lenton, T. (2016). *Earth System science: A very short introduction*. Oxford University Press.

Lepczyk, C. A., Aronson, M. F. J., Evans, K. L., Goddard, M. A., Lerman, S. B., and Macivor, J. S. (2017). Biodiversity in the city: Fundamental questions for understanding the ecology of urban spaces for biodiversity conservation. *BioScience*, 67, pp. 799–807.

Letcher, T. M., ed. (2016). *Climate change: Observed impacts on planet Earth* (2nd edn.). Amsterdam and Oxford: Elsevier.

Levit, G. (2002). The biosphere and the noosphere theories of V. I. Vernadsky and P. Teilhard de Chardin: A methodological essay. *Archives Internationales d'histoire des sciences*, 50/2000: https://web.archive.org/web/20050517081543/http://www2.uni-jena.de/biologie/ehh/personal/glevit/Teilhard.pdf.

Lewis, S. L. and Maslin, M. A. (2015). Defining the Anthropocene. *Nature*, 519, pp. 171–80.

Lightman, A. (2013). *The accidental universe: The world you thought you knew*. New York: Vintage Books.

Lisiecki, L., and Raymo, M. E. (2005). A Pliocene–Pleistocene stack of 57 globally distributed benthic $\delta^{18}O$ records. *Paleoceanography*, 20, p. PA1003, DOI: 10.1029/2004PA001071.

Liu, H. (2016). The dark side of renewable energy. Earth Journalism Network: https://earthjournalism.net/stories/the-dark-sideof-renewable-energy.

Loss, S. R., Will, T., and Marra, P. P. (2013). The impact of free-ranging domestic cats on wildlife of the United States. *Nature Communications*, 4, p. 1396(2013).

Lubick, N. (2010). Giant eruption cut down to size. *Science*: www.sciencemag.org/news/2010/11/giant-eruption-cut-down-size.

Lynas, M. (2011) *The god species: Saving the planet in the age of humans*. New York: Fourth Estate.

Macleod, N. (2014). Historical inquiry as a distributed, nomothetic, evolutionary discipline. *The American Historical Review*, 119, pp. 1608–20.

Malm, A. (2016). *Fossil capital: The rise of steam power and the roots of global warming*. London: Verso Books.

Malm, A. and Hornborg, A. (2014). The geology of mankind? A critique of the Anthropocene narrative. *Anthropocene Review*, 1, pp. 62–9.

Mann, M. and Toles, T. (2016). *The madhouse effect: How climate change denial is threatening our planet*. New York: Columbia University Press.

Mann, M. E., Miller, S. K., Rahmstorf, S., et al. (2017). Record temperature streak bears anthropogenic fingerprint. *Geophysical Research Letters*, 44, DOI: 10.1002/2017GL074056.

Marglin, S. (2010). *The dismal science: How thinking like an economist undermines community*. Cambridge, Mass.: Harvard University Press.

Marglin, S. (2013). Premises for a new economy. *Development*, 56, pp. 149–54.

Marglin, S. (2017) A post-modern economics? Unpublished paper for the workshop "Rethinking Economic History in the Anthropocene," Boston College, March 23–25, 2017.

Marglin, S. and Schor, J. (1990). *The golden age of capitalism: Reinterpreting in postwar experience*. Oxford: Clarendon Press.

Margulis, L. and Sagan, D. (1986). *Microcosmos: Four billion years of microbial evolution*. Berkeley: University of California Press.

Marsh, G. P. (1864). *Man and Nature; Or, Physical Geography as Modified by Human Action*. New York: Charles Scribner (reprinted: ed. D. Lowenthal, Cambridge, Mass.: Belknap Press / Harvard University Press, 1965).

Marsh, G. P. (1874). *The Earth as Modified by Human Action: A New Edition of "Man and Nature."* New York: Charles Scribner; Armstrong & Co.

Martinez-Alier, J. (2002) *The environmentalism of the poor: A study of ecological conflicts and valuation*. Cheltenham and Northampton, Mass.: Edward Elgar Publishers.

Mathesius, S., Hofmann, M., Caldeira, K., and Schellnhuber, H. (2015). Long-term response of oceans to carbon dioxide removal from the atmosphere. *Nature Climate Change*, 5, pp. 1107–13.

McCarthy, C. (2006). *The road*. New York: Vintage International.

McGlade, C. and Ekins, P. (2015). The geographical distribution of fossil fuels unused when limiting global warming to 2 °C. *Nature*, 517, pp. 187–90.

McKibben, B. (2010). *Eaarth: Making a life on a tough new planet*. New York: Henry Holt & Company.

McKie, R. (2018). Portrait of a planet on the verge of climate catastrophe. *The Guardian*: www.theguardian.com/environment/2018/dec/02/world-verge-climate-catastophe.

McNeely, J. (2001). Invasive species: A costly catastrophe for native biodiversity. *Land Use and Water Resources Research*, 1, pp. 1–10.

McNeill, J. R. (2000). *Something new under the sun: An environmental history of the twentieth-century world*. New York: W. W. Norton & Co.

McNeill, J. R. and Engelke, P. (2016). *The great acceleration: An environmental history of the Anthropocene since 1945*. Cambridge, Mass.: Belknap / Harvard University Press.

McNeill, J. R. and McNeill, W. (2003). *The human web: A bird's-eye view of world history*. New York: W. W. Norton & Co.

Meadows, D., Meadows, D., Randers, J., and Behrens, W., III (1972). *The limits to growth*. Washington, DC: Potomac Associates.

Meadows, D., Randers, J., and Meadows, D. (2004). *Limits to growth: The 30-year update*. White River Junction, Vermont: Chelsea Green Publishing.

Meybeck, M. (2003). Global analysis of river systems: From Earth System controls to Anthropocene syndromes. *Philosophical Transactions of the Royal Society*, B358, pp. 1935–55.

Mill, J. (1965 [1948]). Influence of the progress of society on production and distribution. In J. Robson, ed., *Collected works of John Stuart Mill*, vol. III: *The principles of political economy with some of their applications to social philosophy*. Toronto: Routledge & Kegan Paul, pp. 705–57.

Millennium Ecosystem Assessment (2005a). *Ecosystems & human well-being: Synthesis*. Washington, DC: Island Press: www.millenniumassessment.org/documents/document.356.aspx.pdf.

Millennium Ecosystem Assessment (2005b). Overview of the Milliennium [*sic*] Ecosystem Assessment: www.millenniumassessment.org/en/About.html.

Miller, G. H., Gogel, M. L., Magee, J. W., Gagan, M. K., Clarke, S. J., and Johnson, B. J. (2005). Ecosystem collapse in Pleistocene Australia and a human role in megafaunal extinction. *Science*, 309, pp. 287–90.

Minx, J. (2018). How can climate policy stay on top of a growing mountain of data? *The Guardian*: www.theguardian.com/science/political-science/2018/jun/12/how-can-climate-policy-stay-on-top-of-a-growing-mountain-of-data.

Mitchell, T. (1998). Fixing the economy. *Cultural Studies*, 12, pp. 82–101.

Mithen, S. (1996). *The prehistory of the mind: A search for the origins of art, religion, and science*. London: Thames and Hudson.

Mithen, S. (2007). *The singing Neanderthals: The origins of music, language, mind and body.* Cambridge, Mass.: Harvard University Press.

Miyazaki, H. (2014). *Turning point.* Viz Media.

Mol, A. (2002). *The body multiple: Ontology in medical practice.* Durham: Duke University Press.

Mooney, H., Duraiappah, A., and Larigauderie, A. (2013). Evolution of natural and social science interactions in global change research programs. *Proceedings of the National Academy of Sciences of the United States of America*, 110(Supplement 1), pp. 3665–72.

Moore, J. (2015). *Capitalism in the web of life: Ecology and the accumulation of capital.* New York: Verso Books.

Mora, C., Tittensor, D., Adl, S., Simpson, A., and Worm, B. (2011). How many species are there on Earth and in the ocean? *PLoS Biology*, 9, p. e1001127.

Mora, C., Dousset, B., Caldwell, I. R., et al. (2017). Global risk of deadly heat. *Nature Climate Change*, 7, pp. 501–6.

Morera-Brenes, B., Monge-Nájera, J., Carrera Mora, P. (2019). The conservation status of Costa Rican velvet worms (Onychophora): geographic pattern, risk assessment and comparison with New Zealand velvet worms. *UNED Research Journal*, 11, pp. 272–82.

Morrison, K. (2009). *Daroji Valley: Landscape history, place, and the making of a dryland reservoir system.* New Delhi: American Institute of Indian Studies and Manohar.

Morrison, K. (2013). *The human face of the land: Why the past matters for India's environmental future.* Occasional Papers, History and Society Series, 27. New Delhi: Nehru Memorial Museum and Library.

Morrison, K. (2015). Provincializing the anthropocene. [Online] Nature and History: A Symposium on Human–Environment Relations in the Long Term: www.india-seminar.com/2015/673/673_kathleen_morrison.htm.

Morton, T. (2013). *Hyperobjects: Philosophy and ecology after the end of the world.* Minneapolis: University of Minnesota Press.

Morton, T. (2018). The hurricane in my backyard. *The Atlantic*: www.theatlantic.com/technology/archive/2018/07/the-hurricane-in-my-backyard/564554.

Muir, D. C. G. and Rose, N. L. (2007). Persistent organic pollutants in the sediments of Lochnagar. In N. L. Rose, ed., *Lochnagar: The natural history of a mountain lake*, Developments in Paleoenvironmental Research, 12. Dordrecht: Springer, pp. 375–402.

Muller, J. (2018). *The tyranny of metrics.* Princeton University Press.

Murtaugh, P. and Schlax, M. (2009). Reproduction and the carbon legacies of individuals. *Global Environmental Change*, 19, pp. 14–20.

National Institutes of Health (2012). NIH Human Microbiome Project defines normal bacterial makeup of the body. June 13: www.nih.gov/news/health/jun2012/nhgri-13.htm.

National Research Council (1986). *Earth System science: Overview: A program* *for global change.*Washington, DC:The National Academies Press, p. 19: https://doi.org/10.17226/19210.

Nerem, R. S., Beckley, B. D., Fasullo, J. T., et al. (2018). Climate-change-driven accelerated sea level rise detected in the altimeter era. *Proceedings of the National Academy of Sciences of the United States of America*, 115, pp. 2022–5.

Neukom, R., Steiger, N., Gómez-Navarro, J. J., Wang, J., and Werner, J. (2019). No evidence for globally warm and cold periods over the preindustrial Common Era. *Nature*, 571, pp. 550–4.

Nicholson, S. (2013). The promises and perils of geoengineering. In Worldwatch Institute, ed., *Is sustainability still possible? State of the world 2013.*Washington, DC: Island Press, pp. 317–31.

Nicholson, S. and Jinnah, S., eds. (2016). *New earth politics: Essays from the Anthropocene.* Cambridge, Mass.: The MIT Press.

Nickel, E. H. and Grice, J. D. (1998). The IMA Commission on New Minerals and Mineral Names: Procedures and guidelines on mineral nomenclature. *Canadian Mineralogist*, 36, pp. 913–26.

Nilon, C. H., Aronson, M. F. J., Cilliers, S. S., et al. (2017). Planning for the future of urban biodiversity: A global review of city-scale initiatives. *BioScience*, 67, pp. 332–42.

NOAA (n.d.). Climate forcing. NOAA.gov: www.climate.gov/maps-data/primer/climate-forcing.

Nordhaus,T. and Shellenberger, M. (2007). *Break through: From the death of environmentalism to the politics of possibility.* Boston: Houghton Mifflin.

Norgaard, R. (2010). Ecosystem services: From eye-opening metaphor to complexity blinder. *Ecological Economics*, 69, pp. 1219–27.

Norgaard, R. (2013). The Econocene and the delta. *San Francisco Estuary and Watershed Science*, 11.

North–South: A programme for survival (a.k.a. The Brandt Report) (1980): www.sharing.org/information-centre/reports/brandt-report-summary.

Northcott, M. (2014). *A political theology of climate change.* Grand Rapids: William B. Eerdman Publishing Company.

Och, L. M. and Shields-Zhou, G. A. (2012). The Neoproterozoic oxygenation event: environmental perturbations and biogeochemical cycling. *Earth-Science Reviews*, 110, pp. 26–57.

Oliveira, I. de S., Read,V. M. St. J., and Mayer, G. (2012). A world checklist of Onychophora (velvet worms), with notes on nomenclature and status of names. *ZooKeys*, 211, pp. 1–70.

O'Neil, C. (2016). *Weapons of math destruction: How big data increases inequality and threatens democracy.* New York: Crown Publishers.

O'Neill, D. (2015).The proximity of nations to a socially sustainable steady-state economy. *Journal of Cleaner Production*, 108, pp. 1213–31.

Oreskes, N. (2004). The scientific consensus on climate change. *Science*, 306, p. 1686.

Oreskes, N. (2019) *Why trust science?* Princeton University Press.

Oreskes, N. and Conway, E. (2010). *Merchants of doubt: How a handful of scientists obscured the truth on issues from tobacco smoke to global warming.* London: Bloomsbury Press.

Oreskes, N. and Conway, E. (2014). *The collapse of Western civilization.* New York: Columbia University Press.

Orr, D. (2013). Governance in the long emergency. In Worldwatch Institute, ed., *Is sustainability still possible? State of the world 2013.* Washington, DC: Island Press, pp. 279–91.

Orr, D. (2016). *Dangerous years: Climate change, the long emergency, and the way forward.* New Haven: Yale University Press.

Orr, J. C., Fabry, V. J., Aumont, O., et al. (2005). Anthropogenic ocean acidification over the twenty-first century and its impact on calcifying organisms. *Nature,* 437, pp. 681–6.

Ortiz, I. and Cummins, M. (2011). *Global inequality: Beyond the bottom billion – a rapid review of income distribution in 141 countries.* UNICEF Social and Economic Policy Working Paper. New York: UNICEF: www. childimpact.unicef-irc.org/documents/view/id/120/lang/en.

Ostrom, E. (1999). Revisiting the commons: Local lessons, global challenges. *Science,* 284, pp. 278–82.

Ottoni, C., Van Neer, W., and Geigl, E.-M. (2017). The palaeogenetics of cat dispersal in the ancient world. *Nature Ecology & Evolution,* 1, p. 0139(2017).

Parker, G. (2013). *Global crisis: War, Climate change, and catastrophe in the seventeenth century.* New Haven: Yale University Press.

Pauly, D. (2010). *5 easy pieces: The impact of fisheries on marine systems.* Washington, DC: Island Press.

Piketty, T. (2014). *Capital in the twenty-first century.* Cambridge, Mass.: Belknap / Harvard University Press.

Pilling, D. (2018). *The growth delusion.* London: Bloomsbury.

Plastic Oceans International. (2019). Who we are: https://plasticoceans.org/ who-we-are.

Pope, K. (2019). Feeding 10 billion people by 2050 in a warming world. *Yale Climate Connections*: www.yaleclimateconnections.org/2019/02/ warmer-world-more-hungry-people-big-challenges.

Povinelli, E. (2016). *Geontologies: A requiem to late liberalism.* Durham: Duke University Press.

Powell, C. (2013). The possible parallel universe of dark matter. *Discover* (July/ August): http://discovermagazine.com/2013/julyaug/21-the-possible-parallel-universe-of-dark-matter.

Price, S. J., Ford, J. R., Cooper, A. H., and Neal, C. (2011). Humans as major geological and geomorphological agents in the Anthropocene: The significance of artificial ground in Great Britain. In M. Williams, J. A. Zalasiewicz, A. Haywood, and M. Ellis, eds., *The Anthropocene: A new epoch of geological time. Philosophical Transactions of the Royal Society (Series A),* 369, pp. 1056–84.

Prugh, T., Costanza, R., Cumberland, J., Daly, H., Goodland, R., and Noorgard, R. (1999). *Natural capital and human economic survival* (2nd edn.). Boca Raton, Fla.: Lewis Publishers.

Rasmussen, L. (2013). *Earth-honoring faith: Religious ethics in a new key*. New York: Oxford University Press.

Raworth, K. (2017). *Doughnut economics: Seven ways to think like a 21st century economist*. White River Junction, Vt.: Chelsea Green Publishing.

Rees, M. (2003). *Our final hour: A scientist's warning. How terror, error, and environmental disaster threaten humankind's future in this century – on earth and beyond*. New York: Basic Books.

Resplandy, I., Keeling, R. F., Eddebbar, Y., et al. (2018). Quantification of ocean heat uptake from changes in atmospheric O_2 and CO_2 composition. *Nature*, 563, pp. 105–8.

Revkin, A. C. (1992). *Global warming: Understanding the forecast*. New York: Abbeville Press.

Richter, D., Grün, R., Joannes-Boyau, R., et al. (2017). The age of the hominin fossils from Jbel Irhoud, Morocco, and the origins of the Middle Stone Age. *Nature*, 546, pp. 293–6.

Ridley, M. (2010) *The rational optimist: How prosperity evolves*. New York: Harper Collins.

Riginos, C., Karande, M. A., Rubenstein, D. I., and Palmer, T. M. (2015). Disruption of protective ant–plant mutualism by an invasive ant increases elephant damage to savannah trees. *Ecology*, 96, pp. 554–661: https://doi.org/10.1890/14-1348.1.

Robert, F. and Chaussidon, M. (2006). A palaeotemperature curve for the Precambrian oceans based on silicon isotopes in cherts. *Nature*, 443, pp. 969–72.

Robin, L. (2008). The eco-humanities as literature: A new genre? *Australian Literary Studies*, 23, pp. 290–304.

Rocha, J. C, Peterson, G., Bodin, O. and Levin, S. (2018). Cascading regime shifts within and across scales. *Science*, 362, pp. 1379–83.

Roebroeks, W. and Villa, P. (2011). On the earliest evidence for habitual use of fire in Europe. *Proceedings of the National Academy of Sciences of the United States of America*, 108, pp. 5209–14.

Rose, N. L. (2015). Spheroidal carbonaceous fly-ash particles provide a globally synchronous stratigraphic marker for the Anthropocene. *Environmental Science & Technology*, 49, pp. 4155–62.

Ross, C. (2017). Developing the rain forest: Rubber, environment and economy in Southeast Asia. In G. Austin, ed., *Economic development and environmental history in the Anthropocene: Perspectives on Asia and Africa*. London: Bloomsbury, pp. 199–218.

Rothkopf, D. (2012). *Power, Inc.: The epic rivalry between big business and government*. New York: Farrar, Straus, and Giroux.

Royal Society (2009). *Geoengineering the climate: Science, governance and uncertainty*. London: The Royal Society, Science Policy: https://royalso-ciety.org/topics-policy/publications/2009/geoengineering-climate.

Ruddiman, W. F. (2003). The anthropogenic Greenhouse Era began thousands of years ago. *Climatic Change*, 61, pp. 261–93.

Ruddiman, W. F. (2013). Anthropocene. *Annual Review of Earth and Planetary Sciences*, 41, pp. 45–68.

Ruddiman, W. F., Ellis, E. C., Kaplan, J. O., and Fuller, D. Q. (2015). Defining the epoch we live in. *Science*, 348, pp. 38–9.

Rudwick, M. J. S. (2016). *Earth's deep history: How it was discovered and why it matters*. University of Chicago Press.

Rule, S., Brook, B., Haberle, S., Turney, C., Kershaw, A., and Johnson, C. (2012). The aftermath of megafaunal extinction: Ecosystem transformation in Pleistocene Australia. *Science*, 335, pp. 1483–6.

Sachs, J. (2015). *The age of sustainable development*. New York: Columbia University Press.

Samways, M. (1999). Translocating fauna to foreign lands: Here comes the Homogenocene. *Journal of Insect Conservation*, 3, pp. 65–6.

Schor, J. (1998). *The overspent American: Upscaling, downshifting, and the new consumer*. New York: Basic Books.

Schor, J. (2010). *Plenitude: The new economics of true wealth*. New York: Penguin Press.

Schumacher, E. (1973). *Small is beautiful: Economics as if people mattered*. New York: Harper & Row.

Schwägerl, C. (2013). Neurogeology: The Anthropocene's inspirational power. In H. Trischler, ed., *Anthropocene: Exploring the future of the age of humans. RCC Perspectives: Transformations in Environment and Society*, 3, pp. 29–37.

Scranton, R. (2013). Learning how to die in the Anthropocene. *The New York Times*: https://opinionator.blogs.nytimes.com/2013/11/10/learning-how-to-die-in-the-anthropocene.

Scranton, R. (2015). *Learning to die in the anthropocene: Reflections on the end of a civilization*. San Francisco: City Lights Books.

Scranton, R. (2018). *We're doomed. Now what?* New York: Soho Press.

Sen, I. S. and Peuckner-Ehrenbrink, B. (2012). Anthropogenic disturbance of element cycles at the Earth's surface. *Environmental Science and Technology*, 46, pp. 8601–9.

Share the World's Resources (2006). The Brandt Report: A Summary. Share the World's Resources: www.sharing.org/information-centre/reports/brandt-report-summary.

Shellenberger, M. and Nordhaus, T. (2005). The death of environmentalism: Global warming politics in a post-environmental world. *Grist*: https://grist.org/article/doe-reprint.

Sherlock, R. L. (1922). *Man as a geological agent: An account of his action on inanimate nature*. London: H. F. & G. Witherby.

Shiva, V. (2008). *Soil not oil: Environmental justice in an age of climate crisis*. Brooklyn: South End Press.

Shorrocks, A., Davies, J., and Lluberas, R. (2018). *Global Wealth Report 2018.* Zurich: Credit Suisse Research Institute, Credit Suisse AG Group: www.credit-suisse.com/about-us-news/en/articles/news-and-expertise/global-wealth-report-2018-us-and-china-in-the-lead-201810.html.

Sideris, L. (2016). Anthropocene convergences: A report from the field. In R. Emmett, ed., *Whose Anthropocene? Revisiting Dipesh Chakrabarty's "Four theses." RCC Perspectives: Transformations in Environment and Society,* 2, pp. 89–96.

Skidelsky, R. (2009). *Keynes: The return of the master.* New York: Public Affairs.

Skinner, L. C., Fallon, S., Waelbroeck, C., et al. (2010). Ventilation of the deep Southern Ocean and deglacial CO_2 rise. *Science,* 328, pp. 1147–51.

Smail, D. L. (2008). *On deep history and the brain.* Berkeley: University of California Press.

Smil, V. (2011). Harvesting the biosphere: The human impact. *Population and Development Review,* 37, pp. 613–36.

Smit, M. A. and Mezger, K. (2017) Earth's early O_2 cycle suppressed by primitive continents. *Nature Geoscience,* 10, pp. 788–92.

Smith, F., Elliott Smith, R., Lyons, S., and Payne, J. (2018). Body size downgrading of mammals over the late Quaternary. *Science,* 360, pp. 310–13.

Snir, A., Nadel, D., Groman-Yaroslavski, I., et al. (2015). The origin of cultivation and proto-weeds, long before Neolithic farming. *PLoS ONE,* 10, p. e0131422: https://doi.org/10.1371/journal.pone.0131422.

Söderbaum, P. (2000). *Ecological economics: A political economics approach to environment and development.* London: Earthscan.

Solnit, R. (2004). *Hope in the dark: Untold histories, wild possibilities.* New York: Nation Books.

Solnit, R. (2007). *Storming the gates of paradise: Landscapes for politics.* Berkeley: University of California Press.

Solnit, R. (2010). *A paradise built in hell: The extraordinary communities that arise in disaster.* New York: Penguin Books.

Solow, R. (1974). The economics of resources or the resources of economics. *The American Economic Review,* 64, pp. 1–14.

Soo, R. M., Hemp, J., Parks, D. H., Fischer, W. W., and Hugenholtz, P. (2017). On the origins of oxygenic photosynthesis and aerobic respiration in cyanobacteria. *Science,* 355, pp. 1436–40.

Sörlin, S. (2013). Reconfiguring environmental expertise. *Environmental Science & Policy,* 28, pp. 14–24.

Sosa-Bartuano, Á., Monge-Nájera, J., and Morera-Brenes, B. (2018). A proposed solution to the species problem in velvet worm conservation (Onychophora). *UNED Research Journal,* 10, pp. 193–7.

Stager, C. (2012). *Deep future: The next 10,000 years of life on Earth.* New York: Thomas Dunne Books.

Statista (2018). www.statista.com/statistics/268750/global-gross-domestic-product-gdp.

Steffen, W., Sanderson, A., Tyson, P. D., et al. (2004). *Global change and the Earth System: A planet under pressure*. The IGBP Book Series. Berlin, Heidelberg, and New York: Springer-Verlag.

Steffen, W., Crutzen, P. J., and McNeill, J. R. (2007). The Anthropocene: Are humans now overwhelming the great forces of Nature? *Ambio*, 36, pp. 614–21.

Steffen, W., Broadgate, W., Deutsch, L., et al. (2015a). The trajectory of the Anthropocene: The Great Acceleration. *Anthropocene Review*, 2, pp. 81–98.

Steffen, W., Richardson, K., Rockström, J., et al. (2015b). Planetary boundaries: Guiding human development on a changing planet, *Science*, 347, p. 6223.

Steffen, W., Leinfelder, R., Zalasiewicz, J., et al. (2016). Stratigraphic and Earth System approaches in defining the Anthropocene. *Earth's Future*, 4, pp. 324–45.

Steffen, W., Rockström, J., Richardson, K., et al. (2018). Trajectories of the Earth System in the Anthropocene. *Proceedings of the National Academy of Sciences of the United States of America*, 115, pp. 8252–9.

Steffen, W., Richardson, K., Rockström, J., et al. (2020). The emergence and evolution of Earth System science. *Nature*, 1, pp. 54–63.

Steinberg, T. (2010). Can capitalism save the planet? On the origins of Green Liberalism. *Radical History Review*, 2010, pp. 7–24.

Stoppani, A. (1873). *Corso di geologia*, vol. II: *Geologia stratigrafica*. Milan: G. Bernardoni e G. Brigola.

Storm, S. (2017). How the invisible hand is supposed to adjust the natural thermostat: A guide for the perplexed. *Science and Engineering Ethics*, 23, pp. 1307–31.

Strathern, M. (1991). *Partial connections* (updated edn.) Savage, Md.: Rowman and Littlefield.

Subramanian, A. (2017). Whales and climate change: Our gentle giants are natural CO_2 regulators. [Blog] Heirs to Our Oceans: https://h2oo.org/blog-collection/2018/1/27/wzgb1wsr1k2uwpcjvdohk83zydc7pr.

Suess, E. (1875). *Die Enstehung der Alpen*. Vienna: W. Braumüller.

Suess, E. (1885–1909). *Das Antlitz der Erde*, vol. II (Vienna: F. Tempsky, 1888).

Summerhayes, C. P. (2020). *Palaeoclimatology: from Snowball Earth to the Anthropocene*. Chichester: Wiley.

Swindles, G. T., Watson, E., Turner, T. E., et al. (2015). Spheroidal carbonaceous particles are a defining stratigraphic marker for the Anthropocene. *Scientific Reports*, 5, p. 10264, DOI: 10210.11038/srep10264.

Syvitski, J. P. M., Kettner, A. J., Overeem, I., et al. (2009). Sinking deltas due to human activities. *Nature Geoscience*, 2, pp. 681–9.

Terrington, R. L., Silva, É. C. N., Waters, C. N., Smith, H., and Thorpe,

S. (2018). Quantifying anthropogenic modification of the shallow geosphere in central London, UK. *Geomorphology*, 319, pp. 15–34.

Thomas, J. A. (2001) *Reconfiguring modernity: Concepts of nature in Japanese political ideology*. Berkeley and Los Angeles: University of California Press.

Thomas, J. A. (2010). The exquisite corpses of nature and history: The case of the Korean DMZ. In C. Pearson, P. Coates and T. Cole, eds., *Militarized landscapes: From Gettysburg to Salisbury Plain*. London: Continuum, pp. 151–68.

Thomas, J. A. (2014). History and biology in the Anthropocene: Problems of scale, problems of value. *American Historical Review*, 119, pp. 1587–1607.

Thomas, J. A. (2015). Who is the "we" endangered by climate change? In F. Vidal and N. Diaz, eds., *Endangerment, biodiversity and culture*. London: Routledge, pp. 241–60.

Tilman, D. and Clark, M. (2014). Global diets link environmental sustainability and human health. *Nature*, 515, pp. 518–22.

Trenberth, K. E., Cheng, L., Jacobs, P., et al. (2018). Hurrican Harvey links ocean heat content and climate change adaptation. *Earth's Future*, DOI: 10.1029/2018EF000825.

Tsing, A. (2005). *Friction: An ethnography of global connection*. Princeton University Press.

Tsing, A. (2012). On nonscalability: The living world is not amenable to precision-nested scales. *Common Knowledge*, 18, pp. 505–24.

Tsing, A. (2015). *The mushroom at the end of the world*. Princeton University Press.

Tsing, A., Swanson, H., Gan, E., and Bubandt, N. (2017). *Arts of living on a damaged planet: Ghosts and monsters of the Anthropocene*. Minneapolis: University of Minnesota Press.

Tu, W. (1998). Beyond the Enlightenment mentality. In M. Tucker and J. Berthrong, eds., *Confucianism and ecology: The interrelation of heaven, earth, and humans*. Cambridge, Mass.: Harvard University Center for the Study of World Religions, pp. 3–22.

United Nations, Department of Economic and Social Affairs, Population Division (2017). *World population prospects: The 2017 revision*. New York: United Nations: www.un.org/development/desa/publications/world-population-prospects-the-2017-revision.html.

United Nations News (2018). Hunger reached "alarming" ten-year high in 2017, according to latest UN report. UN News: https://news.un.org/en/story/2018/09/1019002.

United Nations, Climate Change (2019). Revenue-neutral carbon tax: Canada: https://unfccc.int/climate-action/momentum-for-change/financing-for-climate-friendly/revenue-neutral-carbon-tax.

US Bureau of Economic Analysis: www.multpl.com/us-gdp-inflation-adjusted/table.

US Global Change Research Program (2018). *Impacts, risks, and adaptation in the United States: The Fourth National Climate Assessment*, vol. II. [Ed. D. R. Reidmiller, C. W. Avery, D. R. Easterling, et al.]. Washington, DC: US Global Change Research Program.

US National Oceanic and Atmospheric Administration (NOAA) (n.d.). Climate forcing. Climate.gov: www.climate.gov/maps-data/primer/ climate-forcing.

Vadrot, A., Akhtar-Schuster, M., and Watson, R. (2018). The social sciences and the humanities in the intergovernmental science-policy platform on biodiversity and ecosystem services (IPBES). *Innovation: The European Journal of Social Science Research*, 31(Supplement 1), pp. S1–S9.

van der Kaars, S., Miller, G., Turney, C., et al. (2017). Humans rather than climate the primary cause of Pleistocene megafaunal extinction in Australia. *Nature Communications*, 8(1).

Varoufakis, Y. (2016). *And the weak suffer what they must?* London: Vintage.

Vernadsky, V. I. (1998 [1926]). *The biosphere*. Trans. from the Russian by D. R. Langmuir, revised and annotated by M. A. S. McMenamin. New York: Copernicus (Springer-Verlag).

Vernadsky, V. I. (1945). The biosphere and the noosphere. *American Scientist*, 33, pp. 1–12.

Vernadsky, V. I. (1997) *Scientific thought as a planetary phenomenon*. Trans. B. A. Starostin. Moscow: Nongovernmental Ecological V. I. Vernadsky Foundation: http://vernadsky.name/wp-content/uploads/2013/02/ Scientific-thought-as-a-planetary-phenomenon-V.I2.pdf.

Vidas, D. (2015). The Earth in the Anthropocene – and the world in the Holocene? *European Society of International Law (ESIL) Reflections*, 4(6), pp. 1–7.

Vidas, D., Zalasiewicz, J., and Williams, M. (2015). What is the Anthropocene – and why is it relevant for international law? *Yearbook of International Environmental Law*, 25, pp. 3–23.

Villmoare, B., Kimbel, W. H., Seyoum, C., et al. (2015). Early *Homo* at 2.8 ma from Ledi-Geraru, Afar, Ethiopia. *Science*, 347, pp. 1352–5.

Visscher, M. (2015a). Green in the new green. *The Intelligent Optimist*, 13, pp. 64–8.

Visscher, M. (2015b). We can have it all. *The Intelligent Optimist*, 13, pp. 69–73.

Vogel, G. (2018). How ancient humans survived global "volcanic winter" from massive eruption. *Science*: www.sciencemag.org/news/2018/03/how-ancient-humans-survived-global-volcanic-winter-massive-eruption.

Vollrath, D. (2020). *Fully grown: Why a stagnant economy is a sign of success*. University of Chicago Press.

Voosen, P. (2017). 2.7-million-year-old ice opens window on the past. *Science*, 357, pp. 630–1.

Wagreich, M. and Draganits, E. (2018). Early mining and smelting lead anomalies in geological archives as potential stratigraphic markers for the base of an early Anthropocene. *The Anthropocene Review*, 5, pp. 177–201.

Walker, J. C. G., Hays, P. B., and Kasting, J. (1981). A negative feedback mechanism for the long-term stabilization of Earth's surface temperature. *Journal of Geophysical Research*, 86, pp. 9776–82.

Walker, M. J. C., Johnsen, S., Rasmussen, S., et al. (2009). Formal definition and dating of the GSSP (Global Stratotype Section and Point) for the base of the Holocene using the Greenland NGRIP ice core, and selected auxiliary records. *Journal of Quaternary Science*, 24, pp. 3–17.

Walker, M. J. C., Berkelhammer, M., Björck, S., et al. (2012). Formal subdivision of the Holocene Series/Epoch: A discussion paper by a working group of INTIMATE (Integration of ice-core, marine and terrestrial records) and the Subcommission on Quaternary Stratigraphy (International Commission on Stratigraphy). *Journal of Quaternary Science*, 27, pp. 649–59.

Warde, P., Robin, L., and Sörlin, S. (2017). Stratigraphy for the Renaissance: Questions of expertise for "the environment" and "the Anthropocene." *Anthropocene Review*, 4, pp. 246–58.

Waters, C. N. and Zalasiewicz, J. (2017). Concrete: The most abundant novel rock type of the Anthropocene. In D. DellaSala (ed.), *Encyclopedia of the Anthropocene*. Oxford: Elsevier.

Waters, C. N., Syvitski, J. P. M., Gałuszka, A., et al. (2015). Can nuclear weapons fallout mark the beginning of the Anthropocene Epoch? *Bulletin of the Atomic Scientists*, 71, pp. 46–57.

Waters, C. N., Zalasiewicz, J., Summerhayes C., et al. (2016). The Anthropocene is functionally and stratigraphically distinct from the Holocene. *Science*, 351, p. 137.

Waters, C. N., Zalasiewicz, J., Summerhayes, C., et al. (2018a). Global Boundary Stratotype Section and Point (GSSP) for the Anthropocene Series: Where and how to look for potential candidates. *Earth-Science Reviews*, 178, pp. 379–429.

Waters, C. N., Fairchild, I. J., McCarthy, F. M. G., Turney, C. S. M., Zalasiewicz, J., and Williams, M. (2018b). How to date natural archives of the Anthropocene. *Geology Today*, 34, pp. 182–7.

Watts, J. (2018). Almost four environmental defenders a week killed in 2017. *The Guardian*: www.theguardian.com/environment/2018/feb/02/almost-four-environmental-defenders-a-week-killed-in-2017.

Weber, M. (1958 [1905]). *The Protestant ethic and the spirit of capitalism*. New York: Scribner.

Weller, R. (2006). *Discovering nature: Globalization and environmental culture in China and Taiwan*. Cambridge University Press.

Wellman, C. H. and Gray, J. (2002). The microfossil record of early land plants. *Philosophical Transactions of the Royal Society B*, 355, pp. 717–32.

Wilkinson, B. (2005). Humans as geologic agents: A deep-time perspective. *Geology*, 33, pp. 161–4.

Wilkinson, R. and Pickett, K. (2009). *The spirit level: Why greater equality makes societies stronger*. New York: Bloomsbury Press.

Wilkinson, T. (2003). *Archaeological landscapes of the Near East.* Tucson: University of Arizona Press.

Wilkinson, T., French, C., Ur, J., and Semple, M. (2010). The geoarchaeology of route systems in northern Syria. *Geoarchaeology,* 25, pp. 745–71.

Williams, M., Ambrose, S., van der Kaars, S., et al. (2009). Environmental impact of the 73ka Toba super-eruption in South Asia. *Palaeogeography, Palaeoclimatology, Palaeoecology,* 284, pp. 295–314.

Williams, M., Zalasiewicz, J., Waters, C. N., and Landing, E. (2014). Is the fossil record of complex animal behaviour a stratigraphical analogue for the Anthropocene? In C. N. Waters, J. A. Zalasiewicz, M. Williams, et al., eds., *A stratigraphical basis for the Anthropocene.* Special Publications, 395. London: Geological Society, pp. 143–8.

Williams, M., Zalasiewicz, J., Waters, C. N., et al. (2016). The Anthropocene: a conspicuous stratigraphical signal of anthropogenic changes in production and consumption across the biosphere. *Earth's Future,* 4, pp. 34–53.

Williams, M., Zalasiewicz, J., Waters, C., et al. (2018). The palaeontological record of the Anthropocene. *Geology Today,* 34, pp. 188–93.

Williams, M., Edgeworth, M., Zalasiewicz, J., et al. (2019). Underground metro systems: A durable geological proxy of rapid urban population growth and energy consumption during the Anthropocene. In C. Benjamin, E. Quaedackers, and D. Baker, eds., *The Routledge companion to big history.* London and New York: Routledge, pp. 434–55.

Wilson, E. (1998). *Consilience: The unity of knowledge.* New York: Alfred A. Knopf.

Witt, A. B. R., Kiambi, S., Beale, T., and Van Wilgen, B. W. (2017). A preliminary assessment of the extent and potential impacts of alien plant invasions in the Serengeti–Mara ecosystem, East Africa. *Koedoe,* 59, p. a1426: https://doi.org/10.4102/koedoe. v59i1.1426.

Wolfe, A. P., Hobbs, W. O., Birks, H. H., et al. (2013). Stratigraphic expressions of the Holocene–Anthropocene transition revealed in sediments from remote lakes. *Earth-Science Reviews,* 116, pp. 17–34.

Wolff, E. W. (2014). Ice sheets and the Anthropocene. In C. N. Waters, J. A. Zalasiewicz, M. Williams, et al., eds., *A stratigraphical basis for the Anthropocene.* Special Publications, 395. London: Geological Society, pp. 255–63.

Working Group on the "Anthropocene," Subcommission on Quaternary Stratigraphy (2019). Results of binding vote by AWG: http://quaternary. stratigraphy.org/working-groups/anthropocene.

World Bank (2018). Gross Domestic Product for world [MKTGDP1WA646NWDB]. Retrieved from FRED, Federal Reserve Bank of St. Louis: https://fred.stlouisfed.org/series/ MKTGDP1WA646NWDB.

World Bank (2019). Fertility rate, total (births per woman) – Sub-Saharan Africa: https://data.worldbank.org/indicator/SP.DYN.TFRT.IN?locations=ZG.

Wrangham, R. (2009). *Catching fire: How cooking made us human*. London: Profile Books.

WWF (2000). *Living planet report 2000*. Gland, Switzerland: WWF – World Wide Fund for Nature (formerly World Wildlife Fund): https://wwf.panda. org/knowledge_hub/all_publications/living_planet_report_timeline/ lpr_2000.

WWF (2016). *Living planet report 2016: Risk and resilience in a new era*. Gland, Switzerland: WWF – World Wild Fund for Nature (formerly World Wildlife Fund): https://wwf.panda.org/wwf_news/?282370/ Living-Planet-Report-2016.

Wynes, S. and Nicholas, K. (2017). The climate mitigation gap: Education and government recommendations miss the most effective individual actions. *Environmental Research Letters*, 12, p. 074024.

Xu, C., Kohler, T. A., Lenton, T. M., Svenning, J. C., and Scheffer, M. (2020). Future of the human climate niche. *Proceedings of the National Academy of Sciences of the United States of America*: www.pnas.org/cgi/ doi/10.1073/pnas.1910114117.

Yamamura, K. (2018). *Too much stuff: Capitalism in crisis*. Bristol: Policy Press.

Yost, C., Jackson, L., Stone, J., and Cohen, A. (2018). Subdecadal phytolith and charcoal records from Lake Malawi, East Africa imply minimal effects on human evolution from the 74 ka Toba supereruption. *Journal of Human Evolution*, 116, pp. 75–94.

Zalasiewicz, J. (2018). The unbearable burden of the technosphere. *UNESCO Courier*, April–June, pp. 15–17.

Zalasiewicz, J. and Williams, M. (2013). The Anthropocene: A comparison with the Ordovician–Silurian boundary. *Rendiconti Lincei – Scienze Fisiche e Naturali*, 25, pp. 5–12.

Zalasiewicz, J., Williams, M., Smith, A., et al. (2008). Are we now living in the Anthropocene? *GSA Today*, 18, pp. 4–8.

Zalasiewicz, J., Cita, M. B., Hilgen, F., et al. (2013). Chronostratigraphy and geochronology: A proposed realignment. *GSA Today*, 23, pp. 4–8.

Zalasiewicz, J., Waters, C. N., and Williams, M. (2014a). Human bioturbation, and the subterranean landscape of the Anthropocene. *Anthropocene*, 6, pp. 3–9.

Zalasiewicz, J., Williams, M., Waters, C. N., et al. (2014b). The technofossil record of humans. *Anthropocene Review*, 1, pp. 34–43.

Zalasiewicz, J., Waters, C. N., Barnosky, A. D., et al. (2015a). Colonization of the Americas, "Little Ice Age" climate, and bomb-produced carbon: Their role in defining the Anthropocene. *Anthropocene Review*, 2, pp. 117–27.

Zalasiewicz, J., Waters, C., Williams, M., et al. (2015b). When did the Anthropocene begin? A mid-twentieth century boundary level is stratigraphically optimal. *Quaternary International*, 383, pp. 196–203.

Zalasiewicz, J., Waters, C. N., Ivar do Sul, J., et al. (2016a). The geological cycle of plastics and their use as a stratigraphic indicator of the Anthropocene. *Anthropocene*, 13, pp. 4–17.

Zalasiewicz, J., Williams, M., Waters, C. N., et al. (2016b). Scale and diversity of the physical technosphere: A geological perspective. *Anthropocene Review*, 4, pp. 9–22.

Zalasiewicz, J., Waters, C. N., Summerhayes, C. P., et al. (2017a). The Working Group on the Anthropocene: Summary of evidence and interim recommendations. *Anthropocene*, 19, pp. 55–60.

Zalasiewicz, J., Waters, C. N., Wolfe, A. P., et al. (2017b). Making the case for a formal Anthropocene: An analysis of ongoing critiques. *Newsletters on Stratigraphy*, 50, pp. 205–26.

Zalasiewicz, J., Steffen, W., Leinfelder, R., et al. (2017c). Petrifying Earth process: The stratigraphic imprint of key Earth System parameters in the Anthropocene. In N. Clark and K. Yusoff, eds., *Theory Culture & Society, Special Issue: Geosocial Formations and the Anthropocene*, 34, pp. 83–104.

Zalasiewicz, J., Waters, C. N., Head, M. J., et al. (2019a). A formal Anthropocene is compatible with but distinct from its diachronous anthropogenic counterparts: a response to W. F. Ruddiman's "Three flaws in defining a formal Anthropocene." *Progress in Physical Geography*, 43, pp. 319–33.

Zalasiewicz, J., Waters, C., Williams, M., and Summerhayes, C., eds. (2019b). *The Anthropocene as a geological time unit*. Cambridge University Press.

Zanna, L., Khatiwala, S., Gregory, J. M., et al. (2019). Global reconstruction of historical ocean heat storage and transport. *Proceedings of the National Academy of Sciences of the United States of America*, 116, pp. 1126–31.

Zehner, O. (2012). *Green illusions: The dirty secrets of green energy and the future of environmentalism*. Lincoln: University of Nebraska Press.

Zelizer, V. (2007). Pricing a child's life. [Blog] *Huffington Post*: www.huffpost.com/entry/pricing-a-childs-life_b_63381.

Index